Ira David Socol

Designed to Fail

A History of Education
in the United States

Appalachian Gateway Press
Copyright 2024 by Ira Socol
ISBN: 979-8-9914708-0-3
First Edition - December 2024
Cover image created in OpenAI's ChatGPT4
Layout design by Dawn Black

Books by Ira David Socol

Timeless Learning: How Imagination, Observation, and Zero-Based Thinking Change Schools (with Pam Moran and Chad Ratliff)

Education Reimagined: A Space for Risk (with Cheryl Walchack Harris and J. Michael Thornton II)

The Drool Room (a novel-in-stories)

for all the kids who need and deserve great learning environments and all the educators desperate to give them those spaces.

I have known Ira Socol for many years and have long appreciated his keen intellect, deep knowledge of education history and policy, and most of all, his unwavering passion to make schooling work for all children. In "Designed to Fail," Socol offers a thoughtful yet unvarnished look at how the American education system came to be and why it continues to fall short for so many students. With righteous anger tempered by scholarly insight, he traces the troubling origins of many educational practices we take for granted, exposing how they were intentionally designed to limit opportunities for marginalized groups. What sets this book apart, however, is that Socol does not merely critique - he also charts a path forward. Drawing on his vast experience as an educator and reformer, he provides concrete ways that schools can be redesigned to truly serve all learners. While acknowledging the magnitude of change required, Socol's vision is ultimately one of hope. He understands the transformative power of education when done right, and this book is a powerful call to create schools worthy of our children. This book is essential reading for anyone who cares about the future of education in America."

— Punya Mishra, Associate Dean of Scholarship & Innovation in the Mary Lou Fulton Teachers College at Arizona State University

"Ira Socol's book is a call to all educational leaders, policymakers, and practitioners to engage in the critical, and often overlooked, task of asking 'why' our educational system operates the way it does. It is through understanding the 'why'—the historical, socio-political, and economic rationales behind our schooling practices—that we can truly begin to envision and enact the change we can't yet even imagine. By examining the roots of our educational beliefs and practices, Socol not only exposes the systemic challenges we face but also inspires us with the resilience and dedication of those working within these constraints. This book is an essential read for anyone committed to understanding the complexities of our educational system and seeking to make it more equitable, inclusive, and effective for all learners. Let us embrace the power of 'why' to fuel our journey forward."

—Melissa Emler, Chief Learning Officer, Modern Learners

"Socol is unapologetic in the fight to build schools for kids, not adults. He pulls back the sheets on several long-held "best practices," which, if you know Socol, he would probably call "worst practices." Socol takes an honest look at our traditional education system and identifies the root cause of several systemic harms imposed on our children. He is not satisfied with tradition as an excuse for stagnation or oppression. Ira is only interested in what works for learning and, more importantly, how to set all kids up for success and get out of their way."

—Ryan Cordia, Founding Principal, Northeast Career and Technical Academy, Las Vegas, Nevada

"We too often consult our own convenience, rather than the comfort, welfare, or accommodation of our children."

– William A. Alcott, 1832

CONTENTS

FOREWORD

by Scott McLeod

Let us begin by traveling back in time. We can start with a young boy in New York. A boy who struggles to read at an early age, long before we knew much about dyslexia, and often is punished quite severely for being academically challenged. Somehow, despite daunting odds, that boy makes his way through the education system. Amazingly, he then passes the New York Police Department exam and serves as a New York City police officer. Now imagine that this young man, after multiple fits and starts, also manages to complete a college degree. He eventually becomes a special educator, closing the circle as he works with children like himself.

A child with special needs. A cop. And a special educator. All inextricably intertwined. Imagine the insights that he has about carceral mindsets and pedagogies. Imagine the experiences that he has working with children and adults who have been failed by our systems. What perspectives on education might he carry? What kind of book might he write?

You're about to find out.

Ira invites us to travel a journey with him. A journey worth taking slowly. A journey worth savoring. This is not a book to be rushed. This is a book of introspective morsels, a book that invites us to pause, ponder each chapter, and reflect deeply. Because what's wonderful about Ira is that, astonishingly, over the years, he has found a way to translate his experiences - and his own contemplations - into an ethos of education centered on the liberation and empowerment of children. Even better, he has a long history of translating these ideas into emancipatory practices for young people in both classrooms and school districts.

In this book, we roam through the past and present of American education, with Ira as a trusted guide. This is not a linear hike, with distinct mileposts, level ground, and clear sunny skies. The history of American schooling is a twisting, grinding passage, with agonizingly slow uphill climbs, a few forward leaps, some cowardly retreats, and setbacks aplenty.

In the first few chapters, Ira explains some of the history behind our educational structures of control, compliance, and conformity. Often based in discriminatory intent, many of the policies and procedures that we implement in schools today have deep, troubling roots. Systems that were built to keep certain people in their place are not easily amended, particularly when they remain dependent on others giving up the power to which they are long accustomed.

As we progress further, Ira invites us to lean into important questions such as *Why do we have 'teaching walls?'* and *Why do we sort children?* and *Why do we so often privilege silence?* Our belief systems about what schools should look like—and feel like—are heavily influenced by historical views of young people, alarmism about growing diversity, protection of privilege, and the elevation of the needs of industry over those of the children in our care.

In the second half of the book, we confront both misinformation and deliberate disinformation as various entities compete for money, power, and control. What's important in learning and teaching—and for life success—becomes highly-contested terrain. In recent decades, external mandates, standardization, and tight academic and behavioral controls have dominated political and policy arenas. When these one-size-fits-all approaches run up against the diversity of humans that show up in our schools each day, the response of policymakers to their inevitable failure has been to double down instead of rethinking their overarching theories of action in light of what we know about humans and learning. The end result of this screw-tightening of control is learning stagnation, student disengagement, and educator departure from the profession.

Finally, Ira walks us through historical anachronisms that continue to shape schooling. Instead of leaning into acceptance, access, attention, and abundance, we continue to limit the experiences, aspirations, and learning outcomes of our young people. Schools that are designed to demoralize and fail certain children usually do. It is a tremendous waste of human capital and a degradation of the interests, skills, and talents of our children, who are desperately longing for something different.

What does all of this mean for us? Well, any expedition worth taking presents us with quandaries, pitfalls, false trails, and mistaken choices along the way. How we confront these dilemmas shapes our ultimate destination. It is difficult to read through this book—and look back over the decades—and not wish that we had traveled some different paths. But the story of American education is an ongoing narrative, and we can elect to change course at any time. We know so much now about learning, teaching, and the ability of young people to do amazing things if we support and let them. Will we choose differently for our children and grandchildren? I hope that we do.

Ira is not just a dreamer. He's a designer and a builder, and he gladly points us toward schools that are doing better by kids. Happy reading.

Scott McLeod, J.D., Ph.D., is a Professor of Educational Leadership, and the Founding Director of CASTLE, at the University of Colorado Denver.

INTRODUCTION

In the late aughts, faced with choosing a dissertation topic for my Ph.D. program at Michigan State University's College of Education, I considered all the projects I could do around Assistive Technology and Universal Design for Learning. I was, after all, a "Special Education Technology Scholar," teaching the college's Assistive Technology courses. However, my real interest in that graduate school experience had become the philosophical "why" of the education system we live with.

My "never miss" moments of that school experience—besides my teaching responsibilities—were once-a-week lunches with the Postmodern Study Group led by Dr. Lynn Fendler (LinkedIn, 2022) and Cleo Cherryholmes (Knapp, 2013). There, we discussed everything: how to see, what to believe, what created truth, how to store root vegetables, and how to make maple syrup. Most importantly, we tried to pull back from the everyday K-12 education in the United States and focus more broadly on what lay behind the curtain. My e-book and audiobook libraries swelled with the works of Michel Foucault (Gutting &

Oksala, 2022), Walter Benjamin (Osborne & Charles, 2021), Svetlana Alpers (Wikipedia contributors, 2023), Jonathan Crary (Wikipedia contributors, 2024), Stephen Toulmin (Wikipedia contributors, 2024), and perhaps above all, Edward Said. (Eagleton, 2004) This was heavy stuff, especially for a grad student who had never taken a philosophy course before and needed to listen to these books on the 90-mile drives to and from campus.

The conversations over those lunches and my private discussions with Fendler, Cherryholmes, Susan Peters (*Susan Jeanne Peters*, n.d.), Yong Zhao (*Education in the Age of Globalization*, n.d.), Rand Spiro (*About Me*, n.d.), and Punya Mishra, (*Punya Mishra's Web*, n.d.) defined my research interest. "Why," I kept asking, "if our schools constantly fail our learners, do we keep doing what we've always done?"

With that question, I dove into Google Books in search of the documents that created our system of schools. I wanted to know what the authors of these structures were saying and thinking as they acted. I wanted to analyze their writings the way we might analyze a novel (if I were to analyze a novel, which is unlikely). I found, at first, the people everyone knows, Thomas Jefferson, Horace Mann, and Henry Barnard, and then I found William Alcott. When I found Alcott, I realized that the battle over what education means, what a classroom means, and what educational technology means had been going on for at least 180 years.

Along the way, I published a five-part blog post series on Google's *Blogger* platform titled Designed to Fail. (*SpeEdChange*, n.d.) Ever since, people – Dr. Pamela Moran included – have asked me to update that research with all I have learned since. This year, 2024, I did that on the Medium platform. (Socol, 2024) This book is an extension and expansion of that effort.

I researched and wrote the dissertation for three years. In the end, my last paragraph was: "I have tried to tell these educators that this is a brutal and endless war. Few things arouse political passions as education does, for it is a struggle for the future. Those who, from Henry Barnard then to the billionaires of today, stand for the economic and social status quo (softened by charity) will always have more resources at hand than Alcott or Dewey or Dr. Moran, but sometimes we do create change. That change, the change in the lives of all of our children, is something we will keep fighting for."

This book is one more part of that fight. It is an argument, not a straight history—but then, there is no such thing as "straight history." Every bit of academic writing is biased, intentionally if the author is self-aware, perhaps unintentionally if they are not. Those who sell you "quantitative research" are no less biased in their storytelling than anyone else because the questions any researcher asks reflect their own or their funders' biases.

So let me say that I view myself as a postmodern and postcolonial thinker. I fully believe in the need to transform society in the United States—and elsewhere—into something more fair, equitable, decent, moral, and kinder. I write from the point of view of a disabled person who, as a student, never has gotten along with school.

Yet, I am also someone who has spent many, many years closely observing schools as they are. That began when I was young and banished to the back of classrooms. It continued through attending a "high school without walls" and multiple universities (Michigan State—twice, SUNY/College at Purchase, Pratt Institute (which had no grades), the New York City Police Academy (with university credits from SUNY), and Grand Valley State University. I have worked in schools in Michigan and Virginia and with schools across the U.S., Canada, and Ireland. Those schools have been in every kind of place and have served every demographic. I have taught, coached, supported, and been an administrator. All of this means I have seen many, many things and implies a certain level of expertise, but "expert" is not a term I want to apply to myself. I am simply an investigator searching for truths.

If this book accomplishes anything, I hope it encourages teachers, administrators, and policymakers to evaluate the "why" behind the things we do while encouraging those interested in research to dive further into the history of education.

I believe that the broader our knowledge base, the less compliant we will be.

Ira Socol, Waynesboro, Virginia, 2024

Sources:

About Me. (n.d.). Retrieved March 9, 2024, from https://postgutenberg.typepad.com/about.html

Education in the age of globalization. (n.d.). Education in the Age of Globalization. Retrieved March 9, 2024, from https://zhaolearning.com/

Gutting, G., & Oksala, J. (2022). Michel Foucault. In E. N. Zalta & U. Nodelman (Eds.), *The Stanford Encyclopedia of Philosophy* (Fall 2022). Metaphysics Research Lab, Stanford University. https://plato.stanford.edu/archives/fall2022/entries/foucault/

Knapp, L. (2013, April 25). News. *News - The Latest at the College of Education - Michigan State University.* https://edwp.educ.msu.edu/news/2013/in-memoriam-cleo-h-cherryholmes/

LinkedIn, O. (2022). About linkedin. *LinkedIn Corporation.* https://www.linkedin.com/in/lynn-fendler-398b6646/

Osborne, P., & Charles, M. (2021). Walter Benjamin. In E. N. Zalta (Ed.), *The Stanford Encyclopedia of Philosophy* (Fall 2021). Metaphysics Research Lab, Stanford University. https://plato.stanford.edu/archives/fall2021/entries/benjamin/

Punya Mishra's web. (n.d.). Retrieved March 9, 2024, from https://punyamishra.com/

Socol, I. D. (2024, February 12). *Designed to Fail: (1): a history of American education.* Teachers on Fire Magazine. https://medium.com/teachers-on-fire/designed-to-fail-1-a-history-of-american-education-b094697d4223

SpeEdChange. (n.d.). Retrieved March 9, 2024, from https://speedchange.blogspot.com/2010/09/designed-to-fail-education-in-america.html

Susan Jeanne Peters. (n.d.). Dignity Memorial. Retrieved March 9, 2024, from https://www.dignitymemorial.com/obituaries/east-lansing-mi/susan-peters-11257508

Wikipedia contributors. (2023, August 19). *Svetlana Alpers.* Wikipedia, The Free Encyclopedia. https://en.wikipedia.org/w/index.php?title=Svetlana_Alpers&oldid=1171205514

Wikipedia contributors. (2024, March 8). *Jonathan Crary.* Wikipedia, The Free Encyclopedia. https://en.wikipedia.org/w/index.php?title=Jonathan_Crary&oldid=1212523306

PROLOGUE

Trinity School sits at the corner of Church Street and Pelham Road in New Rochelle, New York. Constructed in 1955 and expanded multiple times, this public elementary is the successor to that city's first school, a two-story brick 1820s structure that originally housed all grades first through twelfth.

Under a sweeping mid-century entrance canopy, ceramic plaques representing a history of transportation are set into the school's walls. Old ships, trains, planes, and street vehicles head west, 1950s versions of the same head east. What the architects intended when these bits of art were placed is unknown, but for me, small areas of broken glaze on the image of the mid-century railroad locomotive whisper of my struggles with the education system.

The breaks are much smaller than I remember and have blackened with the passage of decades, becoming barely perceptible. In my memory, they are much larger, and the exposed clay is a bright, attention-seizing white. What is muted today was once a loud, desperate scream.

I was somewhere between nine and ten years old when the glaze of that tile was broken, and deep into the third year of a lifelong war with Ellwood Cubberley, a man I would not hear of for four decades.

Cubberley and his co-conspirators invented the schools we all live with and struggle with. This struggle is fought in classrooms, corridors, offices, books, at conferences, and on university campuses. That broken tile might have been the first small victory in that asymmetric conflict between the human child I was and the people who thought my life was clearly "less than."

I have fought this system since I sat in the corner of a second-grade classroom between moments of being yelled at, hit, and locked in the closet by my teacher. My "crimes," in her vision of school, were a failure to conform. I could not read as a seven-year-old was expected to. I could not write as a seven-year-old was expected to. I could not sit for hours as a seven-year-old was expected to. So, I was treated as something less than fully human.

I was hardly alone in that situation. When I began school in a ten-square-mile city with 12 elementary schools, there were many ways a kid could be "less than." Five of those elementaries fed one junior high school, primarily serving the poor and lower-middle-class neighborhoods surrounding the city's downtown. Kids who went there were most likely to end up in vocational programs and lower-level classes once they reached the city's single high school. Six schools served the far more suburban areas further inland and fed a different junior high filled with pathways to high school college prep, honors, and advanced placement courses.

A half-hour walk due north of Trinity School is New Rochelle's Lincoln Park and the historic center of the city's Black community (before World War II, New Rochelle had the highest Black population percentage in the state). Lincoln Park was the site of the city's twelfth elementary, the Black school. If you lived within that highly gerrymandered attendance area, although you did go to the "better" junior high, you went there from a run-down, overcrowded, understaffed school and left unprepared at age 12 to compete with the rich kids for the attention of white teachers.

A United States Supreme Court decision ended that de facto segregation in the early 1960s. (Taylor v. Board of Education of City School District of New Rochelle, 195 F. Supp. 231 (S.D.N.Y. 1961), n.d.) Of those 12 elementary schools, nine had been 99 percent white, one 99 percent Black, and two were integrated—one intentionally by a community effort, the other through a collapse in property values due to Interstate 95's construction through downtown neighborhoods. The school district's settlement with the court was to close Lincoln School and offer parents in that attendance district the opportunity to choose which of the remaining 11 elementaries their children would attend (busing as the solution). Yet, today in New Rochelle (Talk of the Sound News, 2016), a mile away in New York City (Lefty, n.d.), and just about everywhere, our public school systems continue to reinforce the opportunities for those who enter school "ahead," who enter school with privilege, while taking those students who need opportunities most and sentencing them to generational poverty.

"The reason why there are poorly performing schools is because if you put a child in an inferior school then they most likely will do poorly. It simply becomes a cycle, where these people in these schools don't get a proper education and then

have children who later go to the same failing schools. Edu-cation opportunities for everyone will never improve if the schools arc not reformed. I believe that it's not the child's fault, it's the school's fault."—from a New Rochelle student scholar-ship essay. (Talk of the Sound News, 2016)

Education is the most intensely political thing a society does. It is how a culture attempts to craft its future. It is fought over continually by students, teachers, administrators, parents, politicians, scholars, and those with wealth and power. When a society refuses to change education, it is because that society is refusing to change. This is true whether it is Florida refusing to allow Black history ("Florida's New Standards on Black History Curriculum Are Creating Outrage," 2023) or facts about the U.S. Civil War into classrooms, or Oklahoma, Iowa (Akin, 2023), and Indiana (Akin, 2023) refusing to allow any understanding of the range of human gender experiences into school corridors (Akin, 2023), going to court to define "merit" as "what I have prepared my child to be good at" (Politico, 2024), or gaming the system in every way possible to give their "nice white kids" ("Nice White Par-ents," n.d.) the advantages they would probably need to compete if the playing fields were level. (Kohn, 1998)

"...their tone changes a little when I mention having kids. Amer-ican parents have something of a reputation in Europe. We're known for being intense, neurotic, overprotective, obsessed with academic achievement—"the opposite of relaxed," Mat-thias Doepke, a professor of economics at the London School of Economics, told me. Some Europeans worry that American child-rearing norms will take hold there. Yet many of the

parents I've spoken with also express some sympathy, or even pity, for American parents. They seem bewildered by how little support new parents receive in the U.S., and horrified by the prevalence of gun violence in American life." = Stephanie H. Murray, *The Atlantic* (Murray, 2024)

As this book will repeatedly point out, change is always perceived as a threat to those controlling wealth and power. Greed comes almost naturally to those born into the culture of the United States with its myths of individualism and "lifting oneself up by one's bootstraps" and the desperate fear that seems to accompany life in the wealthiest and most powerful nation.

Everyone in our society believes, by virtue of having attended school themselves, that they have real expertise regarding schools despite possessing only snapshots of the experience and glimpses of rumors and news. After all, they've been to school, their kids have been to school, their grandchildren may be attending school, and they constantly hear about schools—as they hear about children and adolescents. These offer Americans an assumption of knowledge about education that they do not have about the military, police, the court system, or the legislative system of government. Those assumptions make real conversations difficult, if not impossible.

The reality is that few know. We don't know because this homogenous and differentiated system eludes everyone, including the U.S. government and almost all the university researchers—past and present.

Whether you are a student, a teacher, a parent, a grandparent, a community member, or a school, district, or state administrator, your understanding of "the system" of education is probably only as deep as what you have experienced personally. You likely don't know how "it" came to be, why "it" came to be, or why "it" remains in place. Yet, most of us who spend our days within the walls of schools struggle with some, if not all, of this system, and far more than a few struggle against it. Still others, in corporate or government offices, "think tanks," legislative chambers, colleges of education, and yes, in homes, work very hard to preserve the essentials of the system and the privileges the system creates.

What we all have in common is a sense that "the school" is, if not a "natural" occurrence, at least inevitable. What we live with day by day is what there is; the system as it exists is all we have. On one side, this leads to either apathy or rage. On the other, to complacency and certainty.

Whether we have succeeded in school or are succeeding, have failed at school or are failing, whatever we know or don't know about the system, we have experienced school in intensely personal ways. School is experienced by individuals who find differing meanings every minute of every school day, for we come from every imaginable kind of home, and some unimaginable to many of our citizens. We come from radically different cultures, from different socioeconomic backgrounds, from different first languages, and with substantial differences in a range of abilities, capabilities, disabilities, and neural genetic designs. No two people ever experience our educational system in exactly the same way; no two classmates ever experience anything in school exactly the same way, making a common understanding so difficult.

But our system was designed. It was built for specific purposes. It was built by humans who had their own agendas for their own times. If we recognize this history, we may see schools as a work of human minds and human hands and not as something unchangeable.

My intentions behind this brief study began in graduate school confusion. As someone who hated school, I wondered why—as study after study reveals our systemic failure—we continue to do what "we have always done." So, I began reading the words of those who created the schools we know: their words, explanations, and inspirations. I began to ask, "If we don't agree with the beliefs or intentions of the system's creators, why are we committed to their design?"

I have been trying to get to this question since I sat terrified in that classroom corner at age seven. Over the years since, with good teachers and terrible teachers, in schools called "good" and schools called "bad," at every level through a Ph.D. program, I have fought with the system as a student, a teacher, an administrator, and a university instructor. I have fought with sullenness and rage, with refusal and disappearance, with deceit, evasion, and, yes, research. I have yelled and cried, begged and wished, argued and listened, experimented and demonstrated. At least once, that rebellion against a system I could not understand became a rock aimed at the building itself. I was ten. That was the only tool I had.

I have found different tools over the years. I have different tools now. This book is one of those. I hope it is a lever that helps pry open the doors to change.

"He carried me toward the school's front doors. As we moved under the concrete canopy I made my last gesture. I still had the rock in my hand. I threw it as hard as I could at the school. It smashed off the ceramic locomotive on the wall. The band teacher stopped for a moment but said nothing. Then he carried me to the Book Room."—Socol, 2007

Sources:

Akin, K. (2023, May 26). Kim Reynolds signs sweeping Iowa education law on book bans, LGBTQ teaching. What it does: *Des Moines Register*. https://www.desmoinesregister.com/story/news/politics/2023/05/26/iowa-governor-kim-reynolds-signs-law-to-ban-school-books-with-sex-acts-gender-identity-lgbtq/70147865007/

Florida's new standards on Black history curriculum are creating outrage. (2023, August 17). *CNN*. https://www.cnn.com/2023/08/17/us/florida-black-history-backlash-reaj/index.html

Kohn, A. (1998, April 2). *Only for My Kid: How privileged parents undermine school reform (*)*. Alfie Kohn. https://www.alfiekohn.org/article/kid/

Lefty, L. (n.d.). *The long fight for educational equity in NYC*. Museum of the City of New York. Retrieved March 9, 2024, from https://www.mcny.org/story/long-fight-educational-equity-nyc

Murray, S. H. (2024, January 5). Why Parents Struggle So Much in the World's Richest Country. *The Atlantic*. https://www.theatlantic.com/family/archive/2024/01/america-failed-parents-rich-countries-raising-kids/677023/

Nice White Parents. (n.d.). *The New York Times*. Retrieved March 9, 2024, from https://www.nytimes.com/column/nice-white-parents

Politico (2024). Supreme Court rejects Thomas Jefferson high school admissions case https://www.politico.com/news/2024/02/20/supreme-court-thomas-jefferson-high-school-admissions-case-00142170

Socol, I. (2007). *The Drool Room*. Lulu.com.

Talk of the Sound News. (2016, October 10). *A Student Perspective: New Rochelle's educational opportunity gap*. Talk of the Sound. https://talkofthesound.com/2016/10/10/a-student-perspective-new-rochelles-educational-opportunity-gap/

Taylor v. BOARD OF ED. OF CITY SCH. DIST. OF NEW ROCHELLE, 195 F. supp. 231 (S.d.n.y. 1961). (n.d.). Justia Law. Retrieved March 9, 2024, from https://law.justia.com/cases/federal/district-courts/FSupp/195/231/1524480/

CHAPTER ONE:

Why do we have the schools we have?

Education in America was designed from the start to fail children.
That is not our fault, but it is our fault if we don't change that system.

In 2001, Linda Darling Hammond wrote "Inequality in Teaching and Schooling: How Opportunity Is Rationed to Students of Color in America" (Smedley et al., 2001) and noted that "Not only do funding systems allocate fewer resources to poor urban districts than to their suburban neighbors, but studies consistently show that, within these districts, schools with high concentrations of low-income and "minority" students receive fewer instructional resources than others in the same district." She added that "tracking systems exacerbate these inequalities by segregating many low-income and minority students within schools (Kozol, 1991; Taylor & Piche, 1991)." (Smedley et al., 2001)

"The end results of these educational inequalities are increasingly tragic," Darling Hammond wrote. "Those who do not succeed in school are becoming part of a growing underclass, cut off from productive engagement in society... working class young people and adults who were prepared for the disappearing jobs of the past teeter on the brink of downward social mobility." She stated an obvious fact, "Meanwhile, schools have changed slowly. Most are still organized to prepare only about 20% of their students for "thinking work" — those students who are tracked very early into gifted and talented, "advanced," or honors courses."

Darling Hammond works at Stanford University. When she wrote the above, her office was in a building built with a huge donation from the man who codified and mythologized the inequities she describes. She likely has had coffee in the building's cafe, an eatery named in celebration of that former dean.

This casual unexamined intersection of knowledge of the problems in education in the United States and a refusal to engage in the history that created those problems is as dangerous in the field of education as it is in all the other discriminatory structures of the nation. Whether the question regards the incredible inequality of voting power in federal elections, racial inequality in generational wealth and opportunity, or the design of public education Darling Hammond and so many others decry, it is impossible to solve these structural issues without facing the facts about the people who built the system and the beliefs that drove their decision making.

"The Department of the History and Art of Education was one of the original twenty-one departments at Stanford University. Ellwood Patterson Cubberley was the department chair from 1898 to 1917. One of his first hires was Lewis Terman, who modified a French intelligence test to create the Stanford-Binet intelligence scale... in 1917 it was renamed the Stanford University School of Education (SUSE). Cubberley became the first dean of the

School of Education and served in that position until 1933. The Graduate School of Education building, funded in large part by a donation from Cubberley, and Cubberley Library were both built in 1938." —(Wikipedia contributors, 2024a)

It is also impossible to create change without facing the forces that sustain these structures, for the ancient systems that drive the failures in today's United States politics, society, and education do work and work very well for some. And those who benefit from these constructs—and have been enriched by the way things have always been—hold the power to block change.

"Schools should be factories in which raw products, children, are to be shaped and formed into finished products. . . man-ufactured like nails, and the specifications for manufacturing will come from government and industry." — Ellwood Cubberley's dissertation 1905, Teachers College, Columbia University (Wikipedia contributors, 2024a)

Over a century ago, Ellwood Patterson Cubberley built a fictitious history of American education. He worked within a worldview conflating Calvinist orthodoxy, age-of-robber-baron capitalism, and eugenics with democracy, equality, and opportunity. Unless we understand the beliefs behind the design of our public education system and the beliefs that keep the school day in thrall to Cubberley's myth, we can never build the schools our children need.

"We want one class to have a liberal education. We want another class, a very much larger class of necessity, to forego

the privilege of a liberal education and fit themselves to perform specific difficult manual tasks." — Woodrow Wilson (Wikipedia contributors, 2024a)

Open any news website, news app, newspaper, or magazine, or watch any news-based television show, and you will find yourself bombarded with opinions on public education. At the same time, corporations and corporate-funded "think tanks" spend billions lobbying legislatures to increase the profits they make from selling their ideas, apps, and products to schools, parents, and students. If that isn't enough, a large number of America's wealthiest, deeply threatened by any progressive movement that might increase their taxes or ask their offspring to compete with others, have more than doubled down on their mission to destroy public education in the United States along with the opportunities great public schools create.

> *"...they won because supporters of comprehensive high schools defined equal education as equal access to different and unequal programs. Guided by the new IQ tests (which did as much as any single thing to convince American educators that tracking was not only possible but preferable) and the rise of guidance and counseling programs (which could match young people with the curriculum track best suited to their"scientifically" determined individual profiles), America entered an era of democratic dumbing down: the equal opportunity to choose (or be chosen for) failing programs."* — Jeffrey Mirel, The Traditional High School: Historical debates over its nature and function (Mirel, 2006)

For so many young people, this is the existential battle they face daily in the mid-21st century.

The technological and economic transformations of this moment have added radical urgency to these struggles, but in truth, almost nothing about our wars over how we move our children from age four to age 18 or 22 has changed since the beginning of the American nation.

It is difficult to see this history because it is rarely taught or discussed outside a few elective university courses. Thus, it is allowed to lie hidden beneath a flood of commentary from pseudo-experts. Some of these pseudo-experts have degrees in education, but most do not. Many are oligarchs — typically with inherited wealth and power — who run investment, technology, or publishing companies. Another significant group are politicians and those who fund their political careers.

The New York Times education section captured February 26, 2024, at 6.30 am.

The key to understanding why these people say what they say lies in understanding that the "American nobility"— like their old European predecessors — believe they are born genetically superior and that their privileged life stems from this eugenic superiority.

This belief in superiority creates a perceived "right" to determine how best to impose personal choices on others. You see this in the 1770s and 1780s with Benjamin Rush—a Revolutionary War medical doctor, Continental Congress member, and treasurer of the United States—who envisioned, along with Thomas Jefferson, education as a critical means of social control. Rush, according to Urban and Wagoner's *American Education: A History* (Wagoner & Urban, 2013), believed "shared understandings and even conformity was considered necessary in order for Americans to enjoy freedom... Rush could see no irony in proclaiming that it was possible (and desirable to convert men into "republican machines,'" proclaiming, "this must be done if we expect them to perform their parts properly in the great machine of the government of the state."

The need for the powerful to have compliant citizens who will "perform their parts properly in the great machine" extends to the 2020s, as billionaire investor Peter Thiel tries to keep young people out of universities so they do not learn about democracy, social responsibility, or non-white cultures. "[B]ack in 1998, author Jeffrey R. Young (*Young is author of a podcast series called "Doubting College," if you wondered about his position*) wrote in 2023, Thiel "had even co-written a book complaining about how, in his view, multiculturalism was leading to group-think, and how he wanted to "reverse the tragic disintegration of American universities and restore true academic excellence."' (*How a Billionaire's Fellowship Spread Skepticism about College's Value (doubting College, Ep. 1)*, n.d.)

"Academic excellence," to those on the far right of global politics, always means "thinking like me" and returning the United States to its pre-Franklin Roosevelt-New Deal "norm." Rush was building a specific type of white protestant republic, which is what Thiel wants back.

"By this means twenty of the best geniuses will be raked from the rubbish annually, and be instructed at the public expense."
—Jefferson (An Academic's Freedom, n.d.) see also: Cameron Addis, Jefferson and Education (Addis, 2012)

When we understand this consistent positioning of those with tremendous wealth and power, we can comprehend what the educational system in the United States was designed to do, why it was designed to do that, and why it is so resistant to change.

In the beginning, there were two voices. As the 1840s began, a period when information and communications would revolutionize American society (the railroad, the telegraph, the steam-powered rotary printing press, machine-made paper, penny newspapers with mass circulations, and steamships), William Alcott and Horace Mann were the two people talking to the young United States about school.

In the 1840s, everything about human communication changed. News that traveled at horse speed could now cross a nation almost instantaneously and plow across the oceans at unimagined speeds.

Alcott, author of *Confessions of a School Master* (1839) (W. A. Alcott, 1969), was a close observer of students and children. He watched students and teachers and saw what was working for them, what made them uncomfortable, what seemed to make learning go, and what seemed to block it. In the 1830s and 1840s, Alcott would re-design the American schoolroom (W. Alcott, 1831), replacing benches and tables (where children squirmed and fatigued because they could not sit back) with desks and chairs. He would blow apart the existing instructional model by bringing the "Black Board" and slate into the room, changing the presentation scheme, and allowing students to make and correct mistakes. (W. A. Alcott, 1842)

Alcott saw student needs as central — "That the general arrangement and appearance of even inanimate things around us, have an extensive influence in forming our character, will hardly be questioned. *Every object, and every individual we see, either renders us more cheerful and happy, or the contrary.* The condition of those objects, therefore, which surround a collection of children, whether the number of those children be five, fifty, or one hundred, must of necessity have a very considerable influence in forming their dispositions, and giving a determination to their future character," he wrote in an 1831 essay on school design. (W. A. Alcott, 1831)

"Even the slate, if it were at their command continually, would become tiresome. To sit still, at times — entirely still — if not continued too long, is one form of doing something; and I consider it as much a part of the teacher's duty to form his pupils to the habit of sitting still, as to teach them spelling and reading. *Not of course an hour at a time, or half an hour, or a quarter, even. To some children, five minutes would be long enough; and to most, ten minutes would he the full extent of what would be useful,*" he added in his book *Slate and Black Board Exercises* because he was working with a view from the ground. (W. A. Alcott, 1842)

Horace Mann, a social reformer historically proclaimed the "father of the American public school," looked at education from a different vantage point. (Wikipedia contributors, 2024d)

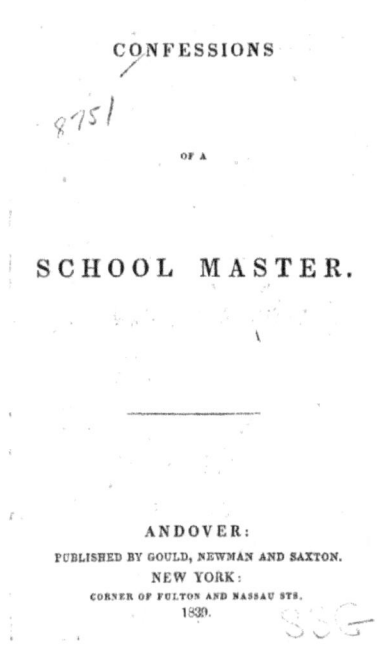

CONFESSIONS

OF A

SCHOOL MASTER.

ANDOVER:
PUBLISHED BY GOULD, NEWMAN AND SAXTON.
NEW YORK:
CORNER OF FULTON AND NASSAU STS.
1839.

1839 edition of Alcott's book

Mann looked down from heaven and saw a nation and a human race in need of perfection. Horace Mann is an incredibly eloquent believer in the potential of our children and our potential to be "better." His vast societal view was charitable and, of course, missionary in style and substance. He would bring education to all in America to correct the social problems of the generations that separated post-revolutionary America from perfection. Yet, he remains a humanist, a believer in human agency: "But it is not every child, nor even a majority of children, who, with any propriety, can be compared to mechanical structures, or to those pliant and ductile materials that are wrought into beautiful forms by the skill of the artisan. Children formed in the prodigality of nature, gifted to exert strong influences upon the race, are not passive; — they are endued with vital and efficient forces of their own. Their capacious and fervid souls were created to melt, and re-cast opinions, codes, and communities as crude ores are melted and purified in the furnace. To the sensitive and resilient natures of such children, an ungentle touch is a sting; a hot word is a living coal," he says in that early lecture.

Mann is Jefferson's successor on public education—without much of the class warfare. He is the person who begins to convince the United States that education must be both a birthright and a societal commitment. However, almost as soon as he begins to move about the nation lecturing, another voice appears—Henry Barnard's.

> *"Had God, then, provided no means by which this part of our nature can be controlled, we should indeed say, that we had been lifted up to heaven in point of privileges, that we might, so much the more certainly, be dashed in pieces by our inevitable fall. But we have not been inexorably subjected to such a doom. If it befalls us, it befalls us with our own consent. Means of escape are vouchsafed; and not of escape only, but of infinite peace and joy.*

> *"The world is to be rescued through physical, intellectual, moral and religious action upon the young."* — Horace Mann, *What God Does, and What He Leaves for Man to Do, in the Work of Education* (1840) (Horace Mann— Secretary to the Board of Education of the State of Massachusetts, 1840)

Before Henry Barnard saw schools as a path to fame and eventual fortune, he was a mercantile-oriented state legislator in Rhode Island with no interest in education. In this way, he is the precursor of all today's pseudo-experts. Like those who trumpet everything from the Science of Reading to vouchers and for-profit charter schools today, Barnard would seize the Public School Movement from Mann before the 1840s would end. He would twist *the father of public education*'s words into something very different. In the end, Horace Mann became, as *so many well-meaning liberals can be,* someone who set out to make a real difference but whose words and image ended up licensed to people and corporations with an entirely different agenda. (*The Unmistakable Tie between Education and Prosperity,* n.d.)

Barnard, like Mann, looked at schools, education, and childhood from 'way above.' But his was not the view from heaven. Rather, his view was from the banker's office, the factory foreman's post, and the mine supervisor.

Year-by-year indoctrination: Education Systems Were First Designed to Suppress Dissent.- image via "Spring Awakening" - Ball State University. (Google Books, n.d.)

At first, he sounds like Mann, although he misses philosophy. "The primary object in securing the early school attendance of children, is not so much their intellectual culture, as the regulation of the feelings and dispositions, the extirpation of vicious propensities, the pre-occupation of the wildeiness of the young heart with the seeds and germs of moral beauty, and the formation of a lovely and virtuous character by the habitual practice of cleanliness, delicacy, refinement, good temper, gentleness, kindness, justice and truth." However, the purposes behind this desired docility are apparent quickly. "By means of such schools, the defective education of many of the youth of our manufacturing population would be remedied, and their various trades and employments be converted into the most efficient instruments of self-culture."

A recent example in the U.S. of the government attempting to hijack school curriculum for political ends was former President Donald J. Trump's 1776 Commission designed to counter the widespread Black Lives Matter protests in the summer of 2020. The commission was charged with promoting "patriotic education," Paglayan said, to supposedly unite Americans. — Christine Clark and Inga Kiderra, University of California — San Diego (Awards & Accolades, n.d.)

In Barnard's world, education was training, not learning. In pursuit of this, Barnard imported the Prussian Model of Education. (Socol, 2018) The Prussian Model was born of that German kingdom's military failings in the Napoleonic Wars. Defeats by the French Levée en masse Army convinced the Prussians to create an educational system designed to indoctrinate children, year-by-year, from age 6 to 16, into full compliance with the state and its military leaders. (The point was, bluntly, to ensure that "no German soldier would ever disobey an order again.") (Wikipedia contributors, 2024b) Barnard wasn't building an army; he was building a compliant workforce to fill factories and mines, so the preparation — year-by-year with age-based grades — was for the assembly lines developing in the gun factories and textile mills of his native New England. He introduced rigid time schedules to schools to prepare the students for the emerging industrial shift work. A little later, he would push for economic efficiencies, lowering teacher pay by replacing male teachers with women while standardizing school buildings and instruction. (Mann had brought a dualism to the "women teacher issue" (*Aspects of the Changing Status of New England Women, 1790-1840*, n.d.) — "*That females are better fitted by nature than males to train and educate young children is a position, which the public mind is fast maturing into an axiom. With economical habits in regard to all school expenditures, it is a material fact, that the services of females can be commanded for half the price usually paid to males. But what is of far higher moment is, that they are endowed by nature with a stronger affection for children; they have quicker sympathies, livelier sensibilities, and more vivid and enduring parental instincts.*" — Common School Journal (Boston), vol. 1, no. 6 (March 15, 1839) — Barnard would use Mann's words while emphasizing the savings and ensuring that women never held decision-making positions within the system.)

Former DC Schools Superintendent Michelle Rhee (Lemann, 2013) *was celebrated by the Obama Administration, by Oprah, and in the media for disparaging the community, its teachers, and children (she even endorsed taping children's mouths shut).* (Warner, 2010) *White politicians and "philanthrocapitalists"* (Hopkinson, 2010) *were furious when led*

by the votes of Black mothers, the District of Columbia fired her and the mayor who hired her. Image, Time Magazine Cover December 8, 2008. ("TIME Magazine Cover: How To Fix America's Schools - Dec. 8, 2008," n.d.)

From this beginning, we see two fundamentally different ways of viewing the purpose of education, or two and a half. And these visions persist today and explain our current battles over schools.

On a weekend night in 2010, this exchange appeared among friends of mine on Twitter:

"Spent last night with cousins, three of whom are teachers — never heard of [the 2010 attacks on education] KIPP, Rhee, ("It Was Hailed as the National Model for School Reform. Then the Scandals Hit," 2018*) or Waiting for Superman. Surprising conversation."* Karen Janowski on Twitter (Janowski, 2010)

"@KarenJan doesn't surprise me one bit. The vast majority of teachers, for better or worse, are blindly focused on their classroom and kids." Jonathan Becker on Twitter ([No Title], n.d.)

Teachers, and most teacher educators, are, as Dr. Becker said, "blindly focused on their classroom and kids." (Jonathan D. Becker, J.D., Ph.D, n.d.) I've worked with hundreds of dedicated, inventive teachers and administrators from Virginia and Massachusetts, San Diego and Florida, Oregon and Pennsylvania. There are tens of thousands more working with students every day, trying to make the changes they can in the lives and learning of our students. "We" are the William Alcotts of today, the Maria Montessoris of today. (Wikipedia contributors, 2024c)

Today's versions of Henry Barnard, those building careers or reputations by ensuring that education works in the service of United States capitalism, are the edu-entrepreneurs, the edu-opinionators, and the edu-politicians from Ron DeSantis to Eric Adams. They all know as little as they care — but they are building their brands on the backs of our most vulnerable. They look down from corporate suites and corruptly furnished political offices and claim that education is failing to produce the compliant workers/citizens their businesses or political contributors need.

These are education's industrialists, with absolutely no sense that a student is different than any other industrially processed part and no sense that a teacher is any different than any industrial worker. For this group, education is measured as industrial processing is measured, parts (students) not successfully processed in any industrial step (grade) are re-processed (retained), and unions for the line workers (teachers) are dangerous because they interfere with the cost structure.

Those committed to human children and those committed to industrial capitalism cannot understand each other because they simply do not see the same thing when they look at "school."

"Historical study of the age-grade efficiency movement which took firm root in North America ... during the early 1900s, in particular the preoccupation of education authorities with "the retardation problem" (the number of scholars over-aged for grade in consequence of their failure to make "normal" annual progress through the course of instruction), importantly contributes to understanding the age-grade homogeneity of modern elementary schools ...seeks to provide comparative insights into measures adopted to reduce retardation in the interests of preserving school order, enhancing pedagogical and bureaucratic "efficiency," improving access to secondary courses, and alleviating the costs of "laggards"

to the state." — Lynne Trethewey— the origin of our "students have fallen behind" theories based on the need to make industrial-style education "efficient." (Trethewey, 1999) https://doi.org/10.2307/370009

That half-step—Horace Mann and the many who sign on with the industrialists—are the missionaries. Their heavenly view, however well-meaning, plays into the industrialists' hands, giving moral cover to brutal colonialism and economic oppression.

And brutal it is. We cannot understand why schools in the United States use age-based grades and standardized tests and why two-thirds of students do badly — consistently — unless we understand why Barnard and his successors built the system they did. The system they built endures, processing our children, as Cubberley noted, in "factories in which raw products, children, are to be shaped and formed into finished products," while discarding "defective" raw materials along the way.

Sources:

Addis, C. (2012). Jefferson and Education. In *The Blackwell Companion to Thomas Jefferson* (pp. 457–473). Wiley Online Library. https://onlinelibrary.wiley.com/doi/pdf/10.1002/97814443446 39#page=473

Alcott, W. (1831). *Essay on the Construction of School Houses* (p. 6). Hilliard, Gray, Littleton, and Wilkins; Harvard University, Harvard Graduate School of Education, Library.

Alcott, W. A. (1842). Slate and Black Board Exercises for Common Schools. *Connecticut Common School Journal (1838-1853)*, *4*(8), 69–84.

Alcott, W. A. (1969). *Confessions of a School Master*. Arno Press.

An Academic's Freedom. (n.d.). Retrieved March 9, 2024, from https://academicsfreedom.blogspot.com/2010/12/raking-geniuses-from-rubbish.html

Aspects of the changing status of New England women, 1790-1840. (n.d.). Retrieved March 9, 2024, from https://www.teachushistory.org/detocqueville-visit-united-states/articles/aspects-changing-status-new-england-women

Awards, & Accolades. (n.d.). *Educate to indoctrinate: Education systems were first designed to suppress dissent*. Retrieved March 9, 2024, from https://today.ucsd.edu/story/education-systems-were-first-designed-to-suppress-dissent

Google Books. (n.d.). Retrieved March 9, 2024, from https://www.google.com/books/edition/Education_Free_and_Compulsory/vrZSPId9H8YC?hl=en&gbpv=1&dq=prussian+education+-suppression+of+dissent&pg=PR1&printsec=frontcover

Hopkinson, N. (2010, September 15). Why Michelle Rhee's Education "Brand" Failed in D.C. *The Atlantic*. https://www.theatlantic.com/politics/archive/2010/09/why-michelle-rhees-education-brand-failed-in-dc/63014/

Horace Mann (Secretary to the Board of Education of the State of Massachusetts.). (1840). *Lecture on Education*.

How a billionaire's fellowship spread skepticism about college's value (doubting college, ep. 1). (n.d.). SoundCloud. Retrieved March 9, 2024, from https://soundcloud.com/edsurge/how-a-billionaires-fellowship-spread-skepticism-about-colleges-value-doubting-college-ep-1?utm_source=www.edsurge.com&utm_campaign=wtshare&utm_medium=widget&utm_content=https%253A%252F%252Fsoundcloud.com%252Fedsurge%252Fhow-a-billionaires-fellowship-spread-skepticism-about-colleges-value-doubting-college-ep-1

It was hailed as the national model for school reform. Then the scandals hit. (2018, March 10). *The Washington Post*. https://www.washingtonpost.com/local/education/dc-school-scandals-tell-me-that-its-not-great-and-that-youre-dealing-with-it/2018/03/10/b73d9cf0-1d9e-11e8-b2d9-08e748f892c0_story.html

Janowski, K. (2010, September 25). *Spent last night with cousins, three of whom are tchrs - never heard of KIPP, Rhee, or Waiting for Superman. Surprising conversation*. Twitter. https://twitter.com/KarenJan/status/25495453479

Jonathan D. Becker, J.d., ph.D. (n.d.). Jonathan D. Becker, J.D., Ph.D. Retrieved March 9, 2024, from https://www.jonbecker.net/

Lemann, N. (2013, May 20). *How Michelle Rhee misled education reform.* The New Republic. https://newrepublic.com/article/113096/how-michelle-rhee-misled-education-reform

Mirel, J. (2006). The Traditional High School: Historical Debates over Its Nature and Function. *Education Next, 6*(1), 14–21.

Smedley, B. D., Stith, A. Y., Colburn, L., Evans, C. H., & Institute of Medicine (US). (2001). *Inequality in Teaching and Schooling: How Opportunity Is Rationed to Students of Color in America.* National Academies Press (US).

Socol, I. D. (2018, August 5). *The Prussian Model and the failure of personal ethics.* Medium. https://irasocol.medium.com/the-prussian-model-and-the-failure-of-personal-ethics-83cf46602c92

The unmistakable tie between education and prosperity. (n.d.). George W. Bush Presidential Center. Retrieved March 9, 2024, from https://www.bushcenter.org/catalyst/freedom/geoffrey-canada-education

TIME Magazine Cover: How To Fix America's Schools - Dec. 8, 2008. (n.d.). *Time.* Retrieved March 9, 2024, from https://content.time.com/time/covers/0,16641,20081208,00.html

Trethewey, L. (1999). Solving "The Retardation Problem" in Primary Education: The Case of South Australia. *History of Education Quarterly, 39*(3), 263–290.

Wagoner, J. L., Jr., & Urban, W. J. (2013). *American Education: A History.* Routledge.

Warner, J. (2010, October 1). Is Michelle Rhee's Revolution Over? *The New York Times.* https://www.nytimes.com/2010/10/03/magazine/03fob-wwln-t.html

Wikipedia contributors. (2024a, January 3). *Stanford University Graduate School of Education.* Wikipedia, The Free Encyclopedia. https://en.wikipedia.org/w/index.php?title=Stanford_University_Graduate_School_of_Education&oldid=1193440949

Wikipedia contributors. (2024b, February 4). *Levée en masse.* Wikipedia, The Free Encyclopedia. https://en.wikipedia.org/w/index.php?title=Lev%C3%A9e_en_masse&oldid=1203180879

Wikipedia contributors. (2024c, March 7). *Maria Montessori.* Wikipedia, The Free Encyclopedia. https://en.wikipedia.org/w/index.php?title=Maria_Montessori&oldid=1212436308

Wikipedia contributors. (2024d, March 8). *Horace Mann.* Wikipedia, The Free Encyclopedia. https://en.wikipedia.org/w/index.php?title=Horace_Mann&oldid=1212463290

CHAPTER TWO:

Why we believe our system is not just good but inevitable.
How our schools became agents of nativist Calvinist
capitalism with eugenics deeply ingrained.

*"We know that the number of children of superior ability is
approximately as large as the number of the feeble in mind,
and also that the future of democratic government hinges
largely on the proper education and utilization of these these
superior children. One child of superior intellectual capacity,
educated so as to utilize his talents, may confer greater benefits upon mankind, and be educationally far more important,
than a thousand of the feeble-minded children upon whom
we have recently come to put so much educational effort and
expense." Ellwood Cubberley 1922* (Cubberley, 1922)

- Why do we have rectangular classrooms with a "teaching wall" at the front?
- Why do we line up student's chairs in rows so often?
- Why do we have lectures?
- Why are all in a class expected to be on the same page of a book?
- Why do we divide learners by age?
- Why do we grade students on a linear scale?
- Why aren't all children included?
- Why do we have notions of tardiness and truancy?
- Why do we have a set daily schedule?
- Why do we line students up when they walk through a hall?
- Why is silence preferred?

Let us begin with just those questions because while any of us might have a hundred more, it's important to understand that these rarely examined norms are neither truly traditional nor research-based. All are structural concepts crafted from religious beliefs, the superiority of white English-speaking protestants to all others, and the desires of the new class of capitalists appearing during the late First (Wikipedia contributors, 2024h) and early Second Industrial Revolutions. (Mokyr, J., & Strotz, R.H., 1998)

We need to ask ourselves if we believe the same things as the designers of our system did. If we don't agree with the designers about the desired outcomes, we must ask why we continue to use their processes.

> Our schools are, in a sense, factories, in which the raw products (children) are to be shaped and fashioned into products to meet the various demands of life. The specifications for manufacturing come from the demands of twentieth-century civilization, and it is the business of the school to build its pupils according to the specifications laid down.
>
> — *Ellwood Patterson Cubberley* —
>
> AZ QUOTES

AZ Quotes (Cubberley, n.d.)

This is important to consider every day if we work in, around, or with schools because far from being "the old way," the schools we have had over the past 200 years are, in fact, a radical experiment in classification, indoctrination, and filtering. And that indoctrination is not the kind Fox News talks about — not at all.

Between 1840 and World War I, the United States went from this: "One error still prevails to a ruinous extent, namely: the neglect of cultivating and developing the powers of the mind, while every thing is attempted to be done by taxing memory with the weight of names and abstractions, allowing no play for thought, and exciting no interest whatever in the child's mind. It seems as if many of our teachers and bookmakers, from the highest to the lowest departments, forget that children have minds, and suppose that the only powers they will ever possess, are to be imparted by teachers, whereas the teacher ought to know that he cannot impart a single iota of power. The most he can do, is, to develop powers already in existence, and because the attempt has been made rather to create than to cultivate, the mind of man has, in many cases, been actually cramped and weakened rather than strengthened at school." — Report of Mr. Lewis, Superintendent of Common Schools of Ohio *(1839)* (Google Books, n.d.-a)

...to schools filled with lockstep curriculum, segregation by born-on-date, segregation by race and social class, rigid beliefs about behavior and dress, opportunities only offered to some students, and the full — if sometimes unconscious — belief that some children, some genetic makeups, and some cultures are inferior to others. That did not happen by accident.

"Darryl George, 18, has not been in his regular classroom in Barbers Hill High School in Mont Belvieu since Aug. 31. Instead, he has either been serving in-school suspension or spending time in an off-site disciplinary program...His Houston-area school district, Barbers Hill, has said George's long hair, which he wears in neatly tied and twisted locs on top of his head, violates a district dress code that limits hair length for boys." — AP News (Lozano, 2024)

"...being an American requires conformity. We will not lose sight of the main goal — high standards for our students — by bending to political pressure or responding to misinformed media reports. These entities have 'lesser' goals that ultimately harm kids." Greg Poole, Superintendent Barbers Hill Independent School District, Texas (Superintendent, n.d.)

Is public education about learning and opportunity? Or training and control? Is it about the "individualism" Americans so often proclaim? Or is it about conformity and compliance, as the Texas superintendent above insists? Is it about equity? Or is it about ensuring educated elites stay above what Marxists call the masses? *The New York Times*)? (Miller et al., 2024)

> *"School has truly become an inexpensive form of police, one whose very authority is supported by the argument that it is a place that helps the individual, and that an individual's interests cannot be separated from social needs"* — Joel Spring, *The Politics of American Education* (Spring, 2010)

The transition from enlightenment to capitalist/Calvinist indoctrination started at the very beginning but became baked into the fabric of education largely through the writings and theories of one man:

"From the point of view of American educational history the most important developments in connection with the Reformation were those arising from Calvinism. While the Calvinistic faith was rather grim and forbidding, viewed from the modern standpoint, the Calvinists everywhere had a program for political, economic, and social progress which has left a deep impress on the history of mankind. This program demanded the education of all, and in the countries where Calvinism became dominant the leaders included general education in their scheme of religious, political, and social reform... In his plan for the schools of Geneva, published in 1538, he outlined a system of elementary education in the vernacular for all. which involved instruction in reading, writing, arithmetic, religion, careful grammatical drill, and training for civil as well as for ecclesiastical leadership." — *Ellwood Cubberley*

Ellwood Cubberley was the most influential person in educational practice from 1910 to 1960. He wrote the textbooks read by aspiring teachers and school administrators. *Public Education in the United*

States: A Study and Interpretation of American Educational History, among many others. (Cubberley, Ellwood Patterson, 1868-1941, n.d.)

> Cubberley's books: *Public Education in the United States: A Study and Interpretation of American Educational History, The Principal and His School: The Organization, Administration, and Supervision of Instruction in an Elementary School, An Introduction to the Study of Education and to Teaching, The History of Education: Educational Practice and Progress Considered as a Phase of the Development and Spread of Western Civilization, State School Administration: A Textbook of Principles, Public School Administration: A Statement of the Fundamental Principles Underlying the Organization and Administration of Public Education*

He was also many things, including an admirer of European fascism, a believer in eugenics, a believer in Anglo-White Supremacy, and an evangelical autocrat. (*Ellwood Cubberley*, n.d.) Among his many despicable beliefs that informed his ideas of educational practice included seeing Eastern European immigrants — Jewish and working class — as a eugenic threat to the nation, describing them as "*largely illiterate, docile, lacking in initiative, and almost wholly without the Anglo-Saxon conceptions of righteousness, liberty, law, order, public decency, and government, their coming has served to dilute our national stock and to weaken and corrupt our political life.*'" Dennis Carlson of Miami University adds, "[Cubberley's] belief that intelligence tests provided an objective assessment of native ability, he was led to conclude that African-Americans were, like Eastern Europeans, largely lacking in intellectual ability." (Carlson, 2009)

Miss Columbia's School (1894 cartoon based on 1869 book) -
California State University Bakersfield (Google Books, n.d.-b)

To understand Cubberley and his mission in full, we need to go back to the 1840s when white America faced a radical new challenge, the arrival of a mass of poor, "uneducated," non-English-speaking and non-Protestant immigrants from the great famine in Ireland. (Date & Great Hunger - History, 2017)

That these immigrants were not Protestant was seen as the biggest problem. These Catholic immigrants came with religious traditions very different than those mythologized arrivals at Plymouth Rock. They didn't all go to Mass at the same time. They didn't use books in the Mass. Their churches were not plain white boxes but spaces filled with many distractions that represented many different teaching methods (stained glass windows, statues, icons, taste, smell, and movement). They definitely did not bring a "Protestant Work Ethic" (Google Books, n.d.-c) with them — and did not see the value in work for work's sake.

(Max Weber noted that Capitalism/Mercantilism may not have arisen without a shift from Catholicism to Calvinism, creating a social order where excess work was considered Godly, and wealth indicated that one was part of God's "elect.") (*History of Work Ethic--4. Protestantism and the Protestant Ethic*, n.d.)

> *"What Weber was arguing was that Calvinism produced a 'spirit' which contributed to the social conditions which in turn produced a class of merchants and bankers who rationalised both the means of production and the flow of finance." — Donald Macleod* (Macleod, n.d.)

None of this was acceptable to the leaders of the time — outside of big-city Democrats who saw potential voters. Even abolitionists — the great left wing of that moment — were anti-immigrant. One belief of the Republican Party has never wavered — it was formed, in significant part, by members of the xenophobic "[Native] American Party" (The Know-Nothings) and has opposed the immigration of "defective foreigners" in every decade.

Thomas Nast, whose cartoons show up so often in our history textbooks, produced many anti-Catholic, and specifically, anti-Irish works - Harper's Weekly 1871 - CUSLAR (Cuslar, 2014)

So public schooling — still rare in many parts of the U.S. at the time, became a popular engine of conversion. These Catholic children would learn English. They would attend class in rectangular white boxes that mimicked Calvinist New England churches. They would be put on a tight schedule, read the Protestant Bible, and learn that working on meaningless assignments was next to Godliness. Which begins to answer all those questions at this chapter's beginning.

"One of the most remarkable features of the American free school is its almost infinite power of assimilation, and this is one of the greatest works which the school does. It draws children from all nations together, and marks them with the impress of nationality. Mr. Pawson says: " The school has more to do than to educate the children: it is the mill, so to speak, into which go children of English, Scotch, Irish, German, Russian, Italian, and Scandinavian parents, and come out Americans. Africa contributes its negroes, and now Asia is sending its Chinese. All must learn English, and the result will soon be that the population of the United States will be the most homogeneous of nations." — Francis Adams. (Adams, 1875)

I began my dissertation on how America's education became what it is with a quote from author and civil rights activist Eamon McCann about The Troubles in the north of Ireland: *"Time tends to impose order on the past. We look back on the early days and think we discern the outline of what comes later...Knowing now how things happened, we assume this is the way it was bound to be...But the trajectory wasn't pre-set. The chaos we felt around us was for real, and rich in possibilities other than those which came to pass."* (Melaugh, n.d.)

The Horatio Alger Myth was a vital part of the conversion of capitalist purpose to Christian National Belief - image: Project Gutenberg: Sink or Swim; Or, Harry Raymond's Resolve by Jr. (Horatio Alger, n.d.)

There is nothing that was inevitable or natural in the way schools came to operate. They were intentionally designed for very specific purposes, purposes with very ugly beliefs lying beneath.

It was one thing for Henry Barnard to design a U.S. education system that would divide children in the most effective way for capitalist industrialism. It was another thing to import a system from authoritarian Prussia designed to foster compliant nationalism and train imperial soldiers. But we would not be living with that system today if not for a system of religious and national mythology embracing that system and making it seem the inevitable result of a progressive, God-inspired nation. (Wikipedia contributors, 2023a)

Politics can and do shift but the essential myths that define a nation create enduring institutions. This is a vital concept for the United States which has barely altered its government structure since 1787 and maintains the voting and representational systems of Queen Anne's 18th century Britain. (Wikipedia contributors, 2024o)

"Like other eugenicists, he feared the immigration of these populations would impact the racial health of the nation: "[T]heir coming has served to dilute tremendously our national stock." Because of this, Cubberley was a proponent of Americanization, the teaching of "American values" in hopes of

removing the culture of immigrants. He promoted a system of education that favored certain populations for their eugenic fitness while exerting control on unwanted groups."—Ben Maldonado, Eugenics on the Farm: Ellwood Cubberley in the *Stanford Daily*, 2020 (Maldonado, 2020)

The United States, lacking a defining specific religion or a native identity, has created and embraced a civil religion based primarily on economic beliefs. The U.S. did not become a nation through the identity formation of "Romantic Nationalism," (Wikipedia contributors, 2024d) because the nation came first. (More traditional Romantic Nationalism is represented by the Irish liberation movement (Wikipedia contributors, 2024i) with its literature (see Declan Kiberd's *Inventing Ireland*), (Kiberd, 1996) sport, and re-embrace of Gaeilge, (Wikipedia contributors, 2024m) or the Zionist movement (Wikipedia contributors, 2024k) with the Maccabiah myths (*Achievements and Challenges*, 2005) and re-establishment of the ancient Hebrew language). (Wikipedia contributors, 2024l) Even the "American Dream" is understood as an economic goal.

That civil religion has become a powerful force in education because in schools, as in economics, it converts arguments for change from political disagreement into heresy.

In 2010, on the blogposts that were the origin of this book, teacher Lisa Parisi commented, *"Seems like we teachers have two choices.... work within the system to help students succeed or fight the system and lose our jobs. Not a good choice either way. And having our government choose people to revamp the system and not choose any educators, is a clear message that the goal is to maintain the system, not help the children."* (Socol, 2010) Lisa sums up the predicament the system creates for teachers. In the same week, teacher William Chamberlain (Chamberlain, n.d.) asked, *"Do you think when teachers are confronted with the reason school is the way it is they will accept it or rebel? Do we simply need to educate teachers about why they teach how they teach?* (Socol, 2010) They may rebel, but the odds against that rebellion winning are long. In the past 300 years, only the French Revolution (Wikipedia contributors, 2024q) permanently altered a society's belief structures. (Wikipedia contributors, 2023c)

There were other choices during the 19th and early 20th centuries. William Alcott and Louisa Parsons Hopkins (Wikipedia contributors, 2024a) stand out as educators who believed in humane, learner-centered learning. Ella Flagg Young (Socol, 2021) — the first woman to be superintendent of Chicago's schools, fought long and hard, along with many progressive women in the 1920s. But their voices were all deemed heretical in a world codified by Cubberley and his predecessors.

> *A pragmatist, [Ella Flagg] Young believed that any student, regardless of ability, should be able to learn. She wasn't a fan of dividing students into grades as much as she was of teachers building relationships with children to tailor their instruction. She wrote a book called Isolation in the Schools, bemoaning a lack of collaboration among teachers, administrators, and students."* — *Education Reform's Forgotten Thought Leader (The 74)* (Stringer, 2018)

The "Civil Religion" of the United States did not arise with the Revolutionary generation; it began to develop when the nascent Second Industrial Revolution joined the uniquely American "Second Great Awakening." (Wikipedia contributors, 2024c) This, historically, coincided with the "invention" of the U.S. public education system, with schools becoming the missions of the new theology.

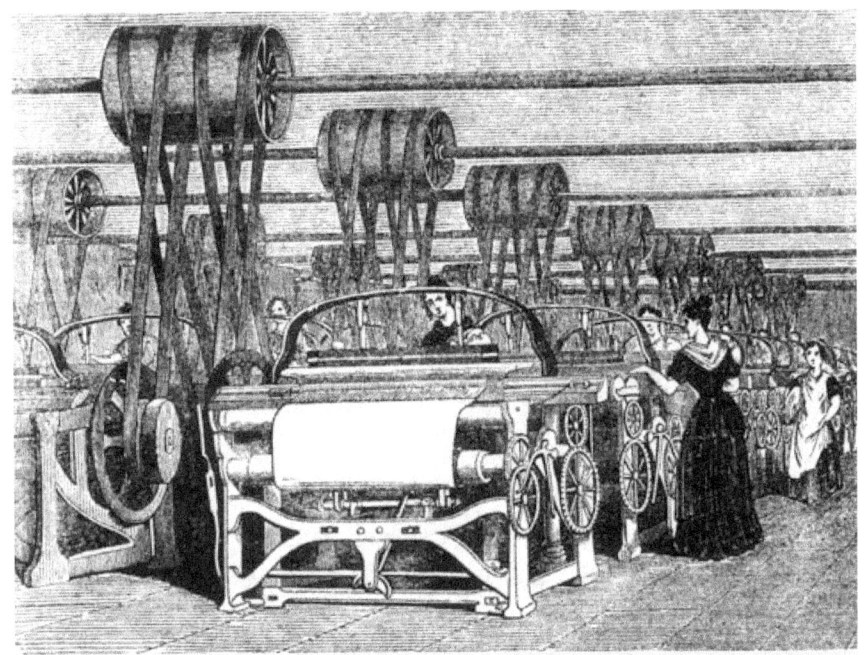

A shift from water power to steam power led the nation into the Second Industrial Revolution. Steam power removed nature from its determining role in the work week. - image via University of Houston (Halton, 1982)

Throughout the 19th Century, as Henry Barnard's system was being "authored," the religion grew alongside it. America was "the last great hope of earth" (Zangwill, 1916), as Lincoln said, with a divine mission. America was "a light unto the world" and the furthest advance of Western civilization. This religion had specific components that were embedded both in the educational system and in the public's attitude toward that system, requiring uniformity of belief and worship — as most Protestant sects do. In turn, this led directly to the "melting pot" concept of American immigration, in which those seeking to join the society would be converted into "Americans." (Wikipedia contributors, 2024e)

*"The fusing process goes on as in a blast-furnace; one genera-
tion, a single year even — transforms the English, the German,
the Irish emigrant into an American. Uniform institutions,
ideas, language, the influence of the majority, bring us soon
to a similar complexion; the individuality of the immigrant,
almost even his traits of race and religion, fuse down in the
democratic alembic like chips of brass thrown into the melting pot."* — Titus Munson Coan (1875) (Coan, 1875)

Schools would be the smelter, replacing the disappearing frontier
that Turner called "the crucible." (Turner, 1920) "The population of
New York City is by no means homogenous," New York Governor — and
later Lincoln's Secretary of State — William Seward said in 1842, "on
the contrary, it is the object of education to make it so." (Harper, 1968)

The civil religion's moral code was essential to the nation's
economic system. Literature played a vital part in this, and it was
transmitted through reading instruction in the schoolhouse, exactly
as the Christian Bible was transmitted through the catechisms of the
Protestant churches.

The "Great Awakenings" of the early and mid-19th century created the concept of the American nation as a "Christian - explicitly Protestant, not Catholic - Nation" in the minds of many. Image of 1819 revival via Wikipedia Commons. (Wikipedia contributors, 2024c)

bee busy buzz sing work

We fly about from flower to flower.
We sing as we work.

 Would you like to know
what we sing?
We sing, " Buzz, buzz."
You will say,
" What a funny way to sing!"
But we do not care what you say.
We are too busy to think about it.
You must not keep us from our work.
What is as busy as a bee?
All day it sings as it works,
" Buzz, buzz, buzz!"

How doth the little busy bee
Improve each shining hour?
It gathers honey all the day
From every bud and flower.

§ bees buzz busy z

60

Busy Bees — the McGuffey Readers (Google Books, n.d.-d)

The McGuffey Readers, the Horatio Alger stories, and the frontier tales of Daniel Boone et al. formed the nation's mythic individual, so different from the communitarian Catholicism and Socialism of late 19th Century continental Europe. In this "America," any joining together of any non-wealthy subgroup was discouraged (whether labor unions (Commons, 1905) or The Grange (*Grange Movement: Patrons of Husbandry*, n.d.)) because "real Americans" worked their way up through individual hard work and moral rightness. This required education to be a competitive environment, where the old peer teaching of the one-room schoolhouse vanished. (*SpeEdChange*, n.d.)

Schools in the U.S. thus attempt to treat all equally as opposed to equitably. We pretend that all are born with the same opportunities and that effort and proper behavior are what matters, what will determine success or failure. This is an educational effort designed to block the revolutionary impulses the 19th-century power structure saw threatening Europe's economic and social structure, where even a Kaiser like Wilhelm II (Wikipedia contributors, 2024f) ruled a nation that was essentially socialist. (*Social Security History*, n.d.)

This leads us to the idea that failure in America's economic system is an individual moral, not a systemic, problem. This is part of a vast wealth preservation scheme that has always been at odds with the thought that public education might indeed open opportunities.

> *"The Horatio Alger myth conveys three basic messages: (1) each of us is judged solely on her or his own merits; (2) we each have a fair opportunity to develop those merits; and (3) ultimately, merit will out. Each of them is, to be charitable, problematic. The first message is a variant on the rugged individualism ethos . . . . In this form, it suggests that success in life has nothing to do with pedigree, race, class background, gender, national origin, sexual orientation — in short, with anything beyond our individual control. Those variables may exist, but they play no appreciable role in how our actions are appraised." — Harlon Dalton.* (Dalton, 1996, p. 261)

Those with wealth, power, and status believe they are superior, and the possibility of increasing competition in public education is devastatingly dangerous to them.

This explains (*see chapter four*) the constant battle to suppress ideas that might make public education both accessible and successful. No matter what actual research shows — those with wealth, power, and status produce a steady drumbeat of arguments as to why their definition of "merit" — born with excess financial and/or social capital — is the only valid definition. (Greene, 2024)

"The tests are not measuring how much students learned or can learn," says Tienken. "They are predominately measuring the family and community capital of the student." — Forbes Magazine, 2024 (Greene, 2024)

This brings us — finally — to Ellwood Cubberley and the permanence of our system. (Wikipedia contributors, 2023b) Cubberley, the Teachers College (*Graduate School of Education*, n.d.) trained teacher educator, stood astride American education in the first half of the 20th Century like a colossus from his chair at Stanford University. (*Stanford Graduate School of Education*, n.d.)

"Let me tell you about the very rich. They are different from you and me. They possess and enjoy early, and it does something to them, makes them soft where we are hard, and cynical where we are trustful, in a way that, unless you were born rich, it is very difficult to understand. They think, deep in their hearts, that they are better than we are because we had to discover the compensations and refuges of life for ourselves. Even when they enter deep into our world or sink below us, they still think that they are better than we are. They are different." — F. Scott Fitzgerald, *The Rich Boy, 1925 (The Rich Boy, n.d.)*

It was Cubberley who wrote the civil religion narrative permanently into the American education system through his books and his deep impact on teacher training. When the history of U.S. education began to be re-investigated after the Second World War, Cubberley's influence was obvious. Teachers College professor Lawrence Cremin (*Lawrence*

Arthur Cremin, n.d.) devoted an entire book to tearing him down (*The Wonderful World of Ellwood Patterson Cubberley*) (Cremin, 1965), but today he is mostly forgotten, and that is a massive mistake. The historiography of our education system matters more than we want to imagine — and no one impacted that more than Cubberley.

Mike Duncan (Wikipedia contributors, 2024b) of the Revolutions Podcast — one of the best contemporary history texts you can engage with — discusses Marxist historical materialism in his episode 10.4 (season 10 being devoted to the Russian Revolution). (Seaquence, 2023b) "Essentially all the prevailing morality," Duncan says, "is the morality of the ruling class imposed on everyone else. Instilling in the exploited class a set of beliefs designed to do little more than rationalize the fact that they are being exploited and why that's fine." This is as true in our educational history as it is in our economic history. Then Duncan explains Cubberley's role (without ever discussing Cubberley or education): "The ruling ideology imprints itself and makes it seem this is the way it's always been and always will be." (Seaquence, 2023b)

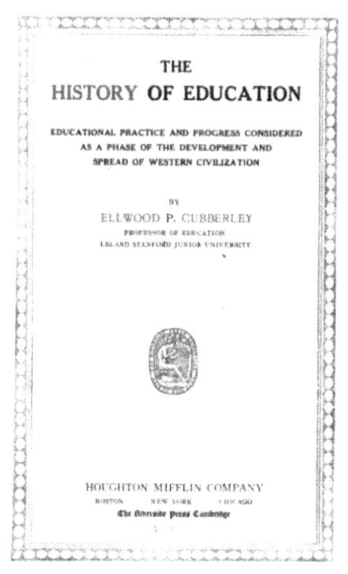

Cubberley's History of Education (Cubberley, 1922)

Thus, many tend to accept the "school as we know it" as inevitable and, thus, what we know must be "the right way."

Like his university-level and political parallel Woodrow Wilson, Cubberley was remaking the world as safe for the white elite. Creating a rational, stable planet for both the business of America and its middle-class joys. What was being done for "the other," whether that was working-class children or Czech independence proponents, was being done for a potent combination of the economic self-interest of the powerful (nations economically and militarily dependent on France, a stable and low-wage workforce) and the "feel good" warmth of liberal accomplishment. (Cohrs, 2006) Thus, Cubberley and Wilson embarked on a systemic re-design of the world — Cubberley through schools, Wilson through borders and government structures — which would be apparently permanent because they were proposed as inevitable. It does not matter whether one is discussing "technique of instruction" (Cubberley, 1922, p. 729) and "the scientific organization of education" (Cubberley, 1922, p. 824) or defensible borders and national self-determination — all are described as products of logical evolution in a "just" universe.

You should really listen to Mike Duncan's "Revolutions" podcasts... start with episode 10.3 (Seaquence, 2023a) *if you're not willing to tackle it all. You do not need to subscribe to Marxist economic theory, historical determinism* (Basu & Brooks, n.d.), *or Marxist literary theory* (Eagleton, 1976) *to appreciate that Karl Marx as a historian.*

Just how enduring this inevitability can be seen in education and politics. In education, "we" continue to pursue the scientific and the "proper technique" (though we now say "evidence-based practice") despite never finding an actual way to measure human learning. In the global political realm, we continue to pursue "self-determination" unless — of course — we don't for reasons of "defensible borders" or the status of allies (Kosovo good (Wikipedia contributors, 2024g), Catalonia bad (Wikipedia contributors, 2024p). Georgia good (Wikipedia contributors, 2024n), South Ossetia bad) (Wikipedia contributors, 2024j).

Our young continue to be called into service for both educational and global military missions and are demonized if they fail to achieve results that remain as impossible now as they were in 1899 or 1917.

As we debate education today, Cubberley, despite the café named for him (*Cubberley Cafe*, n.d.) beneath the College of Education in Palo Alto, has disappeared — and with him, our understanding of the "how" and "why" in our current arguments. Cubberley is only mentioned twice in Tyack and Cuban's *Tinkering toward Utopia*, though we may assume the authors sometimes lunched in the eponymous cafe. (Tyack & Cuban, 1995) In Cuban's massive *How Teachers Taught*, Cubberley is similarly absent (four mentions in 293 pages). (Cuban, 1984) In Richard Altenbaugh's *The American People and Their Education*, Cubberley is not mentioned at all. (Altenbaugh, 2002)

"Since 1900, and due more to the activity of persons concerned with social legislation and those interested in improving the moral welfare of children than to educators themselves, there has been a general revision of the compulsory education laws of our States and the enactment of much new child-welfare... and anti-child-labor legislation....These laws have brought into the schools not only the truant and the incorrigible, who under former conditions either left early or were expelled, but also many children...who have no aptitude for book learning and many children of inferior mental qualities who do not profit by ordinary classroom procedures... Our schools have come to contain many children who... become a nuisance in the school and tend to demoralize school procedure." Gatto quoting Cubberley (Gatto, 2000b)

This is deeply problematic, for it is Cubberley's "victory" over Louisa Parsons Hopkins (Wikipedia contributors, 2024a), Ella Flagg Young, Marie Montessori, and John Dewey that permanized the system and created the canonical text under which almost all of our schools operate. Further from the mainstream of teacher and administrator training, John Taylor Gatto does offer over 30 references to Cubberley in *The Underground History of American Education: A Schoolteacher's Intimate Investigation into the Problem of Modern Schooling*: "Immediate action was called for. Cubberley's celebratory history doesn't examine motives, but does uneasily record forceful steps taken just inside the new century to nip the career of intellectual schooling for the masses in the bud, replacing it with a different goal: the forging of "well-adjusted" citizens." (Gatto, 2000a)

We have yet to escape these now century-old handcuffs that lock us into the worst practices of 1910. If we never achieve that escape, our children will, logically and rationally, reject our schools and our educational system. In the post-pandemic period after 2022, our students have begun to do just that.

Sources:

Achievements and challenges. (2005, August 9). The Jewish Agency. https://archive.jewishagency.org/
  education/israel/achievements/achievements-and-challenges/

Adams, F. (1875). *The Free School System of the United States*. Chapman and Hall.

Altenbaugh, R. (2002). The American people and their Education: A social history. *(No Title)*. https://
  cir.nii.ac.jp/crid/1130282268852824576

Basu, D., & Brooks, C. (n.d.). *The basics of Marxist economics*.
  Retrieved March 11, 2024, from https://jacobin.com/2023/03/
  karl-marx-capital-economics-introduction-profit-surplus-value-labor-deepankar-basu-interview

Carlson, D. (2009). Tales of Future Past: The Living Legacy of Eugenics in American Education. *Journal
  for the Advancement of American Curriculum Studies, 5*, 10.

Chamberlain, W. (n.d.). *Mr. C's Class Blog*. Retrieved March 11, 2024, from https://mrcsclassblog.
  blogspot.com/

Coan, T. C. (1875). A New Country. *The_Galaxy, 19*(1), 463.

Cohrs, P. O. (2006). *The unfinished peace after World War I: America, Britain and the stabilisation of
  Europe, 1919-1932*. https://flore.unifi.it/handle/2158/1155520

Commons, J. R. (1905). *Trade Unionism and Labor Problems*. Ginn.

Cremin, L. (1965). The Wonderful World of Ellwood Patterson Cubberley. *New York, NY*. https://
  books.google.com/books?hl=en&lr=&id=Y9bt9VXe5AoC&oi=fnd&pg=PA8&dq=The+Won-
  derful+World+of+Ellwood+Patterson+Cubberley&ots=jvHqV1cIeW&sig=7CpHGOJDgBJe49W-
  vKNMxivB0rv0

Cuban, L. (1984). *How Teachers Taught: Constancy and Change in American Classrooms, 1890-1980*.
  Longman.

Cubberley Cafe. (n.d.). Yelp. Retrieved March 11, 2024, from https://www.yelp.com/biz/
  cubberley-cafe-stanford

Cubberley, Ellwood Patterson, 1868-1941. (n.d.). Retrieved March 10, 2024, from https://onlinebooks.
  library.upenn.edu/webbin/book/lookupname?key=Cubberley,+Ellwood+Patterson,+1868-1941

Cubberley, E. P. (n.d.). *QUOTES BY ELLWOOD PATTERSON CUBBERLEY*. A-Z Quotes. Retrieved
  March 10, 2024, from https://www.azquotes.com/author/47642-Ellwood_Patterson_Cubberley

Cubberley, E. P. (1922). *A Brief History of Education: A History of the Practice and Progress and
  Organization of Education* (pp. 729, 824). Houghton Mifflin.

Ellwood Cubberley. (n.d.). Eugenics at Stanford. Retrieved March 10, 2024, from https://www.stanfor-
  deugenics.com/ellwood-cubberley

Cuslar. (2014, October 23). *Similar anti-immigrant rhetoric used throughout U.S. history*. Committee on U.S./Latin American Relations. https://cuslar.org/2014/10/23/
  similar-anti-immigrant-rhetoric-used-throughout-u-s-history/

Dalton, H. L. (1996). *Racial Healing: Confronting the Fear Between Blacks & Whites*. Knopf Doubleday
  Publishing Group.

Date, I. P. F., & Great Hunger - HISTORY. (2017, October 17). *Irish Potato Famine*. HISTORY. https://
  www.history.com/topics/immigration/irish-potato-famine

Eagleton, T. (1976). *Marxism and Literary Criticism*. Psychology Press.

Gatto, J. T. (2000a). *The Underground History of American Education Summary* (cleangov.com). https://fastbookx.com/index.php/2019/06/03/the-underground-history-of-american-education-by-john-taylor-gatto/

Gatto, J. T. (2000b). True Believers and the Unspeakable Chautauqua. In *The Underground History of American Education* (p. 129). Odysseus Group. https://ia803006.us.archive.org/13/items/John-TaylorGattoTheUndergroundHistoryOfAmericanEducationBook/John%20Taylor%20Gatto%20-%20The%20Underground%20History%20of%20American%20Education%20Book.pdf

Google Books. (n.d.-a). Retrieved March 10, 2024, from https://www.google.com/books/edition/Connecticut_Common_School_Journal_and_An/twoCAAAAYAAJ?hl=en&gbpv=1&dq=prussian+model+us+schools&pg=PA119&printsec=frontcover

Google Books. (n.d.-b). Retrieved March 10, 2024, from https://www.google.com/books/edition/Miss_Columbia_s_Public_School_Or_Will_it/AnIzAAAAYAAJ?hl=en&gbpv=1&dq=miss+columbia%27s+school&printsec=frontcover

Google Books. (n.d.-c). Retrieved March 10, 2024, from https://www.google.com/books/edition/The_Protestant_Ethic_and_the_Spirit_of_C/6CK2hacFggcC?hl=en&gbpv=1&dq=max+weber+the+protestant+work+ethic&printsec=frontcover

Google Books. (n.d.-d). Retrieved March 10, 2024, from https://www.google.com/books/edition/The_New_McGuffey_First_Reader/fJUAAAAAYAAJ?hl=en&gbpv=1

Graduate school of education. (n.d.). Teachers College - Columbia University. Retrieved March 11, 2024, from https://www.tc.columbia.edu/

Grunge movement: Patrons of husbandry. (n.d.). Retrieved March 11, 2024, from https://www.u-s-history.com/pages/h854.html

Greene, P. (2024, February 10). Research Shows What State Standardized Tests Actually Measure. *Forbes Magazine*. https://www.forbes.com/sites/petergreene/2024/02/10/research-shows-what-state-standardized-tests-actually-measure/

Halton, J. H. (1982). The second industrial revolution. *Wisconsin Medical Journal, 81*(4), 40–42.

Harper, R. C. (1968). *The Course of the Melting Pot Idea to 1910*. University Microfilms.

History of work ethic--4.Protestantism and the protestant ethic. (n.d.). Retrieved March 11, 2024, from http://workethic.coe.uga.edu/hpro.html

Kiberd, D. (1996). *Inventing Ireland*. Harvard University Press.

Lawrence Arthur Cremin. (n.d.). Retrieved March 11, 2024, from https://www.c250.columbia.edu/c250_celebrates/remarkable_columbians/lawrence_arthur_cremin.html

Lozano, J. A. (2024, January 24). *Texas school's punishment of Black student who wears his hair in locs is going to trial*. AP News. https://apnews.com/article/hair-discrimination-school-dreadlocks-1efecc37df77d6bc087d71a1b573bed6

Macleod, D. (n.d.). *Calvinism and economics :: Donald Macleod*. Retrieved March 11, 2024, from https://donaldmacleod.org.uk/dm/calvinism-and-economics/

Maldonado, B. (2020, February 4). *Eugenics on the farm: Ellwood Cubberley*. The Stanford Daily. https://stanforddaily.com/2020/02/04/eugenics-on-the-farm-ellwood-cubberley/

Melaugh, M. (n.d.). *CAIN: Events: Troops: McMonagle, Barney: NO GO - A Photographic Record of Free Derry*. Retrieved March 10, 2024, from https://cain.ulster.ac.uk/events/troops/nogo.htm

Miller, C. C., Mervosh, S., & Paris, F. (2024, January 31). Students Are Making a "Surprising" Rebound From Pandemic Closures. But Some May Never Catch Up. *The New York Times*. https://www.nytimes.com/interactive/2024/01/31/us/pandemic-learning-loss-recovery.html

Mokyr, J., & Strotz, R.H. (1998). *The Second Industrial Revolution , 1870-1914*. Northwestern University. https://faculty.wcas.northwestern.edu/jmokyr/castronovo.pdf

Seaquence. (2023a, September 18). *Mike Duncan's Revolutions - 10.3 - The Three Pillars of Marxism*. Youtube. https://www.youtube.com/watch?v=jHCqjSEMXLE

Seaquence. (2023b, September 18). *Mike Duncan's Revolutions - 10.4 - Historical Materialism*. Youtube. https://www.youtube.com/watch?v=281K_OkxFis

Sink or Swim; Or, Harry Raymond's Resolve by Jr. Horatio Alger. (n.d.). Project Gutenberg. Retrieved March 11, 2024, from https://www.gutenberg.org/ebooks/59517

Social security history. (n.d.). Retrieved March 11, 2024, from https://www.ssa.gov/history/ottob.html

Socol, I. (2010). Designed to Fail - Education in America: Part One. *SpeEdChange*. https://speedchange.blogspot.com/2010/09/designed-to-fail-education-in-america.html?showComment=1285507432292

Socol, I. D. (2021, March 17). *Ella Flagg young — just one of the education leaders we've missed*. Educate. https://medium.com/educate-pub/ella-flagg-young-just-one-of-the-education-leaders-weve-missed-22296bc5bf42

SpeEdChange. (n.d.). Retrieved March 11, 2024, from https://speedchange.blogspot.com/2009/04/ideology-and-education.html

Spring, J. (2010). *The politics of American education*. https://doi.org/10.5860/choice.48-7209

Stanford Graduate School of Education. (n.d.). Stanford Graduate School of Education. Retrieved March 10, 2024, from https://ed.stanford.edu/

Stringer, K. (2018, March 6). *Meet Ella Flagg young, first female school superintendent of a major U.s. city — and ed reform's forgotten thought leader*. https://www.the74million.org/article/meet-ella-flagg-young-first-female-school-superintendent-of-a-major-u-s-city-and-ed-reforms-forgotten-thought-leader/

Superintendent. (n.d.). Retrieved March 10, 2024, from https://www.bhisd.net/departments/superintendent

The Rich Boy. (n.d.). Retrieved March 11, 2024, from https://gutenberg.net.au/fsf/THE-RICH-BOY.html

Turner, F. J. (1920). The Frontier in American History. 1893. *New York: Holt*. http://www.stjohns-chs.org/history/scamillo_courses/ap-united-states-history/turner-frontier-thesis.pdf

Tyack, D. B., & Cuban, L. (1995). *Tinkering Toward Utopia* (p. 10). Harvard University Press.

Wikipedia contributors. (2023a, July 26). *Prussian education system*. Wikipedia, The Free Encyclopedia. https://en.wikipedia.org/w/index.php?title=Prussian_education_system&oldid=1167151370

Wikipedia contributors. (2023b, October 26). *Ellwood Patterson Cubberley*. Wikipedia, The Free Encyclopedia. https://en.wikipedia.org/w/index.php?title=Ellwood_Patterson_Cubberley&oldid=1182023155

Wikipedia contributors. (2023c, December 2). *Secularism in France*. Wikipedia, The Free Encyclopedia. https://en.wikipedia.org/w/index.php?title=Secularism_in_France&oldid=1188021309

Wikipedia contributors. (2024a, February 6). *Louisa Parsons Hopkins*. Wikipedia, The Free Encyclopedia. https://en.wikipedia.org/w/index.php?title=Louisa_Parsons_Hopkins&oldid=1204206486

Wikipedia contributors. (2024b, February 16). *Mike Duncan (podcaster)*. Wikipedia, The Free Encyclopedia. https://en.wikipedia.org/w/index.php?title=Mike_Duncan_(podcaster)&oldid=1208148538

Wikipedia contributors. (2024c, February 18). *Second Great Awakening*. Wikipedia, The Free Encyclopedia.https://en.wikipedia.org/w/index.php?title=Second_Great_Awakening&oldid=1208795446

Wikipedia contributors. (2024d, February 25). *Romantic nationalism*. Wikipedia, The Free Encyclopedia. https://en.wikipedia.org/w/index.php?title=Romantic_nationalism&oldid=1210162269

Wikipedia contributors. (2024e, February 29). *Melting pot*. Wikipedia, The Free Encyclopedia. https://en.wikipedia.org/w/index.php?title=Melting_pot&oldid=1211119951

Wikipedia contributors. (2024f, March 2). *Wilhelm II*. Wikipedia, The Free Encyclopedia. https://en.wikipedia.org/w/index.php?title=Wilhelm_II&oldid=1211426049

Wikipedia contributors. (2024g, March 3). *2008 Kosovo declaration of independence*. Wikipedia, The Free Encyclopedia. https://en.wikipedia.org/w/index.php?title=2008_Kosovo_declaration_of_independence&oldid=1211688407

Wikipedia contributors. (2024h, March 3). *Industrial Revolution*. Wikipedia, The Free Encyclopedia. https://en.wikipedia.org/w/index.php?title=Industrial_Revolution&oldid=1211609798

Wikipedia contributors. (2024i, March 3). *Irish Republican Brotherhood*. Wikipedia, The Free Encyclopedia. https://en.wikipedia.org/w/index.php?title=Irish_Republican_Brotherhood&oldid=1211606385

Wikipedia contributors. (2024j, March 3). *South Ossetia*. Wikipedia, The Free Encyclopedia. https://en.wikipedia.org/w/index.php?title=South_Ossetia&oldid=1211588444

Wikipedia contributors. (2024k, March 4). *Zionism*. Wikipedia, The Free Encyclopedia. https://en.wikipedia.org/w/index.php?title=Zionism&oldid=1211777684

Wikipedia contributors. (2024l, March 6). *Hebrew language*. Wikipedia, The Free Encyclopedia. https://en.wikipedia.org/w/index.php?title=Hebrew_language&oldid=1212223349

Wikipedia contributors. (2024m, March 6). *Irish language*. Wikipedia, The Free Encyclopedia. https://en.wikipedia.org/w/index.php?title=Irish_language&oldid=1212153367

Wikipedia contributors. (2024n, March 7). *Georgia (country)*. Wikipedia, The Free Encyclopedia. https://en.wikipedia.org/w/index.php?title=Georgia_(country)&oldid=1212432841

Wikipedia contributors. (2024o, March 8). *Anne, Queen of Great Britain*. Wikipedia, The Free Encyclopedia. https://en.wikipedia.org/w/index.php?title=Anne,_Queen_of_Great_Britain&oldid=1212522153

Wikipedia contributors. (2024p, March 9). *Catalonia*. Wikipedia, The Free Encyclopedia. https://en.wikipedia.org/w/index.php?title=Catalonia&oldid=1212751146

Wikipedia contributors. (2024q, March 9). *French Revolution*. Wikipedia, The Free Encyclopedia. https://en.wikipedia.org/w/index.php?title=French_Revolution&oldid=1212736456

Zangwill, I. (1916). *The War for the World*.

CHAPTER THREE:

In a system designed to fail 80 percent of its students, only the amazing commitment of educators gets us to where we are today. Why are we so stuck?

Socrates opposed the newest technology of his time: literacy. (Wabash College, n.d.) That opposition sets the stage for millennia of educators refusing to engage in new information and communication technologies. but it is only a symptom of the problem.

> *Socrates: You know, Phaedrus, writing shares a strange feature with painting. The offsprings of painting stand there as if they are alive, but if anyone asks them anything, they remain most solemnly silent. The same is true of written words. You'd think they were speaking as if they had some understanding,*

but if you question anything that has been said because you want to learn more, it continues to signify just that very same thing forever. When it has once been written down, every discourse roams about everywhere, reaching indiscriminately those with understanding no less than those who have no business with it, and it doesn't know to whom it should speak and to whom it should not. And when it is faulted and attacked unfairly, it always needs its father's support; alone, it can neither defend itself nor come to its own support. (Socrates on the Forgetfulness That Comes with Writing, n.d.)

Socrates was not wrong in his objections—arguments become "set in stone" once written down. You can't hold a book and converse with the author. Reading a book is a passive act. Reading lowers the value of memory and robs the reader of both the inflection and the nonverbal cues a listener gets from a speaker. Thus, it is much less trustworthy.

The problem, which is replayed and replayed, is that Socrates was fighting the present and future, fights which are difficult to win. Like elites across history, all the way to those who today would take smartphones away from students, Socrates saw change as a threat to his status, the perceptions of his elite skillset, and perhaps even the lifestyle he had grown accustomed to. Remember, the poor and the powerless may embrace change and transformation—when the presentation promises life improvement—but the rich and powerful see only risks and threats.

Those with wealth, power, and status always depend on the work, efforts, and money of those "below" them. (Revolutionary-era French cartoon, "Le Peuple Sous l'Ancien Régime" via East India Blogging Company) (Baker, 2022)

Social Reproduction isn't a difficult concept to grasp. It simply means structures designed to reproduce the present nature of society in the future. (Or, if you're Florida Governor Ron DeSantis or any of his ilk, to reproduce the society of 1956 in the future.) Schools are obviously a primary engine of that, along with taxation, police procedures, zoning, and more. This is most obvious when parents, teachers, and administrators want schools to be like the school they attended when they say "back to basics" or whenever people complain about anything teenagers do, wear, or listen to.

What we desire, or what we claim to desire, may often be in complete opposition to what we do. We say we want equality of opportunity. We claim (or pretend) to want a meritocracy. We make political statements like "No Child Left Behind." Yet our schools tend to hold tight to those Barnard/Cubberley structures of limitations, inequality of opportunity, and shutting out those who do not seem to be "like us."

SOCIAL REPRODUCTION THEORY

The theory that schools reproduce the social inequities, especially in terms of socioeconomic class and race, that exist in the larger society.

"The basic reproductionist argument was that schools were not exceptional institutions promoting equality of opportunity; instead they reinforced the inequalities of social structure and cultural order found in a given country. How they were understood to do so depended on the theoretical perspective of analysts, the sites they prioritized for study, and a varying emphasis on top-down structural determination versus bottom-up agency by individuals or small groups. Early research on educational reproduction provided structuralist accounts, identifying systematic features of language, culture, and political economy, which were reflected in the conduct and organization of classrooms and curricula and assigned a causal role in perpetuating linguistic, cultural, and economic inequalities."— (Bernstein 1975, Bourdieu and Passeron 1977, Bowles and Gintis 1976)." - James Collins, Social Reproduction in Classrooms and Schools (Collins, 2009)

Slide by Warren Blumenfeld: Social Reproduction Theory and Cultural & Social Capital, 2020) (BlumenfeldFollow, n.d.)

When James Collins wrote, "This is probably because it presents a direct challenge to meritocratic assumptions and seems to dash egalitarian aspirations," he clearly states our refusal to acknowledge the facts. Social Reproduction and the socially reproductive systemic designs of Henry Barnard and Ellwood Cubberley are not discussed in American education—even by the type of elite educational leadership that resides at Stanford University (*Faculty*, 2015) because it is (a) very uncomfortable, (b) challenging to the nation's civil religion discussed in Chapter Two, and (c) because it makes education seem, in deep ways, hopeless.

> *"Although the reproductive thesis is simple to state in academic terms, it has been and continues to be quite unpalatable to many of those who work in schools or educational systems more generally (Rothstein 2004). This is probably because it presents a direct challenge to meritocratic assumptions and seems to dash egalitarian aspirations. Early arguments and analyses of reproduction were also of their era, the 1960s and early 1970s, when economic and social stability seemed more secure than it has in recent decades... By the early 1990s, there was a turning away from arguments about social reproduction and education, whether focused on economic, cultural, or linguistic dimensions. This is puzzling in some respects because the problem of inequality remains a central feature of the contemporary world, within nations and on a global scale (Henwood 2003; Stiglitz 2002), and the centrality of straightforward economic factors in school performance appears little changed over more than 40 years (Coleman 1966, U.S. Dep. Educ. 2001)."—James Collins, Social Reproduction in Classrooms and Schools* (Collins, 2009)

How can we expect to solve the persistent problems if we refuse to engage the basic issues?

In fact, 21st-century "educational reformers" will discuss anything but the systemic structure of the nation's education and its social reproductivity. They will argue for and against teacher training (teachers are not well-trained enough, six weeks of training is all a teacher needs) (Duncan, 2009) for and against increased teacher pay (it is essential, teachers are paid too much), ("D.C. Schools Unveil Teacher-Pay Bonus Plan," 2010) for and against privatization (we must use the business model, federal involvement in education is required), but they will not touch the essential unfairness of American society or its economic system. We don't talk about Social Reproduction because those we choose to treat as "leaders"—from Mark Zuckerburg to Elon Musk to any of that "honor roll" of Stanford ("Economic Diversity and Student Outcomes at Stanford," 2017) and Harvard ("Economic Diversity and Student Outcomes at Harvard," 2017) graduates/dropouts—were all born to generational wealth. None have any interest in anything but Social Reproduction—which will assure their offspring's success without competition from any newcomers.

> *Lululemon founder Chip Wilson, in an interview last month, said he didn't care for the "whole diversity and inclusion thing," arguing that ads showing models with various body types can send the wrong message. "You've got to be clear that you don't want certain customers coming in," said Wilson. ("How a Liberal Billionaire Became America's Leading Anti-DEI Crusader," 2024)*

It is unclear whether these rich kids are completely self-delusional about their privilege or if they have simply been raised to lie in the pursuit of becoming permanent nobility, but it really does not matter. There are no "good intentions" when a Chappaqua-born white guy like Bill Ackman gets vast space in the Washington Post to offer his explanations: "Ackman waves off critics who dismiss him and like-minded titans as wealthy White men clinging to power. And he rejects the idea that anyone should judge him by his new right-wing bedfellows. He says that robust debate, even with people with whom he vehemently disagrees, is exactly what society is currently lacking—the very point of his crusade. If he has a megaphone, he argues, it's only because people want to hear what he has to say." What we have are those with wealth, power, and status broadcasting the self-indulgent views of someone with wealth, power, and status. ("How a Liberal Billionaire Became America's Leading Anti-DEI Crusader," 2024)

Exclusivity is indeed their goal, and exclusivity is about the ability to preserve that generational power—no less so today than in the France of the ancien régime.

All this is why the history of our system, Ellwood Cubberley, and Social Reproduction have vanished from the conversation, from education coursework, and certainly from public consciousness. Even those who should really know better have stopped talking about him (see Tyack and Cuban and other Stanford-based education academics) and often trumpet the memory of Woodrow Wilson—a vicious racist whose international naiveté led directly to World War II—and the "progress" of his age. It is, of course, the progress of the Wilsonian age, the conceits of White American superiority, and our belief in measuring the world against that, which still bedevils us a century later.

Early 20th-century America had better things to do with its lower-class children than educate them. Child coal mine workers in Pennsylvania, 1911 - Lewis Hine photograph (The Child Miners' Photos of Lewis Hine That Appalled America, 1908-1911 - Rare Historical Photos, 2020)

It is important to recall that the system designed was never intended to educate all equally, and the structure developed was designed to ensure that.

When Wilson said, "We want one class to have a liberal education. We want another class, a very much larger class of necessity, to forego the privilege of a liberal education and fit themselves to perform specific difficult manual tasks," we know which groups were automatically consigned to the latter class—African-Americans, Catholics, Latinos, Asians, Native Americans, and anyone who would today be considered "disabled."

The Eton lads get their education, and *so do the kids at Sidwell Friends - photo via Times of London. ("Is Private School
Really Worth It Any More?" n.d.)*

In fact, the system was designed to fail most, dumping three-quar-
ters of students before they ever reached high school. The Prussian
System of age-based grades replaced the individually structured, multiage, peer-tutored one-room schoolhouse model because it would give
schools the means to defeat students who might learn at a different
rate. (Hunt, 2010) In schools before this, "grades" meant the level a
student was working on—essentially a mastery model. When a learner
completed one grade's work, the teacher gave them the next. Time
was not the controller. With the Prussian system, you were expected
to leave if you couldn't keep up. The eight grades had a specific purpose—cut the student body by 80 percent (simple arithmetic—eight
grades, 80 percent failed out), leaving just the elite for high school and
what we'd now call "white collar jobs."

The accompanying industrialized model of mass education was created to consign non-compliant students to the lowest-paying jobs in society. The results were clear. On the verge of the United States' entry into World War II, only 25% of the population had completed high school, and less than 5% had completed college. It would only be after the liberalization of education and the integration of the 1960s that high school graduation rates would cross the 50% mark. Students, then as now, fell behind when measured against the "ideal" standards of "age-based" learning and, unable to catch up in the graded, age-segregated system, dropped out as soon as that was possible or legal.

In the century after 1840, as Wilson, Cubberley, Adams, and Barnard all said, America needed little in the way of 'distributed leadership' and—from the top—wanted less. (*The Distributed Leadership Study*, n.d.) Unschooled tinkerers (Edison, Ford) were one thing, but an educated population—as Germany and France were proving and land-grant education in the U.S. was suggesting—seemed to create socialists, union leaders, and potentially an angrier agricultural class, any of which might overturn the system.

The imported Prussian System, with its age-based steps and grade-level standards, was introduced as a filtering system. As Jefferson had noted at the start of the 19th Century, the separation by age would find the gems and give the rest "an education proportional to the condition and the pursuits of his life" (Sparagana, n.d.) which, in the Social Darwinism of Wilson and Cubberley's time, (Wikipedia contributors, 2024a) meant the capabilities to be a miner, a millworker, a railroad construction crew member, a shipyard worker. Get to eighth grade (or not), and you go to one of those laboring jobs. Get through high school, and you could work on Main Street. (Lewis, 1995) Those five percent who went to college would lead.

Setting the standards for those age-based grades, then as now, was critical to maintaining the nation's class structure. Maintaining the class structure has always been the primary goal of national leadership—and, via the myth of opportunity—that has been sold to voters across the nation for all these years.

> *"All teachers on receiving a new class of children should give special study to the children who appear to be unusually dull or unresponsive in order to discover, if possible, the cause of the appearance. Mental defects amounting to feeble-mindedness in the scientific sense of the term are not always nor even usually the cause of apparent stupidity. Such causes as deafness, nearsightedness, and partial blindness may go unobserved for a time, but, when discovered, afford all necessary explanation. If, after the regular teacher has made a careful study of a case, and has become convinced that the cause of the apparent feeble-mindedness is beyond her power to discover or to remove, the case should be reported to the Superintendent of Public Schools, who will call in the expert services of the teachers of the special classes, and, if he deems it best, authorize the removal of the child to one of the special classes."* - Edwin Seaver, Superintendent of the Boston Public Schools, 1900 (Osgood, 2000)

The target was not just immigrants and not just the children of generational poverty, but, obviously, African American children and anyone who might be tagged with the pathological label of handicapped, (later) retardation, or (later still) disability. Though schools in the American "North" and "West" did often admit "children of color," the structures ensured that they would start "behind," continue "behind," and drop out as soon as possible. For students labeled as obviously genetically damaged—the "slow," the physically "wrong," the mentally "troubled"—the asylum (within the school or outside it) waited whenever the parents could no longer handle the problem at home.

We all know that when grade-level standards are enforced, children must be either retained or passed along as failures. This is the classic definition of "retarded." Once "behind," forever "behind."

The same is true for behavioral standards, which have always been based on white protestant middle-class sensibilities and norms. These still work powerfully to hold Black students, neurodivergent students, and others behind, though the original targets were urban Catholics and the rural poor. Despite our pretenses and the personal actions of many educators, this has not changed. "[T]he top five percent of referring teachers issued an average of over 48 ODRs (Office Disciplinary Referrals) per year—roughly one ODR every four school days," a study by Liu, Penner, and Gao published in 2023 found. "That is several times greater than the rates of their average-referring colleagues, who issued less than one ODR for every two months of school. Top referrers accounted for 34.8 percent of all ODRs." (Liu et al., 2023) The problem is that neither administrators nor teacher peers of these "top referrers" intervene. They don't interfere because this kind of failure by design is fully accepted.

"[in the North] at first the States made no efforts to educate Negroes," Dubois wrote in a 1911 report, "It was claimed at the time that technically the public schools were open to Negroes, but no inducements were offered to make them attend, and the abstract right was rarely tested... In Ohio, the Negroes were excluded from white schools in 1828, and practically no provision made for them save through benevolence until 1849." He does add, "From about 1835 on it became general for the Northern States to support wholly a separate system of Negro schools. They were usually poorer than the whites, worse taught and worse equipped, and wretchedly housed. Beginning with Massachusetts, in 1855, the separate schools have been abolished in nearly all Northern States." (Du Bois & Dill, 1911)

> *"[in 1870] in the whole United States 79.9 percent of the Negroes were illiterate... This mass of ignorance existed too by the nation's own will. After feeble and hesitating opposition to the slave trade in some quarters, the United States proceeded deliberately to import a mass of Negroes and train them in ignorance. The unwritten law of the land was that Negroes should receive no instruction. In the North this custom gradually was given up, but with the cotton gin in the South it crystalized into [written] law.—W.E.B. Dubois* (Du Bois & Dill, 1911)

Those beginnings of integration proved illusory, of course. 108 years later, in 1963, the United States Supreme Court backed a circuit court decision against the New Rochelle (New York) School Board: "This Court found that the school board, in 1930, had gerrymandered the district in which the Lincoln School was located in order that a large portion of its white students would be excluded and permitted to attend the nearby Webster and Mayflower schools; that within the four years following, the boundaries of the Lincoln district were manipulated so as to incorporate the ever-increasing Negro population; that until 1949, the Board assured the continuance of Lincoln School as a Negro school by permitting white students resident within the district to transfer to schools outside the district... this Court was constrained to find that the deliberate efforts to maintain the Lincoln School as a segregated educational institution worked a deprivation of the equal protection of the laws constitutionally proscribed by the Fourteenth Amendment... The conduct of responsible school officials has operated to deny to Negro children the opportunities for a full and meaningful educational experience guaranteed to them by the Fourteenth Amendment."

In 1963, nine years after Brown vs Board of Education (*Brown v. Board of Education (1954)*, 2021), a school system next to the City of New York was crowding almost all of the Black community's elementary-age children into one outdated, poorly repaired, and understaffed school, ensuring that these children would be far behind when they entered the city's integrated secondary schools. (Goodenow & Ravitch, 1983)

Grade-level standards were developed to ensure those not prepared to begin formal schooling in a certain economic and cultural situation, along with those deemed "inferior"—then and now—could never find ultimate success in public schools. It is difficult to imagine how, if the age-based standards are accurate measures of anything, the majority of children could be "below grade level." Since all of our achievement levels, from the IQ test through every large assessment, are based on an "age-based norm"—shouldn't that "norm" at least be the median?

Yes, it is "a median," but not "the median." The age-based standards are developed based on upper-middle-class white children living in suburbs or expensive urban neighborhoods and functioning "normally"—that is, without "disability," without language issues, without safety issues, without poverty issues, without family stress, etc. The class Wilson and Cubberley were willing to educate in the days of the Great War, are still the socio-economic class we create schools for. (*The Great War*, n.d.)

This is exactly what the powerful get out of an education system designed to fail: They get (a) to control the measuring devices and design them for themselves, and they get to (b) reduce economic competition.

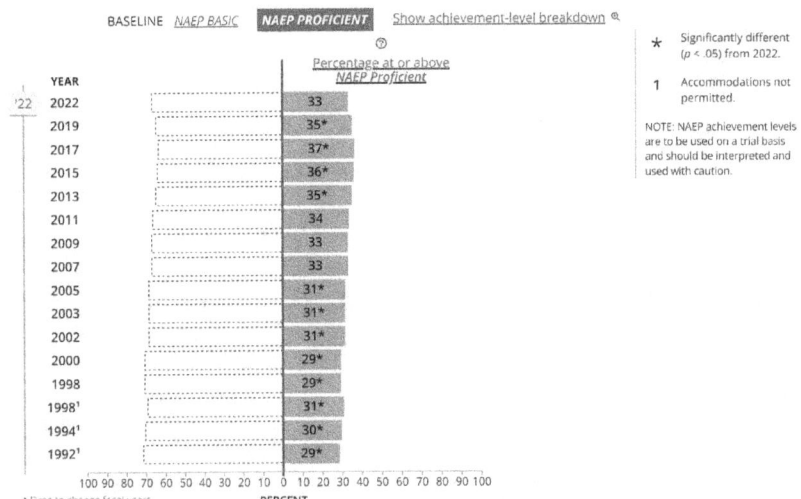

67% of Fourth Graders are below "proficient" in reading. How is "proficient" defined for this age? At the peak, 63% were "proficient."

FIGURE | Trend in fourth-grade NAEP reading average scores

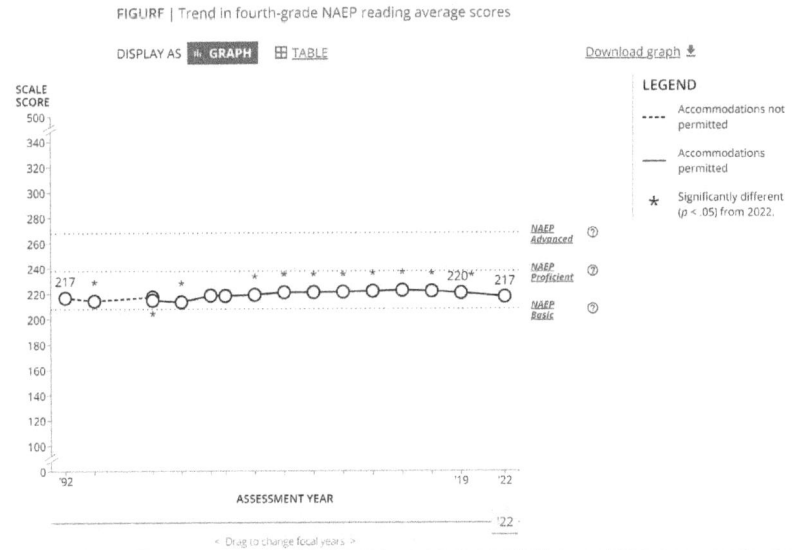

(Grade 4 National Results, n.d.) The total variation—across all our supposed evidence-based research over 30 years—is 6

points on a 400-point scale. (Grade 4 National Results, n.d.)
Since NAEP tests different students in different schools in dif-
ferent districts each year—the data is truly worthless, but is
used as a club to enforce conformity.

By establishing "measuring sticks" that declare their own superiority, the wealthy and powerful—the Ivy Leaguers (Halberstam, 2002) of
America—get to win before the race they so enjoy is run. And by winning, they get to preserve the fruits of victory for themselves and their
offspring—the best schools, the Ivy League educations, the top-paying
jobs in the economy, and the agenda-setting jobs in government.

As for those top university admissions, "the odds of getting into the
pool of credible candidates for admission to a selective college or university are six times higher for a child from a high-income family than
for a child from a poor family; they are more than seven times higher
for a child from a college-educated family than they are for a child who
would be a first-generation college-goer," While at Ivy League and
'Ivy equivalent" institutions, "Low-income students constituted about
11 percent of those admitted to the nineteen institutions that were
studied; first-time college goers made up 6 percent. Students who fit
both categories made up just 3 percent of enrollment at these schools,
even though such students represent roughly 19 percent of the U.S.
college-age population."

In simple terms, the system works remarkably well for those who
currently have wealth and power. When people decry the educational
system in the United States, they are really not discussing Scarsdale, New
York, Greenwich, Connecticut, Sidwell Friends in Washington, Evanston,
Illinois, Santa Barbara, California, or St. Ann's in Brooklyn. All of these
schools do fine, public or private, unionized or not, with longer or shorter
school days/years and no matter the teacher pay structure.

Who is your measuring stick built for? Girls meet in a collaboration flex space. The room was once a librarian's office—but she gave it to her kids. (photo: Ira Socol)

The schools that are struggling—and educators, from William Alcott to all those I've worked with since 1995, know this—because of a lack of resources and/or having differing resources—in the students' homes (Lareau, 2000), in the community (Brooks-Gunn et al., 1997), and in the school itself. (Heyns, 1997) The students "in trouble" do not enter with fewer skills; they enter with different skills built to function in a different environment. An environment and skillset discounted completely by those in power.

Here is the "colonial" issue, as I wrote about both in a post titled "Pygmalion" (*SpeEdChange*, n.d.-a) and in that 2011 history: "The English child raised on the estate in Essex, with parents speaking "The Queen's English," (Wikipedia contributors, 2024b) begins that "race to the top" halfway there. (*SpeEdChange*, n.d.-b) This child knows the language, the rules of rugby, the proper way to drink tea. The child growing up in Derry or Bombay, Lagos or Port Elizabeth comes with differing language, differing sports, and differing eating habits. If school is about the British language, British customs, and British manners, the children from "the colonies" begin way behind. Unless that kid from Essex falls asleep under a tree, as in *The Tortoise and the Hare*, with no one to wake him up, it is inconceivable that the colonial kids will ever catch up. The best they can hope for, if they run all their lives, is to be second-class Brits."

"[Paul] Tough [and] his researchers search their known world among children they do not know at all—and that is a problem for the story Tough wants to tell. First, he tells us that kids in a Chicago juvenile detention facility have much smaller vocabularies than other students, but we have no way of knowing whether that is true or not. The vocabularies of the jailed teens were not measured, instead, they were asked about white middle class vocabulary. I could easily devise a test based on South Side Chicago street vocabulary that middle-class AP students would fail, but there just isn't any validity in either assessment."—Ira Socol (Socol, 2019)

Similarly, the child raised in Scarsdale, Greenwich, Santa Barbara, or at Sidwell or St. Ann's begins the race more than halfway there. They know the language, the rules of classroom play (including how to bully), and the proper way for a parent's note to excuse them from work or school itself. If they mess up, they have the resources to escape any trouble. Children attending urban and rural schools, wracked by poverty, know how to navigate city streets, how to function on a highly adult level, how to be their own caregivers, and how to communicate in a wide range of circumstances. But they do not know what that first group of kids knows, and if they get into trouble, they are on their own, and if they are abused, there is often a strong thread of victim blaming. So, unless the kids in Scarsdale or Greenwich or Santa Barbara, or at Sidwell or St. Ann's die, the best these colonial kids can be, if they run all their lives, is second-class Americans.

"There is pushback against the movement to treat public institutions and the precious people in them like factories. And when the impacted public is treated as an obstacle and not a part-ner to urban reform, it gives the whole effort colonial and paternalistic smell." (Hopkinson, 2010) DC Schools Superin-tendent Michelle Rhee was the toast of the "ed reform crowd," loved by the Obama administration, wealthy white parents, the national media, and Walmart, but completely de-human-izing to Black children. Here, she is pictured laughing about taping poor kids' mouths shut. Her education-reformer audi-ence laughs with her. (Zucker, 2010)

The problem is, if these "colonial" schools leveraged these differing entry abilities and supported differing learning paths with equitable resources, then the path to homogeneity, to the "one America"—behav-ing consistently no matter what race or ethnicity or national origin, would not come into existence. Remember Francis Adams? "The school has more to do than to educate the children: it is the mill, so to speak, into which go children of English, Scotch, Irish, German, Russian, Italian, and Scandinavian parents, and come out Americans. Africa contributes its negroes, and now Asia is sending its Chinese. All must learn English, and the result will soon be that the population of the United States will be the most homogeneous of nations." Back in 2010, Barack Obama's Secretary of Education opened an "Education Nation" conversation by saying, "What the president fundamentally gets is we have to educate our way to a better economy." Not a society with equal opportunity, not an equitable society, not even a "better society." What all in power want is higher Wall Street profits.

> *But here's the thing. There are other facts out there. One is that children in poverty don't come to school knowing less, they know different. Another is that kids in poverty learn just as fast as any other kid. A third is that kids in poverty are every bit as curious as any child. And a fourth is that kids in poverty often demonstrate more advanced judgment than their suburban counterparts. A fifth is that—given the chance—kids in poverty will describe their world with vivid imagery, in art, in music, in writing, that can be far superior to anything a suburban middle class kid can do.* —Ira Socol (Socol, 2016)

> *Rural high-poverty middle school kids build rolling treehouses to remake their cafeteria and learn math. Are you only measuring things that make the children of winners into winners? - photo: Ira Socol*

If the colonial children could leverage what they bring to school, if they might find their own path to success rather than stumbling along in another's wake, well, they might not just compete; they might come out on top (see Irish Literature within the English language for proof of this). This is what scares those at the top.

So, that path is blocked. While "white" kids get creativity and stories in their early grades, teaching them about the world and giving them dreams, "poor" kids get scripted instruction, (*Making Schools Work with Hedrick Smith . School-by-School Reform . Scripted Lessons*, n.d.) chants (Betlach, n.d.), and memorization. If they ever get past that, they find themselves so far behind their "white" peers that continuing the race likely seems genuinely hopeless.

This hopelessness is a bottomless well unless we remove the colonialist context from our minds and practices.

If knowledge is power, then when schools or universities only offer a European-centric curriculum as the valued knowledge, students from other backgrounds and experiences can feel devalued. Similarly, when educational institutions have policies or procedures related to discipline or conduct that only recognize some norms of behavior and presentation of students of certain backgrounds over others, those who are "othered" will feel that they do not belong. —Amy Stuart Wells (Wells, 2020)

"The educational market is now flooded with materials that educators use to teach or promote diversity. There are subject-area and skills-based programs, training manuals, games, texts, sales-oriented Web sites, and videos for teachers, teacher educators, and school administrators. These materials claim to provide multicultural content for students and professional development and to effectively teach core subjects in "failing urban schools," using programs that meet state and federal grant requirements for "research-based" practices," Ellen Swartz wrote in 2009. She adds that "it is not surprising that this model of diversity remains shackled to the dominant discourse of "otherness." pointing out that we remain engaged in "hegemonic discourse." (Swartz, 2009)

Swartz pushes for "an emancipatory model, built with tenets drawn from African, Diasporan, and Indigenous worldviews and scholarship." I would add poverty and neurodiversity to that list since those represent significant minorities in our schools.

Whole Language and Language-Minority Students: A Natural Fit

By Kevin Clark

We first read the world, then the word.

—*Paulo Freire*

Near the end of 1992, a handful of teachers and administrators in the West Contra Costa Unified School District, Richmond, California, gathered one rainy morning and asked a simple question, the answer to which would affect nearly 400 elementary teachers and thousands of language-minority students. The question: How are we best going to provide English-language development to our increasing population of second-language learners?

At first glance the question seems innocuous enough but underneath strikes at the heart of teaching and learning: What do teachers need to

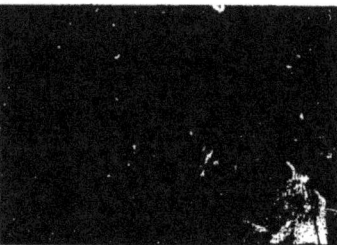

Cyndi Thompson elicits the Hmong word for *coconut* from a student.

basic tenets are that (1) all learning is social; (2) language is learned through use; and (3) purpose and intention drive learning.

For hundreds of elementary teachers in the West Contra Costa Unified School District, whole language was about to become the pillar of a theory-

• Show teachers what they are expected to do. A videotape of the strategies they were asked to try was provided.

• Engage teachers in critically analyzing the instructional outcomes for language-minority students that addressed social/affective, cognitive/academic, linguistic, and metacognitive areas (Sanchez, 1990).

• Ask teachers to implement the strategies as demonstrated and bring the results to a second group meeting for debriefing.

• Provide ongoing assistance by providing constructive feedback and coaching and listening to their concerns.

ELD Instructional Sequence

In the "Reading Wars," the political goal seems largely to increase privilege... thus in the "Science of Reading," there is an absolute refusal to consider culture or prior knowledge. (Clark, 1994)

The essentialness of breaking the "white-middle-class-Calvinist-neurotypical is normal" model schools have used since the beginning requires emancipation from what Swartz says are the "dominant narratives [that] exist in all disciplines" when the "historical systemic forces in inequitable societies exercise hegemonic influences [determining] whose knowledge counts and whose interests are served by particular versions of history." That emancipation won't come easily because the threat to those whose privilege includes their "prior knowledge" of a world they have self-described is massive.

And when the threat to privilege is massive—the counter-revolutionary response is massive. It will come from the right, and it will come from the left. And those battles across history are the focus of Chapter Five.

> "History is a record of conflicts between the ideal and external forms which were fixed by custom and law. There is a perennial strife between those who are loyal to forms as against the idea, and those who are loyal to the ideas against the form. There are those who seem to think that the external condition of things is the law, and therefore unassailable. Especially prone to hold this view are those who are a part of the fixed system." Arnold Tompkins, professor of pedagogy, University of Illinois (Tompkins, 1895)

Sources:

Baker, J. (2022, November 30). *French Revolution political cartoons: Telling truth to power*. East India Blogging Co. https://eastindiabloggingco.com/2022/11/29/french-revolution-political-cartoons/

Betlach, K. (n.d.). *Teaching in the 408*. Retrieved March 13, 2024, from https://roomd2.blogspot.com/2005/11/one-coin-two-sides.html

BlumenfeldFollow, W. (n.d.). *Social Reproduction Theory and Cultural & Social Capital*. SlideShare. Retrieved March 12, 2024, from https://www.slideshare.net/wblumen/social-reproduction-theory-and-cultural-social-capital

Brooks-Gunn, J., Duncan, G., & Lawrence Aber, J. (1997). *Neighborhood Poverty: Context and Consequences for Children*. Russell Sage Foundation.

Brown v. Board of Education (1954). (2021, September 29). National Archives. https://www.archives.gov/milestone-documents/brown-v-board-of-education

Buck, R. T., David, N., & Truitt, M. (1961). Public School Segregation_ Does the Fourteenth Amendment Require. Kent State Law Review, 38(2), 169–184.

Carnevale, A. P., & Rose, S. J. (2003). SOCIOECONOMIC STATUS, RACE/ETHNICITY, AND. Century Foundation.

Clark, K. (1994). ELL students: Literacy development and language development. *Be Outreach*, *3*(spring), 24–26.

Collins, J. (2009). Social Reproduction in Classrooms and Schools. *Annual Review of Anthropology*, *38*(1), 33–48.

D.C. schools unveil teacher-pay bonus plan. (2010, September 10). *The Washington Post*. http://www.washingtonpost.com/wp-dyn/content/article/2010/09/10/AR2010091006604.html

Du Bois, W. E. B., & Dill, A. G. (1911). *The Common School and the Negro American*. Periodicals Service Company.

Duncan, A. (2009, August 16). Do Teachers Need Education Degrees? *The New York Times*. https://archive.nytimes.com/roomfordebate.blogs.nytimes.com/2009/08/16/education-degrees-and-teachers-pay/

Economic diversity and student outcomes at Harvard. (2017, January 18). *The New York Times*.

Economic diversity and student outcomes at Stanford. (2017, January 18). *The New York Times*.

Faculty. (2015, July 27). Stanford Graduate School of Education. https://ed.stanford.edu/faculty/profiles

Goodenow, R. K., & Ravitch, D. (1983). *Schools in Cities: Consensus and Conflict in American Educational History*. Holmes & Meier.

Grade 4 national results. (n.d.). Retrieved March 13, 2024, from https://www.nationsreportcard.gov/reading_2009/nat_g4.asp?tab_id=tab2&subtab_id=Tab_1

Halberstam, D. (2002). *The Best and the Brightest*. Random House Publishing Group.

Heyns, B. A. D. (1997). *Does Money Matter? The Effect of School Resources on Student Achievement and Adult Success*. 26(4), 488–489.

Hopkinson, N. (2010). Why Michelle Rhee's Education 'Brand' Failed in D.C.
The Atlantic https://www.theatlantic.com/politics/archive/2010/09/
why-michelle-rhees-education-brand-failed-in-dc/63014/

How a liberal billionaire became America's leading anti-DEI crusader. (2024, February 10).
The Washington Post. https://www.washingtonpost.com/technology/2024/02/10/
bill-ackman-end-dei-industry/

Hunt, T. C. (2010). *Encyclopedia of Educational Reform and Dissent.* SAGE.

Is private school really worth it anymore? (n.d.). *The Times.* Retrieved March 11, 2024, from https://
www.thetimes.co.uk/article/is-private-school-worth-it-k66lncxd9

Lareau, A. (2000). *Home Advantage: Social Class and Parental Intervention in Elementary Education.*
Rowman & Littlefield.

Lewis, S. (1995). *Main Street: The Story of Carol Kennicott.* Penguin.

Library of Congress, Aesop fables. (n.d.). Retrieved September 3, 2024, from https://read.gov/
aesop/025.html

Liu, J., Penner, E. K., & Gao, W. (2023). Troublemakers? The Role of Frequent Teacher Referrers in
Expanding Racial Disciplinary Disproportionalities. *Educational Researcher* , *52*(8), 469–481.

Making schools work with Hedrick Smith . School-by-school reform . Scripted lessons. (n.d.). Retrieved
March 13, 2024, from https://www.pbs.org/makingschoolswork/sbs/sfa/lessons.html

Nation's Report Card (2009) from https://www.nationsreportcard.gov/reading_2009/
nat_g4.asp?tab_id=tab2&subtab_id=Tab_1#tabsContainer

Osgood, R. L. (2000). *For "children who Vary from the Normal Type": Special Education in Boston,
1838-1930.* Gallaudet University Press.

Socol, I. D. (2016, December 16). *You must see your school as a home of opportunity.* Medium. https://
irasocol.medium.com/you-must-see-your-school-as-a-home-of-opportunity-6c7532b43e6f

Socol, I. D. (2019, March 6). *The Limits of "Traditional" Research — or — Why I want to be Oscar
Humlum when I grow up.* Student Voices. https://mystudentvoices.com/the-limits-of-traditional-
research-or-why-i-want-to-be-oscar-humlum-when-i-grow-up-6c471ef009d8

Socrates on the Forgetfulness that Comes with Writing. (n.d.). Retrieved March
12, 2024, from https://newlearningonline.com/literacies/chapter-1/
socrates-on-the-forgetfulness-that-comes-with-writing

Sparagana, J. (n.d.). *Educational theory of Thomas Jefferson.* Retrieved March 13, 2024, from https://
www.newfoundations.com/GALLERY/Jefferson.html

SpeEdChange. (n.d.-a). Retrieved March 13, 2024, from https://speedchange.blogspot.com/2011/07/
pygmalion.html

SpeEdChange. (n.d.-b). Retrieved March 13, 2024, from https://speedchange.blogspot.com/2010/09/
designed-to-fail-education-in-america_28.html

Swartz, E. (2009). Diversity: Gatekeeping Knowledge and Maintaining Inequalities. *Review of Educational Research, 79*(2), 1044–1083.

The child miners' photos of Lewis Hine that appalled America, 1908-1911 - Rare Historical Photos.
(2020). https://rarehistoricalphotos.com/child-miners-lewis-hine/

The distributed leadership study. (n.d.). Retrieved March 13, 2024, from https://distributedleadership. northwestern.edu/

The Great War. (n.d.). American Experience | PBS. Retrieved March 13, 2024, from https://www.pbs. org/wgbh/americanexperience/films/great-war/

Tompkins, A. (1895). *The Philosophy of School Management*. Ginn.

Wabash College. (n.d.). *Socrates on technology*. Wabash College. Retrieved March 12, 2024, from https://www.wabash.edu/news/story/1452

Wells, A. S. (2020). Racial, Ethnic, and Cultural Diversity Across K–12 and Higher Education Sectors: Challenges and Opportunities for Cross-Sector Learning. *Change: The Magazine of Higher Learning*, *52*(2), 56–61.

Wikipedia contributors. (2024a, March 2). *Social Darwinism*. Wikipedia, The Free Encyclopedia. https://en.wikipedia.org/w/index.php?title=Social_Darwinism&oldid=1211479016

Wikipedia contributors. (2024b, March 12). *Received Pronunciation*. Wikipedia, The Free Encyclopedia. https://en.wikipedia.org/w/index.php?title=Received_Pronunciation&oldid=1213357520

Zucker, P. (2010, December 29). Michelle Rhee and Masking Tape. Where is the Outrage? *HuffPost*. https://www.huffpost.com/entry/michelle-rhee-and-masking_b_801339

CHAPTER FOUR:

Revolution and Counter-Revolution:
Those with Wealth and Power have No Incentive to
Help Make Public Education Work.

A failing educational system benefits those who currently have wealth and power. They don't want to share either of those things, nor do they want their children to have to compete with others who may have much more talent, creativity, and ambition. They win—they keep our public education in conservative turmoil—because they have the wealth and the power.

Barricades in Berlin during the Revolutions of 1848. The ideals of those revolts were smashed, yet the events determined the next 100 years, and 100 years later, the aspirations were largely realized. - image (Hoecker & Dornemann, 2011)

*If you have listened to the **Revolutions podcast** you know it is a sobering experience to understand the failure of revolutions—failure usually created by a counter-revolution of the rich and powerful.* (Revolutions, n.d.-a)

Whether we discuss France in 1815 or 1848, Ronald Reagan's U.S. Department of Education in the 1980s (Jarding, 2016), Arne Duncan's U.S. Department of Education in the 2010s (Barnum, 2015), or Ron DeSantis' educational purges of the 2020s, it is all as it has always been. (Cineas, 2023)

Those historical facts, however, should not dissuade us. Because often we creep forward, and after a counter-revolution, we may actually find ourselves a bit down the road, building on our progressive past and helping to develop the next group of humans interested in using schools to enable human opportunity.

That happens in both global politics and education. The French monarchists overplayed their hand (repeatedly), and the last king of France fled the country in 1848. The Austrian Emperor Franz Joseph overplayed his hand in 1849 and not only lost control of Hungary in 1867, but he became effectively, if not historically, the last emperor of a dissolved nation. People like Arne Duncan, Joel Klein, and the Democrats for Education Reform (DFER) (M. T. Cunningham, 2021) tried to steal public education and have ended up mostly forgotten and discredited—despite media attempts to keep up the facade. (Stefano, 2023)

Obama Chief of Staff Rahm Emanuel and Education Secretary Arne Duncan used "school reform"—privatization—as a key fund-raising tool. image: Steven Singer (Rahm Emanuel's Non-Apology Apology for Being a School Privatization Cheerleader, 2019)

Yet there is something else that blocks revolutionary success, and for this, it is worth looking at the European Revolutions of 1848 (These are the subject of untold numbers of history books, but the most digestible form is probably the 33 chapters of Series 7 of Duncan's Revolutions Podcasts). (Revolutions, n.d.-b) Part 7.33 of that series points out that a primary cause of the ultimate failure of the movements that swept Europe in that year was the unwillingness of the "liberal conservatives"—who were fighting for representative government and civil rights—to continue working with the "radical left"—which was seeking socio-economic changes to benefit workers and the poor. (Wikipedia contributors, 2024e) When the "liberal conservatives" initially gained power, they refused to go along with the social agenda—rights to jobs, housing, and food—of the "radical left." That split the forces of revolution and made the job of the counter-revolutionaries easy.

Of course, they refused to go along. The "liberals" of that time, whether French, Hungarian, or German, were people with wealth and status. Upending the economic order threatened their wealth and status, and humans are—and always have been—motivated primarily by self-interest. *Those who transcend that form the tiny minority that are our heroes.* Yes, you do see coalitions form, but whether that was in France in that revolutionary year of 1848, in Russia in 1905, or even in the United States in the transformational year of 1968, those coalitions typically involve the poor and powerless going along with the aspirations of middle-class liberal reformers—civil rights, improved democracy, ending wars—with those reformers pulling away when the agenda of the powerless—land redistribution (or rezoning in contemporary American terms), income redistribution, minority equality—appears on the horizon.

> *"These senators don't actually care about protecting kids, they just want to control information," one teenager posted. "If congress wants to protect children, they should pass a ... privacy law," another teenager said."*—Washington Post ("Online Safety Legislation Is Opposed by Many It Claims to Protect," 2024)

Education is the most political thing we do; it is the fight for our future (Socol, 2020), and in the U.S. public education is a tool for the maintenance of economic power. Education is either about social reproduction or about opportunity. Those with wealth, power, and status prefer Social Reproduction for self-interest and parental self-interest. Those without—unless they've been co-opted by those who stoke religious/pseudo-religious hatred—desire opportunity. And there is no group with less power than children who lack the right to vote or even the right to voice in most decision-making situations.

For professors, segregation begins at home

Christopher Emdin, Pamela Moran, and Ira David Socol

January 21, 2019

Schools are intensely segregated in many of the nation's (outwardly progressive) college towns.

"...when they become parents, many academics start building their children's college application portfolios literally from birth, paying for language immersion preschools, early music

lessons, summer enrichment opportunities, and more." (For Professors, Segregation Begins at Home, 2019)

What this means is that those who are liberal or leftist but who have wealth, power, and/or status are never quite "all-in" on education as opportunity, nor are they "all-in" on hearing student voices if those voices—now labeled as "immature"—collide with adult beliefs on anything from school schedules to international conflicts.

Yes, professors of education promote progressive ideas, but they do that from segregated enclaves closed to opportunity—Palo Alto, California; Cambridge, Massachusetts; Ann Arbor, Michigan; Boulder, Colorado; Evanston, Illinois; even places like East Lansing, Michigan and State College, Pennsylvania. (*For Professors, Segregation Begins at Home*, 2019) Those places also rank high in "intensive" and "expert" parenting, where exaggerations of logic and research are used to block negotiation during intergenerational conflict. (*Raising Successful Kids*, 2019)

They do all that while ensuring their children have every conceivable advantage over their children of have-nots.

It is not just professors. We can look at the websites for two New York City public schools separated by two miles and many demographics. There is PS 20, "The Clinton Hill School," (PS 20 the Clinton Hill School — Cluster Specialists, n.d.) serving what are now the highly upscale parts of Fort Greene in Brooklyn (which was far less upscale when I lived there), with dance, art, music, and French among the offerings. There is PS 124—not an impoverished community but a place lacking in status—which has a dance teacher and an intervention teacher, but not art, music, or French, and where the website begs for contributions.

"Regardless of their stated beliefs, many academics are disin-clined to tear down these policies and practices, from which they have benefited enormously. It's no secret that many people residing in highly educated college communities have deeply internalized beliefs about intelligence and merit, as defined by performance on standardized achievement tests. The path to their own elite opportunities began with their selection into advanced ability groups in elementary reading and math, to their assignment to gifted and talented programs in the middle grades, to their enrollment in tiered courses in high school."—Emdin, Moran, and Socol, 2019 (*For Professors, Segregation Begins at Home*, 2019)

The parents of PS 20 kids are far left by national political standards. Their member of Congress is Hakeem Jeffries, (Wikipedia contributors, 2024f), and their State Assembly member is the Democratic Socialist Phara Souffrant Forrest (Wikipedia contributors, 2024a), who received 99.4 percent of the vote in the last election. Nevertheless, they send their children to a school filled with opportunities unavailable to most Brooklyn children, and they aggressively fund-raise and lobby the Board of Education to maintain that inequity.

Thus, when it comes to fundamental—revolutionary—change, changing funding mechanisms and teacher pay, changing attendance boundaries, altering the school year, adding UDL technologies and strategies for every child, giving every child the learning opportunities wealthy "gifted" kids get—you will find that there is no coalition backing you.

"Why would I want more kids to get an advanced diploma? Then my kid's diploma would be worth less."—A University of Virginia faculty member at a local school board meeting.

Does it all seem hopeless now? Yes and no. As noted, the Revolutions of 1848 unleashed all kinds of ideas that—down the road—could not be stopped. Whether nationalism is good or bad is an important question, but it seems highly superior to loyalty to a monarch by inheritance. Democracy—at least the "republican" (or "constitutional monarch") kind—is better than absolutism. The concept of civil rights is better than authoritarianism. Socialism, though controversial in the United States, makes most developed nations safe places to raise a child.

While the names Alcott, Hopkins, Young, Dewey, Holt, and Post-man are largely forgotten, their work remains out there. A small but significant cadre of people—like myself—who experienced something better, know that something different is better, and understand that the necessary radical change is possible. That group forms the societal memory that we need to pull progressive theories off the dusty shelves and celebrate those efforts. They remind us of our long history of trying to do right for our children and help us remember that we do have wins—and that even if those wins are small, they change the lives of children.

Some moments create the environment for change and progress, often coinciding with technological changes, particularly in information and communications technologies. We live in one of those moments, so we must fight now.

Historical clashes happen; even if they don't look like revolutionary victories, they can be steps forward. The history of the world is a record of progress and regression, followed by progress and regression. Individual moments may feel like bleak defeats, but the arc of history does bend toward the right things. We are always building on the work of those who came before. A short and selective history of those challenges to the status quo follows.

Louisa Parsons Hopkins vs the Prussian School

The late 19th century was a battleground between "education for learning" and "education as training." Critically, this battle was playing out on a rapidly changing field—much as we experience today. "When the men of my time graduated, Franklin Pierce was President," Charles Francis Adams wrote in 1883. "No united Germany and no united Italy existed. The railroad and the telegraph were in their infancy; neither nitro-glycerine nor the telephone had been discovered. The years since then have been fairly crammed with events. A new world has come into existence, and a world wholly unlike that of our fathers—unlike it in peace and unlike it in war. It is a world of great intellectual quickening, which has extended until it now touches a vastly larger number of men, in many more countries, than it ever touched before." (Adams, 1883)

As schooling became more common and was endowed with public support—at least across the northern United States and in large cities—a battle for purpose appeared. Would schools remain that engine of assimilation and economic preparation? Or would schools be something else? Writing in 1976, Carl Kaestle and Maris Vinovskis noted that the history of education had changed since 1955, with new "questions about the initial and continuing purposes of public schooling. A new critical view has emerged, emphasizing economic realities rather than political ideals. Revisionist historians emphasize class and cultural conflict, bureaucracy, and the schools' role in inculcating 'submissive attitudes."

Meyer, Tyack, Nagel, and Gordon (1979) touched on the ideology involved, "[W]e argue that the spread of schooling in the rural North and

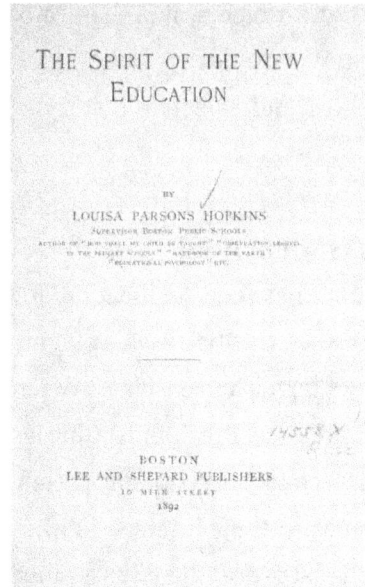

THE SPIRIT OF THE NEW
EDUCATION

BY
LOUISA PARSONS HOPKINS

BOSTON
LEE AND SHEPARD PUBLISHERS
1892

The spirit of the new
education (Hopkins, 1892)

West can best be understood as a social movement implementing a commonly held ideology of nation-building. It combined the outlook and interests of small entrepreneurs in a world market, evangelical Protestantism, and an individualistic conception of the polity." (Meyer et al., 1979)

I would note that while I often refer to "industrial schooling" in that the form of mass public education followed industrial processing practices, the development of the system pre-dates most U.S. industrialization (though New England led the way in both industry and public education—so there is a link). More important was—as argued in Chapter One—converting those on societal margins into "true" Americans—protestant, hard-working, compliant citizens of a developing mercantile empire.

The Prussian Model, imported by Barnard, was created as a citizenship tool in pre-industrial proto-Germany. It operated like a factory, but its purpose—in America as in the German states—was to create a defined type of human adult.

The counter-argument at the time came from the humanist side, which was committed to emerging Victorian concepts of childhood and emerging views on psychology emphasizing curiosity and natural growth. (H. Cunningham, 2012)

The teacher has the child-nature constantly before him to observe; he is bound to observe it carefully, that he may be able to handle it wisely and to meet its needs."—Louisa Parsons Hopkins, 1886 (Hopkins, 1886)

Louisa Parsons Hopkins was a Massachusetts educator trained in psychology. If we were to remove her praise for Puritan life, she would fit in with today's progressive leaders. She focused her work on early child development and the value of kindergarten at one end of the process and the relevance of hands-on work to adolescents at the other.

I am more and more convinced that children should be led into these pleasant paths of natural observation very early, while they have a marked love for it, to find that the revelation of knowledge is direct to each one that hungers and thirsts for it, and it is the first business of the teacher to create this hunger by putting appetizing food before the scholar, not cramming it down his throat in doses of books; let him look at the beautiful fruit until his mouth waters for it; let him taste it by so much as he can put into his own mouth at once, and he will learn to love it, and will not be satisfied but with more and more as he is able to digest it. The teacher is with him, not to examine for him, not to force the result of another's observation upon him, not even to examine him, but to direct his senses, to stimulate his desire, to present the essential points of the object before him, and to preserve an underlying method in his observations of which he is as yet unconscious; so there will be little need of mere recitation. Will the child forget a secret of nature which she herself has revealed to him? Never; he is more receptive and patiently observant then he will ever be again if this opportunity is neglected."—Louisa Parsons Hopkins, 1887 (Hopkins, 1887)

Hopkins was not a winner either, but her beliefs and writings became the foundation of John Dewey's work and thus informs many progressive educational concepts to the present.

Ella Flagg Young and John Dewey vs. the Carnegie Commission

"The dull routine of trying to form habits by wearisome repetitions, the discouraging process of trying to overcome the enemy, the old habit, only to find it upon the first lapse of vigilance rein stated in full sway, must give way to a higher type of activity. The individual must, under the stimulus of interest in a consciously originated and defined end, utilize inherited and acquired tendencies and powers in organizing and reorganizing for its attainment. The satisfaction that comes with exercise along lines that are peculiar to the individual will be secured by everyone, in greater or less degree, through automatic action . But whether this shall reduce the life to a narrow mechanism that stifles and dwarfs , or shall expand the life into a developing process that inspires and enlarges, depends upon the origination and construction of the end or aim by which the tendency is called into action."—Ella Flagg Young, *Isolation in the School*, 1901 (Young, 1901)

If Hopkins informed Dewey's work, Ella Flagg Young was a "senior partner" (ignored due to gender bias) in their work together at the University of Chicago and the University of Chicago Lab School. (Lagemann, 1996) She became Superintendent of the Chicago Public Schools and a leader in the development of the high school—but a leader in conflict with Cubberley and the Carnegie Commission.

"...after visiting many high schools within the last few months, high schools in different cities, I may say one is justified in criticizing the high school; everywhere there prevails the idea that our work must be so done that when the boys and the girls graduate they must be slightly in touch with every subject known to man, but they need not necessarily think and speak with continuity and exactness in any one of the multitude."—Ella Flagg Young, 1910 (Young, 1910)

"The Carnegie Unit, also known as the credit hour, became the basic unit of measurement both for determining students' readiness for college and their progress through an acceptable program of study," Silva, White, and Toch wrote in a 2015 Carnegie Foundation publication. "Over time, the Carnegie Unit became the building block of modern American education, serving as the foundation for everything from daily school schedules to graduation requirements, faculty workloads, and eligibility for federal financial aid."

"...after visiting many high schools within the last few months, high schools in different cities, I may say one is justified in criticizing the high school; everywhere there prevails the idea that our work must be so done that when the boys and the girls graduate they must be slightly in touch with every subject known to man, but they need not necessarily think and speak with continuity and exactness in any one of the multitude."—Ella Flagg Young, 1910 (Young, 1910)

The 1906 work of the Carnegie Foundation for the Advancement of Teaching expanded on the 1890 Committee of Ten's notions of a shattered curriculum (which it deemed "the only comprehensive work-

ing theory of secondary education which has thus far been proposed.")
by attaching the notion of "seat time"—120 hours per high school
course—to a curriculum developed by an entitled few "elite" educators.
(National Education Association of the United States. Committee of
Ten on Secondary School Studies, 1894)

The New York Times Magazine, July 17, 1910: Young led Chicago schools and the NEA. (Friedman, 2010)

These developments, created without any noticeable research base
beyond a few observations and conversations, built the boring, irrelevant secondary schools our children rebel against today.

Young argued against curricular division, "the flitting from subject
to subject," and for cross-curricular courses and mixing ages—more

mature students with younger—as well as "the necessity for developing the social life, the social method of attack in the schools." She also advocated for experiences as a primary learning tool.

Year	CLASSICAL THREE FOREIGN LANGUAGES (one modern)		LATIN-SCIENTIFIC TWO FOREIGN LANGUAGES (one modern)	
I	Latin	5 p.	Latin	5 p.
	English	4 p.	English	4 p.
	Algebra	4 p.	Algebra	4 p.
	History	4 p.	History	4 p.
	Physical Geography	3 p.	Physical Geography	3 p.
		20 p.		20 p.
II	Latin	5 p.	Latin	5 p.
	English	2 p.	English	2 p.
	*German (or French) begun	4 p.	German (or French begun)	4 p.
	Geometry	3 p.	Geometry	3 p.
	Physics	3 p.	Physics	3 p.
	History	3 p.	Botany or Zoölogy	3 p.
		20 p.		20 p.
III	Latin	4 p.	Latin	4 p.
	*Greek	5 p.	English	3 p.
	English	3 p.	German (or French)	4 p.
	German (or French)	4 p.	Mathematics { Algebra 2 / Geom. 2 }	4 p.
	Mathematics { Algebra 2 / Geom. 2 }	4 p.	Astronomy ½ yr. and Meteorology ½ yr	3 p.
		20 p.	History	2 p.
				20 p.
IV	Latin	4 p.	Latin	4 p.
	Greek	5 p.	English { as in classical 2 / additional 2 }	4 p.
	English	2 p.	German (or French)	3 p.
	German (or French)	3 p.	Chemistry	3 p.
	Chemistry	3 p.	Trigonometry and Higher Algebra or History	3 p.
	Trigonometry and Higher Algebra or History	3 p.	Geology or Physiography ½ yr. and Anatomy, Physiology, & Hygiene ½ yr.	3 p.
		20 p.		20 p.

The 1892 Committee of Ten established the high school curriculum. (Report of the Committee of Ten 1892.pdf, n.d.) The 1906 Carnegie Commission locked "seat time."

MRS. ELLA YOUNG INVENTS PRONOUN

"He'er, "His'er" and "Him'er"
as Combination of Genders
Used in Address.

MAKES PRINCIPALS GASP.

History is full of surprises. Non-gendered pronouns are old, so apparently are plagiarism charges against women leaders. "I have simply solved a need that has been long impending. The English language is in need of a personal pronoun of the third person, singular number, that will indicate both sexes." Young said, though later admitting, "Fred L. Pond... [a Chicago insurance broker] is the inventor of the new pronoun, [having] announced his coinage of he-er, his-er, and him-er in a letter to the Mansfield, Ohio, News-Journal on March 21, 1911. (Baron, n.d.)

In many ways, most of our secondary students would be happier in Young's schools than in the schools they currently attend. Young's ideas didn't stand a chance because the Carnegie time-equals-credit plan came with a huge bribe. Educators could be part of a pension plan—but only if their schools kept kids bored for 120 hours per course.

"If we could plan our courses of study so that in each course there were three subjects upon which we expect the boys or girls to put all the intensity of power possible and then if there were a line of work which would be not so much for the training in precision of thought as for awakening them to the social environment and to the movements of society, and also for developing the artistic and aesthetic side of the nature, we should improve upon the marsh-like results of the pres-

ent extensive study courses. In that fourth course intensive
preparation should not be expected, but the type of work that
arises naturally out of the genuine social, intellectual inter-
course between educated men and women on one hand and
boys and girls of high-school age on the other should be the
outcome."—Ella Flagg Young, 1910 (Young, 1910)

Progressive Women vs Ellwood Cubberley

Cubberley's machine was in full swing in the 1920s. His textbooks dominated every teacher-training Normal School and every educational administrative course. (Wikipedia contributors, 2024g) The division of the curriculum and the day into disconnected irrelevant units of "seat time" was extended to younger learners through the development of Junior High School. (Briggs, 1920) IQ tests were all the rage, and a belief in eugenics permeated everything.

"Known as the father of intelligence testing in the United
States, [Henry H.] Goddard used a perversion of Binet's intel-
ligence scale to rank those he considered feebleminded into
varying degrees of mental incompetence: idiots (pre-verbal),
imbeciles (illiterate), and morons (highfunctioning).33 For
Goddard, morons, or those with mental ages of eight through
twelve,34 posed the gravest eugenic threat because of the ease
with which they could pass for normal and reproduce." DePaul
Law Review, 2006 (*De Paul Law Review*, 2004)

But not everyone was on board the Stanford University train.

"Today, we must not only extend knowledge, but apply knowl-edge to man's service, toward the end that each individual may be set free to make the highest use of his own powers. This means patient work in re-examining our old theories and practices; it means a change in attitude and view-point, and for every one of us many readjustments. There is misunder-standing and lack of experience everywhere. The industrial laborer threatens, then strikes, refusing to work—the pupil laborer shirks, then rebels and refuses to learn, not because the tasks are too difficult or are in themselves unpleasant but both sets of laborers refuse because the conditions under which they work impede the powers which would permit them to release and give expression to that inner urge which motivates every task."—Helen Parkhurst, 1924 (*Progressive Education*, 1924)

The Progressive Education Association (*History*, n.d.) was driving the other way, pushing a movement "of "reconstruction," looking to make education more of an experience through the *addition* of "new qualities" and "new values" (Breed). Previously, American elementary education was structured in a way that put more value on quantity than quality; classes were made up of a greater number of children, none of whom regularly received individualized support, and things were done in a set way, according to lesson plans. With Progressive education, ideally, every student was allowed to pursue his or her interests within the classroom setting. Teachers were to be more like teammates than disciplinarians and encouraged to implement activities like reading, creative writing, and dramatics that allowed their pupils more individual freedom."

"Progressive teachers will encourage the use of all the senses, training the pupils in both observation and judgment and, instead of hearing recitations only, will spend most of the time teaching them how to use the various sources of information, including life activities, as well as books"—Progressive Education Association in the Baltimore Sun

Many of the proponents were women—though they always seemed to need the cover of a male association president. Their journals show a very high percentage of women authors, including Helen Parkhurst, (Wikipedia contributors, 2023b) the founder of Manhattan's progressive Dalton School, (Wikipedia contributors, 2024c) Lucia Burton Morse, and Beatrice Ensor. (Wikipedia contributors, 2023a)

The progressives did not win the battle before World War II, but they did set the stage for new thinking on school buildings, pedagogy, and curriculum which gained traction in the postwar era.

What's essential to learn? *"...in order to give a child a mastery of the common essentials, we must know what the common essentials are, and we must know how to present them effectively to children. By a common essential we mean a knowledge or skill which is essential to everyone, a knowledge or skill which is used by practically everyone who possesses it. The knowledge of square root is not a common essential, because only a few people use it. The knowledge that 7 and 8 are 15 is a common essential because everybody uses it."*—Carleton Washburn, 1924

A classroom in Winnetka, Illinois' Crow Island School (1940).
Open, flexible, complex, sunlit spaces connected to the outside.
Now beautifully restored. (Kothari, 2021)

Raymond Callahan and John Holt vs. Soviet Education

The 1950s and early 1960s held real promise for learners. Dewey's books were almost as widely read as Cubberley's, schools were built with huge windows and flexible furniture, field trips became common, kindergarten neared universality (outside the South), northern schools were increasingly integrated, and the U.S. Supreme Court invalidated "separate but equal" education. But the counter-revolution began when Sputnik happened at the midpoint of this mid-century moment.

Speaking of the creed of a slave, as with Barnard's infatuation with authoritarian Prussia, the American power elite determined that the authoritarian Soviet Union had an education model that needed to be copied. "But the difference between what they learn and the atmosphere in which they learn it," wrote *Life Magazine*, "measures the frightening scale of the problems the U.S. now faces in its public schools." (Time Inc, 1958)

Scarsdale, New York's Heathcote Elementary School (1955) continually linked inside and outside while rejecting the simple rectangle for room design.

"*Raymond Callahan's lively study exposes the alarming lengths to which school administrators went, particularly in the period from 1910 to 1930, in sacrificing educational goals to the demands of business procedures. He suggests that even today the question still asked is: "How can we operate our schools?" Society has not yet learned to ask: "How can we provide an excellent education for our children?"*"—University of Chicago [expressing that university's split between their economic and educational theories] (Callahan, 1964)

The "golden age" of education imagined by Ron DeSantis and other right-wing voices, wasn't a success by their measuring sticks. It wasn't authoritarian enough, and as a film like *Blackboard Jungle* suggests, all the kids were not fully attentive despite the lack of mobile phones. (Wikipedia contributors, 2024b)

SCHOOLBOYS POINT UP A U.S. WEAKNESS

If only Chicago could be more like Stalingrad. Life Magazine, 1958. (Time Inc, 1958)

In a nation that supposedly hated communism—the hero worship of Soviet education stands out. (Suenobu, 2007)

Raymond Callahan attacked the concept of educational efficiency in his brilliant 1964 book, Education and the Cult of Efficiency, asking if "efficient teaching" had any positive relationship with student learning and if "being efficient" was in any way associated with building either skills or knowledge. (Callahan, 1964)

At the same time, John Holt began publishing his education studies based on his teaching experiences in the late 1950s. *How Children Fail* is an incredibly persuasive attack on the norms of education, then and now. "Fear, boredom, and resistance—they all go to make what we call stupid children," Holt wrote. "The idea of painless, nonthreatening coercion is an illusion. Fear is the inseparable companion of coercion and its inescapable consequence. If you think it your duty to make children do what you want, whether they will or not, then it follows inexorably that you must make them afraid of what will happen to them if they don't do what you want." He continues, "We don't have to make human beings smart. They are born smart. All we have to do is stop doing the things that made them stupid." (Holt, n.d.)

The running battle between humane education and brutal "efficiency" ("sit down and take the test") would continue to the 1980s when Ronald Reagan drove a full-frontal attack on anyone not extremely wealthy—including America's children and adolescents.

> *"This idea that children won't learn without outside rewards and penalties, or in the debased jargon of the behaviorists, "positive and negative reinforcements," usually becomes a self-fulfilling prophecy. If we treat children long enough as if that were true, they will come to believe it is true. So many people have said to me, "If we didn't make children do things, they wouldn't do anything." Even worse, they say, "If I weren't made to do things, I wouldn't do anything... It is the creed of a slave."*—John Holt, *How Children Fail* (Holt, n.d.)

Integration, Whole Language, New Math, and Neil Postman vs the Reagan Right

The Reagan administration continues to live in the heads of Americans as the carefully constructed myth it always was. Reagan didn't lower taxes, he raised them on every wage earner. Reagan didn't improve the lives of the middle class (Smith, 2013); he destroyed it by attacking unions (Schwarz, 2021) and wrecking the mortgage market. (Wikipedia contributors, 2024d) He did not begin to improve our schools. His education department (featuring the now remorseful Diane Ravitch) crushed whatever progress the progressives of 1950–1980 had achieved.

"In an open classroom, you need to structure things according to each kid's needs."—Life Magazine, 1971

Despite the Sputnik panic, multiple things coalesced in the late 1960s and drove a fundamental change in educational opportunity. School integration began—both north and south. Lyndon Johnson's War on Poverty—which made life in what we now call "Red States" a reasonable thing (adding electricity and refrigeration to homes, for example)—offered people health care, nutrition, and housing. State universities—with costs borne almost entirely by the governments (up to 90 percent)—expanded dramatically. And pedagogical changes were welcomed—from relevant reading instruction featuring whole language and balanced literacy, the "new math" focused on process and concepts instead of memorization, to the now falsely maligned open classrooms and "schools-without-walls."

Students Flock to Philadelphia 'School Without Walls'

"For the first time," said one parent, [my son] is actually being educated. He has learned more in his first session than in all his previous years of school. For the first time he likes school."—*The New York Times,* 1973 (Stevens, 1970)

"There is no way to help a learner to be disciplined, active, and thoroughly engaged unless he perceives a problem to be a problem or whatever is to-be-learned as worth learning, and unless he plays an active role in determining the process of

solution."— Neil Postman and Charles Weingartner, Teaching as a Subversive Activity—

I attended a Postman-designed alternative high school without walls in New Rochelle, New York. (Postman & Weingartner, 1969)

These shifts offered those on the margins—Black, Brown, Neurodivergent, Impoverished, Rural, and Urban—chances at success that had not existed before. Because we've now reached the era of statistical analysis above all else, we can use "the establishment's" favorite kind of assessment to show the success:

Figure 11. Trend in NAEP reading average scores and score gaps for White and Black 17-year-old students

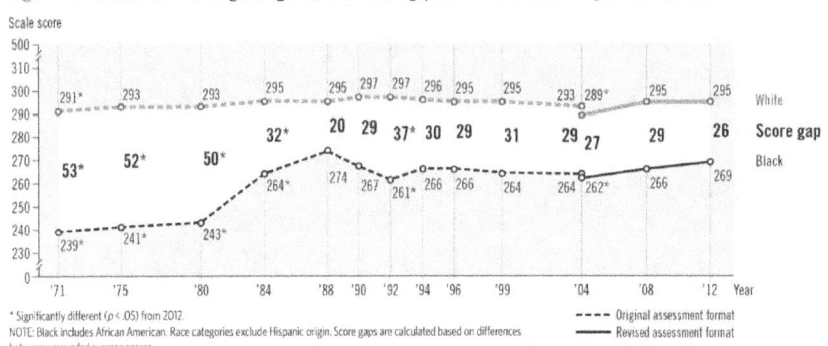

* Significantly different (p < .05) from 2012.
NOTE: Black includes African American. Race categories exclude Hispanic origin. Score gaps are calculated based on differences between unrounded average scores.

---- Original assessment format
—— Revised assessment format

For those entering their high school senior year, the smallest reading achievement gap was achieved by those entering school in the mid-1970s, the high point of open education theories. (NAEP 2012 Executive Summary.pdf, n.d.)

As Reaganism began to have influence, as the experiments in accessible education were shut down, the gap widened.

For those whose elementary experience began in the radically different opportunities of the mid-1960s and 1970s, the gains at the end of high school—for those traditionally "filtered out" were both remarkable and unmatched. For those at the top, nothing went down (and went up slightly).

Progressive strategies were the problem for those behind the "Reagan [Counter] Revolution." America's move toward equitable outcomes and equal opportunity threatened their dominance and generational wealth seizures. As they worked hard to halt the Johnson administration-created War on Poverty, America's conservatives insisted that education promoting increased opportunity stopped (the same argument made today) because "merit" had to be defined as being wealthy and white.

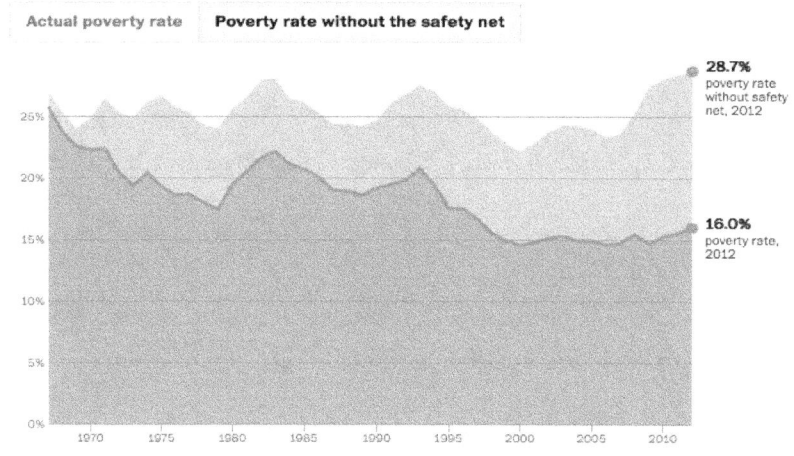

Poverty rate with/without "Great Society" programs. Graphic, Washington Post (2014) ("The Best Case That the War on Poverty Has Failed," 2014)

The same curve is obvious among those reaching middle school. The growth in achievement for those "at risk" was greatest with "New Math," "Whole Language," and open classrooms, which pushed that stubborn "achievement gap" to historically low levels.

For both African-American and white students, the 1970s were the high point of achievement. The political narrative sold to the nation is quite different, whether the seller is the Republican Party or *The New York Times*, but that's why, here, I am using their "facts" and not just the observational data, which indicates happier, more engaged, more likely to stay-in-school students. ("Opinion," 2023)

Figure 9. Trend in NAEP reading average scores and score gaps for White and Black 13-year-old students

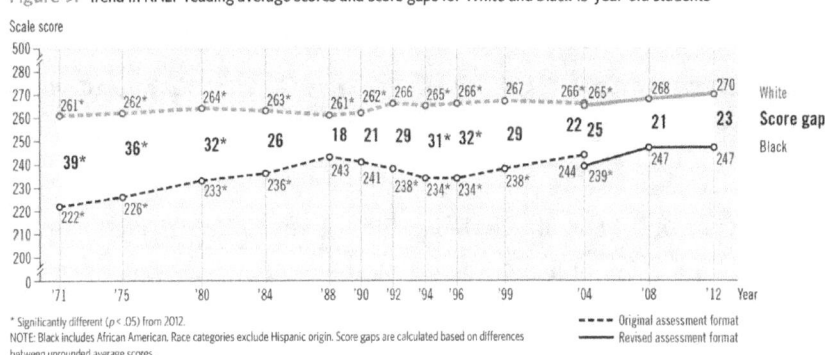

* Significantly different (p < .05) from 2012.
NOTE: Black includes African American. Race categories exclude Hispanic origin. Score gaps are calculated based on differences between unrounded average scores.

‑ ‑ ‑ Original assessment format
——— Revised assessment format

For children entering school between 1970 and 1978, the reading achievement gap was cut in half on the NAEP measurements by age 13, to a level not matched since. (NAEP 2012 Executive Summary.pdf, n.d.)

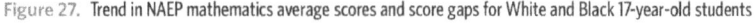

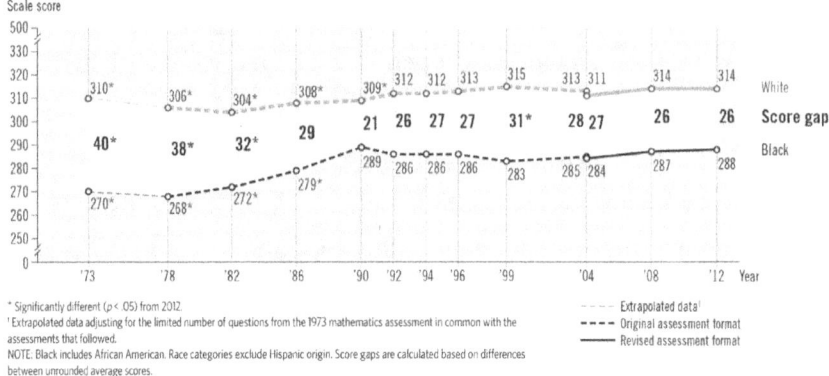

* Significantly different (p < .05) from 2012.
† Extrapolated data adjusting for the limited number of questions from the 1973 mathematics assessment in common with the assessments that followed.
NOTE: Black includes African American. Race categories exclude Hispanic origin. Score gaps are calculated based on differences between unrounded average scores.

- - - - Extrapolated data†
- - - Original assessment format
——— Revised assessment format

The same evidence is clear in mathematics, the much-maligned "New Math" led to the smallest historic racial achievement gap - 21 points in 1990. (NAEP 2012 Executive Summary.pdf, n.d.)

"Is every bit of the above debatable?" I wrote in 2014, "of course. It's especially debatable within the context of my argument. Three significant shifts were occurring—racial integration, open education, and dramatic anti-poverty programs all coalescing, and augmented by a fourth, the rapid expansion of very inexpensive university opportunities. What was the most important factor? Was there a most important factor?" (*Why We Think 1970s Open Education Failed, and Considering What the Truth Really Is*, n.d.)

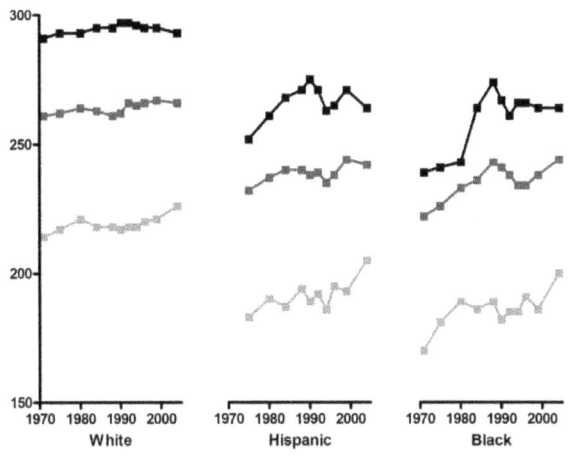

| 1970 1980 1990 2000 | 1970 1980 1990 2000 | 1970 1980 1990 2000 |
| White | Hispanic | Black |

The peak of equality of outcomes in reading (17-year-olds in the darkest line), came for those students most impacted by the open education movement. The "back to basics" focus beginning in the Reagan years raised elementary and middle school test scores but lowered high school achievement. The same pattern is produced today by the "Science of Reading"-driven "Mississippi Miracle," which has raised third-grade test scores but has left eighth-grade black students nowhere. Ten percent of Black students reach proficiency, and for black students achieving advanced, the percentage "rounds to zero." (2022 NAEP.pdf, n.d.)

REPORTING GROUPS	PERCENTAGE OF STUDENTS	AVG. SCORE	PERCENTAGE AT OR ABOVE *NAEP* BASIC	*NAEP* PROFICIENT	PERCENTAGE AT *NAEP* ADVANCED
Race/Ethnicity					
White	41	267	78	35	3
Black	49	240	49	10	#
Hispanic	6	247	59	17	1
Asian	1	‡	‡	‡	‡
American Indian/Alaska Native	#	‡	‡	‡	‡
Native Hawaiian/Pacific Islander	#	‡	‡	‡	‡
Two or More Races	3	265	78	32	2
Gender					
Male	51	249	58	20	1
Female	49	257	68	24	2
National School Lunch Program					
Eligible	76	247	57	16	1
Not eligible	24	271	81	41	4

Rounds to zero.
‡ Reporting standards not met.
NOTE: Detail may not sum to totals because of rounding, and because the "Information not

The narrative constructed by those in power was that "70s education failed." Whether it was a full-scale success is debatable (full implementation remained rare even at its height), but no evidence suggests failure.

Just as our narrative on the War on Poverty leaves out all its dramatic successes—because it is more important today for Amazon not to pay taxes—the lies about this progressive period are used to ensure that those on the margins will be forever blocked in their pursuit of equity. As the coming century will prove in the next chapter.

"The Science of Reading" in 1960 at left, and Bank Street's inclusive Whole Language Model (1970) at right. The Dick and Jane Reading series is often mislabeled as "whole language" but the vocabulary construction is purely phoneme-based. The Bank Street Readers were geared both to relevance and context.

Sources:

2022 NAEP.pdf. (n.d.).

Adams, C. F. (1883). *A College Fetich: An Address Delivered Before the Harvard Chapter of the Fraternity of the Phi Beta Kappa, in Sanders Theatre, Cambridge, June 28, 1883.* Lee and Shepard.

Barnum, M. (2015, July 22). *Arne Duncan's wrong turn on reform: How federal dollars fueled the testing backlash.* https://www.the74million.org/article/arne-duncans-wrong-turn-on-reform-how-federal-dollars-fueled-the-testing-backlash/

Baron, D. (n.d.). *Heer, hiser, himer: Pronouns in the news, 1912 edition.* Retrieved March 20, 2024, from https://blogs.illinois.edu/view/25/612401423

Briggs, T. H. (1920). *The Junior High School.* Houghton Mifflin.

Callahan, R. E. (1964, March). *Education and the Cult of Efficiency.* University of Chicago Press; pu3430623_3430810. https://press.uchicago.edu/ucp/books/book/chicago/E/bo24046474.html

Cineas, F. (2023, February 15). *What DeSantis is doing to Florida schools, explained.* Vox. https://www.vox.com/policy-and-politics/23593369/ron-desantis-florida-schools-higher-education-woke

Cunningham, H. (2012). *The Invention of Childhood.* Random House.

Cunningham, M. T. (2021). Democrats for Education Reform and the Inside Job. In M. T. Cunningham (Ed.), *Dark Money and the Politics of School Privatization* (pp. 137–167). Springer International Publishing.

De Paul Law Review. (2004). De Paul University School of Law.

For professors, segregation begins at home. (2019, January 21). Kappan Online. https://kappanonline.org/professors-college-towns-segregation-emdin-moran-socol/

Friedman, D. (2010, July 16). *Women triumph in national educational association.* SundayMagazine.org. https://sundaymagazine.org/2010/07/16/women-triumph-in-national-educational-association/

History. (n.d.). PEN - Progressive Education Network. Retrieved March 20, 2024, from https://progressiveeducationnetwork.org/history/

Hoecker, B., & Dornemann, V. (2011). *Wir sind Deutschland!: Ein illustrer Streifzug durch die deutsche Geschichte* (1st ed.). Lappan.

Holt, J. C. (n.d.). *How Children Fail Quotes.* Retrieved March 20, 2024, from https://www.goodreads.com/work/quotes/560026-how-children-fail

Hopkins, L. P. S. (1886). *Educational Psychology: a Treatise for Parents and Educators.* Lee and Shepard.

Hopkins, L. P. S. (1887). *How Shall My Child be Taught?: Practical Pedagogy, Or, The Science of Teaching Illustrated.* Lee and Shepard.

Hopkins, L. P. S. (1892). *The Spirit of the New Education.* Lee and Shepard.

Jarding, S. (2016, April 11). The unwitting father of the American progressive movement? Ronald Reagan. *HuffPost.* https://www.huffpost.com/entry/the-unwitting-father-of-t_b_9657198

Kothari, D. (2021, August 31). *Crow Island School, Illinois by Eero Saarinen.* RTF | Rethinking The Future. https://www.re-thinkingthefuture.com/case-studies/a5035-crow-island-school-illinois-by-eero-saarinen/

Lagemann, E. C. (1996). Experimenting with Education: John Dewey and Ella Flagg Young at the University of Chicago. *American Journal of Education*, *104*(3), 171–185.

Meyer, J. W., Tyack, D., Nagel, J., & Gordon, A. (1979). Public Education as Nation-Building in America: Enrollments and Bureaucratization in the American States, 1870-1930. *The American Journal of Sociology*, *85*(3), 591–613.

NAEP 2012 Executive Summary.pdf. (n.d.).

National Education Association of the United States. Committee of Ten on Secondary School Studies. (1894). *Report of the Committee of Ten on Secondary School Studies: With the Reports of the Conferences Arranged by the Committee*. National Education Association.

Online safety legislation is opposed by many it claims to protect. (2024, February 1). *The Washington Post*. https://www.washingtonpost.com/technology/2024/02/01/online-safety-hearing-opposition/

Opinion. (2023, November 18). *The New York Times*. https://www.nytimes.com/2023/11/18/opinion/pandemic-school-learning-loss.html

Postman, N., & Weingartner, C. (1969). *Teaching as a Subversive Activity* (p. 3). Dell Publishing.

Progressive Education. (1924). The Association.

PS 20 the Clinton hill school — cluster specialists. (n.d.). PS 20 The Clinton Hill School. Retrieved March 20, 2024, from https://www.ps20.org/clusterteachers

Rahm Emanuel's non-apology apology for being a school privatization cheerleader. (2019, February 10). Gadflyonthewallblog. https://gadflyonthewallblog.com/2019/02/10/rahm-emanuels-non-apology-apology-for-being-a-school-privatization-cheerleader/

Raising successful kids. (2019, April 16). Harvard Gazette. https://news.harvard.edu/gazette/story/2019/04/harvards-ronald-ferguson-explores-how-to-raise-successful-children/

Report of the Committee of Ten 1892.pdf. (n.d.).

Revolutions. (n.d.-a). Revolutions. Retrieved March 20, 2024, from https://thehistoryofrome.typepad.com/revolutions_podcast/

Revolutions. (n.d.-b). Revolutions. Retrieved March 20, 2024, from https://thehistoryofrome.typepad.com/revolutions_podcast/2017/07/701-the-volcano.html

Schwarz, J. (2021, August 6). *The murder of the U.S. middle class began 40 years ago this week*. The Intercept. https://theintercept.com/2021/08/06/middle-class-reagan-patco-strike/

Smith, A. W. (2013). *Ronald Reagan & the great social security heist: How Reagan gave birth to the looting of social security*. Ironwood Publications.

Socol, I. D. (2020, June 4). *Education is the most political thing we do, it is the fight for our future*. Age of Awareness. https://medium.com/age-of-awareness/education-is-the-most-political-thing-we-do-it-is-the-fight-for-our-future-315b85dc51d

Stefano, J. (2023, August 30). *Americans want education reform. Why don't Democrats?* Newsweek. https://www.newsweek.com/americans-want-education-reform-why-dont-democrats-opinion-1823149

Stevens, W. K. (1970, January 23). Students Flock to Philadelphia "School Without Walls." *The New York Times*. https://www.nytimes.com/1970/01/23/archives/students-flock-to-philadelphia-school-without-walls.html

Suenobu, K. (2007). *Life: Band 11* (A. Klepper, Trans.). Heyne.

The best case that the war on poverty has failed. (2014, February 19). *The Washington Post*. https://www.washingtonpost.com/news/wonk/wp/2014/02/19/the-best-case-that-the-war-on-poverty-has-failed/

Time Inc. (1958). *LIFE*. Time Inc.

Why we think 1970s Open Education failed, and considering what the truth really is. (n.d.). Retrieved March 21, 2024, from https://speedchange.blogspot.com/2014/02/why-we-think-1970s-open-education.html

Wikipedia contributors. (2023a, October 1). *Beatrice Ensor*. Wikipedia, The Free Encyclopedia. https://en.wikipedia.org/w/index.php?title=Beatrice_Ensor&oldid=1178088875

Wikipedia contributors. (2023b, December 14). *Helen Parkhurst*. Wikipedia, The Free Encyclopedia. https://en.wikipedia.org/w/index.php?title=Helen_Parkhurst&oldid=1189808296

Wikipedia contributors. (2024a, February 11). *Phara Souffrant Forrest*. Wikipedia, The Free Encyclopedia. https://en.wikipedia.org/w/index.php?title=Phara_Souffrant_Forrest&oldid=1206119820

Wikipedia contributors. (2024b, February 23). *Blackboard Jungle*. Wikipedia, The Free Encyclopedia. https://en.wikipedia.org/w/index.php?title=Blackboard_Jungle&oldid=1209712413

Wikipedia contributors. (2024c, March 6). *Dalton School*. Wikipedia, The Free Encyclopedia. https://en.wikipedia.org/w/index.php?title=Dalton_School&oldid=1212073471

Wikipedia contributors. (2024d, March 14). *Savings and loan crisis*. Wikipedia, The Free Encyclopedia. https://en.wikipedia.org/w/index.php?title=Savings_and_loan_crisis&oldid=1213712227

Wikipedia contributors. (2024e, March 16). *Mike Duncan (podcaster)*. Wikipedia, The Free Encyclopedia. https://en.wikipedia.org/w/index.php?title=Mike_Duncan_(podcaster)&oldid=1214007340

Wikipedia contributors. (2024f, March 17). *Hakeem Jeffries*. Wikipedia, The Free Encyclopedia. https://en.wikipedia.org/w/index.php?title=Hakeem_Jeffries&oldid=1214251623

Wikipedia contributors. (2024g, March 19). *Normal school*. Wikipedia, The Free Encyclopedia. https://en.wikipedia.org/w/index.php?title=Normal_school&oldid=1214547735

Young, E. F. (1901). *Isolation in the School*. University of Chicago Press.

Young, E. F. (1910). The Public High School. *The School Review, 18*(2), 73–83.

CHAPTER FIVE:

How the Segregationists Triumphed in the 21st Century.
The Destruction of Public Education Began with Some of the
Best of Intentions and Some of the Worst.

Since the 1954 Brown vs. Board of Education Supreme Court decision, many in the United States have been committed to turning back the clock. This effort began in the South, where, rather than integrate, public schools were shut down while white students were sent to "Segregation Academies" also known as white-flight schools. (Porter et al., 2014) The controversy spread to the North after federal courts began to insist that de facto segregated schools be integrated. Racist and opportunistic politicians fueled opposition to "forced busing" that moved white working-class students to traditional black schools (black students joining in white schools was more acceptable, as long as they remained in the minority). Boston, as an example, exploded with racial violence in opposition to busing for integration. (Wikipedia contributors, 2024c)

A newly conservative Supreme Court filled with Nixon and Reagan appointees began whittling away at school integration decisions, (*Riddick by Riddick v. Sch. Bd. Of City of Norfolk, 627 F. Supp. 814 (E.d. Va. 1984)*, n.d.), (Sippy, 2021), and Southern suburban parents began separating their white schools from otherwise integrated school districts. (Taylor et al., 2019)

What seemed surprising at the turn of the 21st century was how "liberal" politicians began to be fully seduced into endorsing the Segregation Academy model.

Child Development-Based Education vs No Child Left Behind and the Corporations

The vote in the United States Senate on the bill creating "No Child Left Behind" was 87 to 10. Strom Thurmond, Mitch McConnell, Hillary Clinton, and Ted Kennedy all voted "Yea." (*U.S. Senate: U.S. Senate Roll Call Votes 107th Congress - 1st Session*, 2023) Few things are more indicative of the idea that inclusive education will never have elite support than this near unanimity.

If the children of people experiencing poverty, of minorities, or those with disabilities were doing poorly in public schools—and they often were—something must have been causing that. Leaders considered three possible answers to this question: eugenics, school organization and teacher unionization, and accountability. Either minority students lacked something essential, or teachers and administrators were lazy and overpaid, or because we weren't sufficiently harsh in grading schools, schools didn't care enough to do the hard work.

Quoting "father of eugenics" Francis Galton, University of Pennsylvania scholar Angela Duckworth blamed the students and the non-white cultures they were raised in. (Duckworth et al., 2007) These people—African-Americans, Hispanics, and African Immigrants—all lacked "grit." They could not persist in the face of obstacles.

"It reminds me of a study done of taxi drivers in 1997," Duckworth has often told this story of African Immigrant cab drivers in New York City. "When it's raining, everybody wants a taxi, and taxi drivers pick up a lot of fares. So if you're a taxi driver, the rational thing to do is to work more hours on a rainy day than on a sunny day because you're always busy so you're making more money per hour. But it turns out that on rainy days, taxi drivers work the fewest hours. They seem to have some figure in their head—"OK, every day I need to make $1,000"—and after they reach that goal, they go home. And on a rainy day, they get to that figure really quickly." (Perkins-Gough & Duckworth, 2013)

Note two things. First, Duckworth declares that the Calvinist belief in the moral value of excess work is "rational." Second, she applies that construct to show that certain cultures are inherently flawed, and her work explains how schools must drive out those flawed cultures. For this cultural genocide approach—a favorite from the European treatment of North American natives—she received a Macarthur Foundation "genius" grant and became a TED Talk/YouTube star.

"Terms like "prejudice" and "racism" often miss the full scope of racial devaluation in our society, implying as they do that racial devaluation comes primarily from the strongly prejudiced, not from "good people" like [teachers]. But the prevalence of racists—deplorable though racism is— misses the full extent of [his] burden, perhaps even the most profound part. He faces a devaluation that grows out of our images of society and the way those images catalogue people. The catalogue need never be taught. It is implied by all we see around us..."—Claude Steele, 1992. (Steele, 1992)

Many Republican state legislators, while certainly not dismissing Duckworth's racist beliefs, found it easy to target teachers' unions and school administrators by passing anti-union laws and bills allowing white state government takeovers of public schools in black-majority cities. These efforts have continued throughout the century. (Dodd, 2023)

Neither of these theories could be readily accepted—or at least voiced—by the political left. However, like other successful American members of the elite, they were happy to accept Duckworth's belief in their "cultural superiority." They could embrace the third cause, a lack of accountability. If only schools had to declare how they were doing publicly, they'd do it better.

Obviously, the causes of underachievement could not be a national refusal to invest in the needs of integrated schools, solutions to persistent generational poverty, nor the early end to Lyndon Johnson's "Great Society" initiatives (replaced by the Nixonian "benign neglect"), (Alterman, 2022) nor zoning, substandard housing, poor and expensive medical care, nor a lack of national child care and parental leave. If it had been any of those things, real and costly solutions would have been required.

All NCLB required of those with power was the distribution of lucrative contracts to test development companies whose lobbyists were everywhere in Washington. "NCLB is distinctive in that it requires, not simply permits, some local school systems to contract with private providers for services," Patricia Burch, Joseph Donovan, and Matthew Steinberg wrote for *Kappan* in 2006. (Burch et al., 2006) "Across the U.S., test publishers, software companies, and research firms are swarming to take advantage of the revenues made available by NCLB." And, the authors indicated, even in the first few years of the law, those revenues were massive. "Schools and local governments," they noted in that year, "now spend approximately \$48 billion per year to purchase products and services from the private sector." That included "one of the four largest companies in the area of test development and preparation [generating] sales of \$4.4 billion and a profit of \$560 million in 2003... [while] for-profit tutoring companies took in \$4 billion in revenue" in that same year. (Burch et al., 2006)

"The more people see how NCLB actually works, the more it becomes clear that NCLB is not a tool for solving a crisis in public education, but a tool for creating one"— (Meier & Wood, 2004)

NCLB ranked schools based on a single type of test, and the tests were written based on the prior knowledge of the wealthy and white by companies led by white Ivy League (and Stanford and Duke) graduates. A look at the top executives of the College Board (as of March 5, 2024) demonstrates the diversity of experience and thought they have assembled, with alma maters listed as Yale, University of Michigan, Yale, Northwestern, George Washington, Duke, Stanford, William & Mary, Brigham Young, University of Chicago, Harvard, University of Virginia, Brown, University of Maryland, and Syracuse. (*Our Leadership*, n.d.) In a nation in which "less than 1 percent of American college students attend the 12 elite colleges," as stated by *The New York Times* in 2023 (counting the Ivies plus Duke, Stanford, MIT, and the University of Chicago, but not Northwestern or "public Ivies" such as the Universities of Michigan and Virginia), the 15 leaders of the primary path to the top universities must count institutions like Michigan (18 percent of applicants admitted), Virginia (19 percent), Brigham

Young (67 percent), Maryland (44 percent), Northwestern (7 percent), George Washington (49 percent), and Syracuse (52 percent) as their "outreach" to underserved populations. (Bhatia et al., n.d.)

Nowhere on their list are any land-grant universities, no matter how limited their admissions are—Michigan State (88 percent), Kentucky (95 percent), Ohio State (53 percent), Virginia Tech (57 percent), nor any HBCUs—Howard (53 percent), Coppin State (45 percent), Tuskegee (30 percent), nor any urban publics such as Brooklyn College (CUNY—55 percent), University of Buffalo (SUNY—68 percent), not even UCLA with a 9 percent admissions rate. (all admission rates from *US News and World Report*—March 6, 2024). (*The Best National Universities in America*, 2024)

In terms of opportunities created—the expressed goal of the liberals who voted for NCLB—their efforts are a radical failure, as the Reagan era was before. "Even after decades of affirmative action, black and Hispanic students are more underrepresented at the nation's top colleges and universities than they were 35 years ago," *The New York Times* reported in 2017. "The share of black freshmen at elite schools is virtually unchanged since 1980. Black students are just 6 percent of freshmen but 15 percent of college-age Americans." (Ashkenas et al., 2017) Those are the statistics from before the United States Supreme Court banned the consideration of race in college admissions. They did not ban universities from considering the lack of need for financial aid in admissions decisions, nor legacy admissions.

This elite lock-out extends into real-life power dynamics. "Although fewer than 1% of college students attend the highly selective, private "Ivy-Plus" colleges," *Forbes* reported in 2023, "they eventually account for 15% of those in the top 0.1% of the income distribution. They also make up a quarter of U.S. Senators, half of all Rhodes scholars, and three-fourths of Supreme Court justices appointed in the last half-century." (Nietzel, 2023) Forbes indicated that the elites' preferences for students from wealthy backgrounds were actuated through legacy admissions, Olympic sports recruiting, and an application process that focuses on "non-academic factors like extracurricular activities, leadership capacity, and personal traits," and that, "those who attend private high schools tend to obtain much higher non-academic ratings (but similar academic ratings) than students attending public high schools." (Nietzel, 2023)

All of this is defended endlessly. If elites do better than others after attending elite universities, it must be the education provided, not the inherent privileges. *Forbes*, while admitting bias, will still protect the concepts. "SAT/ACT scores and holistic academic ratings were highly predictive of post-college outcomes. According to the authors, "despite having potential biases that may favor high-income students, SAT/ACT scores remain one of the best predictors of students' post-college outcomes among available indicators."" (Nietzel, 2023)

In the *post hoc ergo propter hoc* world of wealth and power, because our kids do well, the system works because our kids are superior. (Wikipedia contributors, 2024a)

With all of this in place, the wealthy and powerful sent their kids to highly progressive private schools, from Dalton in Manhattan and St. Ann's in Brooklyn, Sidwell Friends in Washington DC and Imagination Lab School in Palo Alto, to Montessori elementary schools everywhere and Avenues—The World School (wherever rich executives gather), and elite public schools such as Thomas Jefferson High School in Fairfax, Virginia and New York City's Stuyvesant High, all but the publics exempt from the accountability standards, those in power doubled-down on locked down scripted curriculum, aggressive behavior control that criminalized black students, and endless test-prep for the children unable to escape.

No rows, no government tests, no 120 hours—Avenues, The World School—tuition $65,850 per year. (Avenues, n.d.)

The privileged students prospered as their parents and grandparents found new ways to profit from the nation's disinvestment in children.

This class war is fought with the deep support of media owned by the wealthy—especially *The New York Times, Washington Post,* and television networks. And this war has deadly results for the marginalized NCLB was most supposed to help.

"NCLB, as it was known, is the worst federal education legislation ever passed by Congress. It was punitive, harsh, stupid, ignorant about pedagogy and motivation, and ultimately a dismal failure. Those who still admire NCLB either helped write it, or were paid to like it, or were profiting from it."— (Ravitch, 2018)

Because NCLB (and its state continuations) and the media partners put so much pressure on schools and school districts, any student behind in any tested subject had all opportunity stripped away so they could be "remediated." That remediation is almost a requirement in "at-risk" schools where any child's failure can put teacher and administrator jobs on the line. It occurs less often when the few white/wealthy kids not keeping up won't hurt the school's status. (see: Crisafulli, No Educator Left Unscathed: How No Child Left Behind Threatens Educators' Careers) (Crisafulli, 2006)

White and "Gifted" (#16 "gifted" Children, 2008)

With curiosity-driven, learner-centered education for the kids of the powerful and a social boot camp for the marginalized being the new normal, it is no surprise that "Gifted and Talented" education extends these divisions into every school corridor and classroom where a mix of demographics exist. In these "integrated" schools, "gifted" most often means white, neurotypical, and above the school population's median income. (Long et al., 2023) "Students who qualified for free/reduced-price lunch (FRPL), EL, and Black or Latinx students were between two to eight times less likely to be identified as gifted compared to non–free/reduced-price lunch, non-EL, and White or Asian students," Long, McCoach, Siegle, Callahan, and Gubbins determined in their 2023 paper. "However, between 50% and 100% of gifted identification disparities could be explained by student-level differences in early academic achievement, which is consistent with an opportunity gap explanation of underrepresentation." (Long et al., 2023) The divide and damage—opportunities for the rich, tests, test-prep, and harsh discipline—for profit—for the poor—wasn't just seen in the public/private split, but in school districts neighboring each other and within school districts, as a small swath of Brooklyn containing PS 20, PS 124 demonstrates. To fully understand the dynamics of early 21st-century educational wealth, we must stretch the area a bit to include the Commodore Barry Public Housing Project and the elevated Brooklyn-Queens Expressway (Interstate 278). In addition to the divide created by parent wealth discussed previously, the world of for-profit charter schools—which shift taxpayer school funding to corporate investors and highly paid executives—adds a vicious twist.

The New York Times calls poor children lazy—a favorite pastime in the "newspaper of record."—*"As access to devices has spread, children in poorer families are spending considerably more time than children from more well-off families using their television and gadgets to watch shows and videos, play games and connect on social networking sites, studies show. This growing time-wasting gap, policymakers and researchers say, is more a reflection of the ability of parents to monitor and limit how children use technology than of access to it."* —Matt Richtel in *The New York Times* (Richtel, 2012) (see my thoughts on Richtel's bias) (*SpeEdChange*, 2012)

Just six blocks from the high privilege of PS 20's students, "Success Academy Fort Greene" (which now appears to have closed) was co-located with Middle School 265 (now McKinney Secondary School of the Arts). Part of two nationwide trends, hyper-colonization of education and profiteering via charter schools and vouchers, Success Academy was embraced by conservative mayors Bloomberg (2002-2013) and Adams (2022-?) and tolerated by the more centrist DeBlasio (2014-2021) while enriching its chief executive Eva Moskowitz ($981,770 in compensation in 2022) (Suozzo et al., n.d.) and building a management bureaucracy that now fills three and a half floors, 94,000 square feet, in a Wall Street skyscraper. (Four other executives earned over $400,000 in 2022, with five others over $250,000.) (Nehring, 2024)

Overall, in 2022, Success Academies took in almost $189 million, almost entirely from taxpayer money for public education, while spending just under $93 million—a profit of $96 million for this "non-profit." (Suozzo et al., 2013)

Success Academies, much like KIPP Academies, are an expression of what those in power want education to be for the poor and marginalized. Based on the same colonial theories that drove the U.S.'s "Indian Boarding Schools," (*U.S. Indian Boarding School History*, n.d.) Canada's "Residential Schools" (Mosby & Millions, 2021), as well as native language-denying British schools in Wales and Ireland, these schools combine test-prep that pleases government scorekeepers and the *Washington Post* with cultural conversion to compliance with white middle-class etiquette. Mosby and Millions in *Scientific American* August 2021 quoted the goal of the Canadian Residential Schools, "Kill the Indian, and save the man... [with a] focus was on manual labour, religious instruction and cultural assimilation." (Mosby & Millions, 2021)

Whether KIPP's "SLANT" [Sit up straight. Listen. Ask and answer questions. Nod for comprehension. Track the speaker with your eyes.] or Success Academies' deep focus on silence with "hands folded in

[your] lap" (*Effectively Keep Students Engaged with SLANT*, 2014) the primary purpose is easily seen as making minority young people less threatening to those gentrifying U.S. cities. "During the time your class was observed, there were several scholars who did not meet the school's posture expectations," a Success principal emailed a teacher in 2023. "In addition, scholars were unfocused and playing with loose items on their desks during instruction. playing with his pen cap..." (Camperi, 2023)

"That Brutal Charter School Video Shows That Rich People Love No-Excuses Discipline ... for Other People's Kids" was the headline for a 2016 *Slate* article by *New York Times* reporter Michelle Goldberg. (Goldberg, 2016) The video revealed classroom psychological abuse and persistent suspension of even kindergarten students at a Success Academy school in a fast-gentrifying Brooklyn community—a community also profiled in the *Times'* "Nice White Parents" podcast series. (Gill, 2015) That school, and the one in Fort Greene, were found to have "Got to Go" lists (Katz, 2016) of students they wanted out because their testing failures might damage the schools' claims to what is defined as "achievement." (Taylor, 2015)

"Charter schools are a popular cause among elites in New York, particularly on Wall Street," Goldberg continues, quoting Diane Ravitch, "Hedge fund managers supply the millions that enable charters to thrive. They are big givers to charters, and they are big givers to political candidates who support charters," before noting the obvious, "If you look around a neighborhood like [the one surrounding that Success Academy school], you'll see that in many cases, when rich people are educating their own children, only the most progressive, touchy-feely methods will do." (Latham, 2023)

"[Success Academy] is a data-driven institution, just like the entire rest of the American education system. This is not a surprise. What was a surprise, though, was the lengths the school goes to attain its desired data. For nearly three months leading up to the NY State English and Math tests (January to March), the students are not learning anything. I feel the need to emphasize that again before I explain: for three months, students attending a school are not learning anything in their time there. What they are doing, instead, is practicing taking multiple-choice tests, day in and day out. This is, ironically, called "Think" season."—Livia Camperi, 2023 (Camperi, 2023)

Learner-Centered Learning vs the Anti-Education Coalition

Paralleling the previous battle, yet outliving it, is the coalition against public education. This pressure group includes the segregationist core— parents who will not tolerate more than a handful of minority students in their children's schools, the politicians who have always catered to that crowd, from George Wallace and Lester Gordon to Ron DeSantis, Donald Trump, and hundreds of state legislators, the profiteers from above who know that if public education is fully privatized they can skim hundreds of billions from classrooms, religious fundamentalists offended by secular education, and American "individualist" thinkers who do not even believe in public roads or fire departments—much less schools—those who see extreme capitalism as their religion.

The attacks from this coalition are directed from state houses, corporate offices, right-wing think tanks, university economics depart- ments, and lobbyists hired by a dizzying array of for-profit organizations that want more and more of the golden goose their efforts have created.

This array includes the testing industry, the test prep industry, the remediation industry, and both online and in-person for-profit private and charter school operators.

Sarah Stitzlein: "EMOs [Educational Management Organizations] are for-profit, private companies that run schools by executive authority, often replicating school models established elsewhere. EMOs are... corporations that manage and run nearly all aspects of a school, from hiring teachers to the selection of curricula... EMOs are primarily profit driven. I want to stress that while these schools do have goals of educating children, their funding and governance structures prioritize profit, relying upon profit to function and exist. EMOs endorse and embody neoliberal ideologies championed by such school choice pioneers as Milton Friedman, Fredrich von Hayek, John Chubb, and Terry Moe... EMOs uniquely begin with the explicit goal of competing in the US free-market economy to make a profit." (Stitzlein, 2013)

W. Brett Robertson 2015: "Charter school researchers have begun to use geographic information systems (GIS) to analyze the particular geography of charter schools in order to illuminate how their distribution across districts and regions may have implications for student sorting. As charter schools proliferate in urban districts, new charter schools open while traditional public schools close. These changes can have implications for school stratification by race, socioeconomic status and achievement. This stratification, in turn, can influence the academic opportunities and outcomes of students at schools where there is concentrated advantage or disadvantage." (Robertson, 2015)

Shifting public education fully away from both the public purpose of national improvement and the language of equality of outcomes represents the triumph of the right-wing University of Chicago economics movement. Milton Friedman had long pursued the privatization of education for reasons of both economic segregation of children and because he and his colleagues could not comprehend any situation in the world in which the profit motive would not be a good thing. He began from one primary point that public education had begun to "fail" as soon as school integration was introduced in the mid-1950s. (Friedman, 1997) "The quality of schooling is far worse today than it was in 1955. There is no respect in which inhabitants of a low-income neighborhood are so disadvantaged as in the kind of schooling they can get for their children," Friedman wrote in 1997, making the white middle-class assumption that the schools he attended in the 1920s in Rahway, New Jersey were (a) good, (b) inclusive in some way, and (c) a norm. (Friedman, 1997) This triple fallacy, combined with a distrust of government based on ideology instead of facts and a penchant for lying (the biggest school districts he railed against as a new development all existed when he was a child), allowed Friedman to see a new way to take tax revenue from public purposes and put it into private pockets. With NCLB in place and a measurement system constructed to make public schools look bad, Friedman's cohort could easily seduce the Wall Street hedge-fund managers behind the New Schools Venture Fund (Barkan et al., 2011), their co-conspirators in the Democrats for Education Reform campaign finance group (Meltzer, 2018), the foundations of the super-rich (Eli Broad (Haefele, 2021) and Mark Zuckerberg (Weber & Baker, 2017)), as well as White Houses both right-wing—George W. Bush's administration—and center-left—Barack Obama and his Chicago basketball pal Arne Duncan. There was both money to be had and political points to score.

"To justify their campaign, ed reformers repeat, mantra-like, that U.S. students are trailing far behind their peers in other nations, that U.S. public schools are failing. The claims are specious. Two of the three major international tests—the Progress in International Reading Literacy Study and the

Trends in International Math and Science Study—break down student scores according to the poverty rate in each school. The tests are given every five years. The most recent results (2006) showed the following: students in U.S. schools where the poverty rate was less than 10 percent ranked first in reading, first in science, and third in math. When the poverty rate was 10 percent to 25 percent, U.S. students still ranked first in reading and science. But as the poverty rate rose still higher, students ranked lower and lower. Twenty percent of all U.S. schools have poverty rates over 75 percent. The average ranking of American students reflects this. The problem is not public schools; it is poverty. And as dozens of studies have shown, the gap in cognitive, physical, and social development between children in poverty and middle-class children is set by age three."— Joanne Barkan, 2011 (Barkan et al., 2011)

If the fault lies with public schools, there is no reason to address poverty, and addressing poverty is a massive threat to those currently concentrating wealth and power in their own hands. For the rich, the mantra that "the public schools are failing" is a profitable defense of the political system that keeps their superiority and economic prosperity intact.

The New York Times
https://www.nytimes.com › pandemic-school-learning-loss   ⋮

Opinion | The Startling Evidence on Learning Loss Is In

Nov 18, 2023 — The State of Virginia took a big swing at the problem of **learning loss** when it announced what is being described as a statewide tutoring program ...
Magical thinking · Opinion · The Pandemic Erased Two...

The New York Times
https://www.nytimes.com › learning-loss-school-districts   ⋮

See How Your School District Is Recovering From ...

7 days ago — Look up data from the first detailed national study of **learning loss** and academic recovery since the pandemic ... © 2024 The **New York Times** ...

The New York Times
https://www.nytimes.com › interactive › 2024/01/31 › pa...   ⋮

Students Are Making a 'Surprising' Rebound From ...

Jan 31, 2024 — Overall in math, a subject where **learning loss** has been greatest ... Bob Miller for The **New York Times**. When it comes to success, no one ...

The New York Times
https://www.nytimes.com › education-learning-loss   ⋮

What Our Schools Can Do to Reverse Learning Loss

Dec 9, 2023 — What Our Schools Can Do to Reverse **Learning Loss**. Readers discuss an editorial about how to address declining test scores and chronic ...

The New York Times
https://www.nytimes.com › 2023/09/05 › opinion › covi...   ⋮

We Can Fight Learning Loss Only With Accountability and ...

Sep 5, 2023 — ... **learning loss** has been eerily quiet. Responsibility for reversing ... Follow The **New York Times** Opinion section on Facebook, Twitter (@NYTopinion) ...

The New York Times
https://www.nytimes.com › learning-loss-test-results-covid   ⋮

American Students Outperformed Much of the World ...

Dec 13, 2023 — By now, you've probably registered the alarm that pandemic **learning loss** has produced a "lost generation" of American students.

The New York Times
https://www.nytimes.com › 2023/05/11 › opinion › pand...   ⋮

Parents Don't Understand How Far Behind Their Kids Are ...

May 11, 2023 — Within school districts, **learning loss** was similar across racial groups. Change in math scores for Black students. 1 year. gain. Black students ...

The constant drumbeat of The New York Times *on how badly poor kids are doing. Will they get dance, music, art, or maker labs to help them succeed?* (Google search image captured by Ira Socol)

Though research (Apple, 2007) —and Diane Ravitch—have discredited NCLB (Hess, 2022), the wealthy and powerful have simply renamed the issue so they can carry on. Almost daily, *The New York Times* proclaims how poor kids, and Black and Brown kids, have "lost their learning." This calls for more remediation and, obviously, less opportunity. (Miller et al., 2024)

Will this impact private schools? No. Religious schools that get vouchers? No. Scarsdale kids? Palo Alto kids? The kids in rich communities in Austin, Texas? No. This obsession punishes only our most vulnerable children. They will lose out on everything that brings kids to school, creates world-opening opportunities, and allows children to demonstrate their unique skills, talents, and knowledge.

This divide is a design feature, not an unwanted side effect. "Reform efforts previously geared toward improving the system of public education have been superseded by the efforts of venture philanthropies and foundations like Gates, Walton, and Broad to remake education into a private market," Gregory Tewksbury of CUNY wrote in 2016. "The power of these institutions politically, socially and economically to reshape the educational landscape in America raises fundamental questions about the role of wealthy elites and their influence on democracy and education." (Gregory Tewksbury, 2016) (Tewksbury, 2016)

"The students most at risk are those in poor districts, whose test scores fell further during the pandemic. Though the new data shows that they have begun to catch up, they had much more to make up than their peers from higher-income families, who are already closer to a recovery." The New York Times advocates—without saying it—to remediate poor kids instead of opening opportunities.

Beginning in the 2020s, other assaults on public schools joined these privatization efforts, the "anti-woke" (Wertheimer, 2023) attacks by Republican voters and politicians (Hatfield, 2023) that set out to eliminate critical inquiry and citizenship development—two cornerstones of education for many, a now non-euphemistic effort to make schools hostile places for Blacks (*"Texas Insists on Discriminating against Black Hair,"* 2024), Latinos, (Gomez, 2023),students with disabilities or neurodiversity (Vallas et al., 2017), and any young person not locked into historic cisgender roles (Riedel, 2024), and finally a voucher system aimed at shifting school funds away from public schools (*The Facts Are In. Instead of Promoting Choice, Much of the Nearly $400 Million for Expanded Ohio School Vouchers Went to Those Already Attending Private Schools:* Editorial, 2024) to unaccountable private and religious schools (Walker, 2024) —even when no student made that switch. (Cowen, 2023b)

"[T]he real issue today is that they come at a cost of funding traditional public schools," Michigan State University professor Josh Cowen wrote in 2023. "As voucher systems expand, they cannibalize states' ability to pay for their public education commitments. Arizona, which passed universal vouchers in 2022, is nearing a genuine budget crisis as a result of voucher over-spending. Six of the last seven states to pass vouchers have had to slow spending on public schools relative to investments made by non-voucher states... For many rural students who live far from the nearest private school, vouchers are unrealistic in the first place, meaning that when states cut spending on public education, they weaken the only educational lifeline available to poorer and more remote communities in some places." (Cowen, 2023a) This stripping of funds from public education continues a long-term trend—since the Reagan Administration—of right-wing attempts to "starve the beast," eliminate government services by shifting funds to the private sector. (Wikipedia contributors, 2024b)

Countering these efforts has been a groundswell of efforts in and out of public schools to humanize education and return to the more equitable practices of the 1970s. There are more alternatives offered in public schools where the political mood allows (Socol et al., 2018) including public Montessori schools (Montessori Public, 2016), alternative high schools (CodeRVA, 2018), lab schools (STEAM Academy, n.d.), new learner-centered assessment structures (CDLI - Defenses of Learning, n.d.), and programs modeled on the "forest kindergarten" (Appalachian Forest School, n.d.) concept. Of course, wealthy suburban school districts—those never threatened by low state test scores, often keep progressive concepts such as project-based learning, maker work, and explorations as central to their work. (Bloomfield Hills Public Schools, n.d.)

We do what we can.

This cycle of revolution and counter-revolution will never stop. Nor will the battle between education as opportunity and education as training. In 2024, as the Carnegie Foundation finally pushes against the "Carnegie Unit"—or credit for time sitting on your ass, as it should be known—the American right is shifting into full counter-revolution mode. (Planning And Evaluation Committee on the Ryan White Care Act Data for Resource Allo, 2004)

On the website "Real Clear Education," anti-education crusader Max Eden (*January 18, 2024: Evidence Mounts That Pre-K Harms Kids, July 24, 2023: Trauma-Deformed Pedagogy, June 13, 2023: Do These Books Belong in Public School Libraries? You Be The Judge, et al*) quotes Daniel Buck—the classic white male ex-teacher elevated to "expert" by a right-wing think tank—as saying that altering the Carnegie Unit "could choke out our already wilting commitment to tradition, rigorous academics." (*Max_Eden_83_Prop.pdf*, n.d.) Buck works at the for-profit charter school advocate Thomas B. Fordham Institute, where he seemingly sits around with fellow well-paid conservatives and works to maintain our national wealth divide. (The Thomas B. Fordham Institute, n.d.)

Even the inventors of the Carnegie Unit know the damage these ancient practices have done. Image: Carnegie Foundation (Tavenner, 2023)

In this La-La-Land of wealth, conspiracy theories are promulgated actively. "Conservative parents are already deeply skeptical of big tech and education-establishment-driven social engineering efforts. They won't take kindly to the prospect of classroom cameras datamining their kids to grade them on character skillsets defined by progressive do-gooders," writes Eden—and he can sell this straw man to his wealthy audience and those who follow them on X and TruthSocial, because, if not counting hours sitting on your ass, how could learning ever be assessed?

The kids of Fordham Institute funders may not be very smart, creative, or even effective, but if they have not been trained to sit still quietly before they are five, mom and dad will pay for a questionable disability diagnosis (something poor parents cannot afford) and let their kids game the system right through the SATs and their legacy admission to an Ivy League university.

Revolutions get crushed. Revolutions often get crushed before they can be fully born. Inequity is baked into the human experience.

"Them that's got shall get. Them that's not shall lose. So the bible said and it still is news," sang Billie Holiday in 1941, and today is not so different—but it is different. (BillieHolidayVEVO, 2022)

We keep fighting, not because we fully believe that we can change the world, but because we know we can help at least some children. And each of our revolutionary attempts moves us forward, if only by the lessons we learn.

Sources:

#16 "gifted" children. (2008, January 23). Stuff White People Like. https://stuffwhitepeoplelike. com/2008/01/22/17-gifted-children/

Alterman, J. B. (2022, September 21). *Benign Neglect*. Center for Strategic and International Studies. https://www.csis.org/analysis/benign-neglect

Appalachian Forest School. (n.d.). App Forest School. Retrieved March 30, 2024, from https://www. appforestschool.com/

Apple, M. W. (2007). Ideological Success, Educational Failure?: On the Politics of No Child Left Behind. *Journal of Teacher Education, 58*(2), 108–116.

Ashkenas, J., Park, H., & Pearce, A. (2017, August 24). Even With Affirmative Action, Blacks and Hispanics Are More Underrepresented at Top Colleges Than 35 Years Ago. *The New York Times*. https://www.nytimes.com/interactive/2017/08/24/us/affirmative-action.html

Avenues. (n.d.). Avenues. Retrieved March 30, 2024, from https://www.avenues.org/ny/2021/ discover-the-upper-division-at-avenues

Barkan, J., Eva Gold, Jeffrey R. Henig, and Elaine Simon, Walzer, M., & Hochschild, J. (2011, January 1). *Got dough? How billionaires rule our schools*. Dissent Magazine. https://www.dissentmagazine.org/article/got-dough-how-billionaires-rule-our-schools/

Bhatia, A., Miller, C. C., & Katz, J. (n.d.). Study of Elite College Admissions Data Suggests Being Very Rich Is Its Own Qualification. *The New York Times*.

BillieHolidayVEVO. (2022, January 14). *Billie Holiday - God Bless The Child (Audio)*. Youtube. https://www.youtube.com/watch?v=mp349H8G0XQ

Bloomfield Hills Public Schools. (n.d.). Bloomfield Hills Public Schools. Retrieved March 30, 2024, from https://www.bloomfield.org/

Burch, P., Donovan, J., & Steinburg, M. (2006). The New Landscape of Educational Privatization in the Era of NCLB. *Phi Delta Kappan, 88*(2), 129–135.

Camperi, L. (2023, March 31). *The cruel dystopia of success academy - Livia camperi*. Medium. https://liviacamperi.medium.com/the-cruel-dystopia-of-success-academy-53524cfc53d0

CDLI - Defenses of Learning. (n.d.). Retrieved March 30, 2024, from https://sites.google.com/jefferson. kyschools.us/jcpsdl/resources/defenses-of-learning

CodeRVA. (2018, April 3). CodeRVA Regional High School. https://coderva.org/

Cowen, J. (2023a, December 8). *Dark Money Vouchers Are Having a Moment*. Washington Spectator. https://washingtonspectator.org/the-year-in-review-dark-money-vouchers-are-having-a-moment/

Cowen, J. (2023b, December 12). As an education researcher, the data show school vouchers would harm Tennessee students. *Tennessean*. https://www.tennessean.com/story/opinion/ contributors/2023/12/12/tennessee-school-vouchers-data-betsy-devos-bill-lee-private-schools-tuition-increases/71844211007/

Crisafulli, T. P. (2006). No educator left unscathed: How no child left behind threatens educators' careers. *Brigham Young University Education and Law Journal, 2006*, 613–637.

Dodd, E. (2023, April 8). Ron DeSantis and the Florida GOP want to make it harder for public-sector unions to collect dues — with exceptions for police and firemen. *Business Insider*. https://www.businessinsider.com/desantis-florida-republicans-union-bill-targets-teachers-not-police-2023-4

Duckworth, A. L., Peterson, C., Matthews, M. D., & Kelly, D. R. (2007). Grit: perseverance and passion for long-term goals. *Journal of Personality and Social Psychology*, *92*(6), 1087–1101.

Effectively keep students engaged with SLANT. (2014, April 3). KIPP NJ Blog. https://blog.kippnj.org/2014/04/03/effectively-keep-students-engaged-with-slant/

Friedman, M. (1997). Public schools: Make them private. *Education Economics*, *5*(3), 341–344.

Gill, L. (2015, December 21). *Ft Greene-area district wants ban on new Success charter schools*. Brooklyn Paper. https://www.brooklynpaper.com/ft-greene-area-district-wants-ban-on-new-success-charter-schools/

Goldberg, M. (2016, February 12). *Brutal charter school video shows that rich people love no-excuses discipline … For other people's kids*. Slate. https://slate.com/human-interest/2016/02/success-academy-undercover-video-shows-no-excuses-discipline-at-its-ugliest.html

Gomez, G. R. (2023, November 21). *Gov, AG and schools ask court to reject Horne's lawsuit against dual-language instruction*. Arizona Mirror. https://azmirror.com/2023/11/21/gov-ag-and-schools-ask-court-to-reject-hornes-lawsuit-against-dual-language-instruction/

Haefele, M. (2021, May 7). *Remembering Eli Broad's charter school crusade*. Capital & Main. https://capitalandmain.com/remembering-eli-broads-charter-school-crusade-0507

Hatfield, J. (2023, June 5). *Partisan divides over K-12 education in 8 charts*. Pew Research Center. https://www.pewresearch.org/short-reads/2023/06/05/partisan-divides-over-k-12-education-in-8-charts/

Hess, F. (2022, October 6). *20 years ago, NCLB kinda, sorta worked. That's the problem*. Education Next. https://www.educationnext.org/20-years-ago-nclb-kinda-sorta-worked-thats-the-problem/

Katz, M. (2016, April 30). *Success Academy Hit With More Criticism Over Infamous "Got To Go" list*. Gothamist. https://gothamist.com/news/success-academy-hit-with-more-criticism-over-infamous-got-to-go-list

Latham, T. (2023, April 25). *Billionaire Ken Griffin Donates $25 Million to NYC's Success Academy Charter Schools*. Robb Report. https://robbreport.com/lifestyle/finance/ken-griffin-success-academy-donation-1234835048/

Long, D. A., McCoach, D. B., Siegle, D., Callahan, C. M., & Gubbins, E. J. (2023). Inequality at the Starting Line: Underrepresentation in Gifted Identification and Disparities in Early Achievement. *AERA Open*, *9*, 23328584231171535.

Max_Eden_83_Prop.pdf. (n.d.).

Meier, D., & Wood, G. (Eds.). (2004). *Many Children Left Behind: How the No Child Left Behind Act Is Damaging Our Children and Our Schools* (p. 65). Beacon Press.

Meltzer, E. (2018, April 15). *Colorado Democrats overwhelmingly reject Democrats for Education Reform at state assembly*. Chalkbeat. https://www.chalkbeat.org/colorado/2018/4/14/21104748/colorado-democrats-overwhelmingly-reject-democrats-for-education-reform-at-state-assembly/

Miller, C. C., Mervosh, S., & Paris, F. (2024, January 31). Students Are Making a "Surprising" Rebound From Pandemic Closures. But Some May Never Catch Up. *The New York Times*. https://www.nytimes.com/interactive/2024/01/31/us/pandemic-learning-loss-recovery.html

MontessoriPublic. (2016, March 23). *Public Montessori*. MontessoriPublic. https://www.montessori-public.org/public-montessori/

Mosby, I., & Millions, E. (2021, August). Canada's Residential Schools Were a Horror. *Scientific American*. https://www.scientificamerican.com/article/canadas-residential-schools-were-a-horror/

Nehring, A. (2024, January 4). *Success academy expands HQ to 94K SF at 120 Wall Street*. Commercial Observer. https://commercialobserver.com/2024/01/success-academy-expands-headquarters-120-wall-street/

Nietzel, M. T. (2023, July 24). How The Admission Practices Of Elite Colleges Perpetuate The Advantages Of The Wealthy. *Forbes Magazine*. https://www.forbes.com/sites/michaeltnietzel/2023/07/24/how-the-admission-practices-of-elite-colleges-perpetuate-the-advantages-of-the-wealthy/

Our leadership. (n.d.). Retrieved March 30, 2024, from https://about.collegeboard.org/leadership

Perkins-Gough, D., & Duckworth, A. L. (2013). The significance of grit. *Educational Leadership: Journal of the Department of Supervision and Curriculum Development, N.E.A, 71*, 14–20.

Planning And Evaluation Committee on the Ryan White Care Act Data for Resource Allo. (2004). *Measuring what matters: Allocation, planning, and quality assessment for the Ryan white care ACT*. National Academies Press. https://www.carnegiefoundation.org/our-work/measuring-what-matters/

Porter, J. R., Howell, F. M., & Hempel, L. M. (2014). Old Times Are Not Forgotten: The Institutionalization of Segregation Academies in the American South. *Social Problems, 61*(4), 576.

Ravitch, D. (2018, January 8). Today is the anniversary of the worst federal education law ever passed. *HuffPost*. https://www.huffpost.com/entry/no-child-left-behind-anniversary_b_5a538591e4b003133eca7a05

Richtel, M. (2012, May 30). Wasting Time Is New Divide in Digital Era. *The New York Times*. https://www.nytimes.com/2012/05/30/us/new-digital-divide-seen-in-wasting-time-online.html

Riddick by Riddick v. Sch. Bd. Of City of Norfolk, 627 F. supp. 814 (E.d. va. 1984). (n.d.). Justia Law. Retrieved March 30, 2024, from https://law.justia.com/cases/federal/district-courts/FSupp/627/814/1973888/

Riedel, S. (2024, February 28). *A top Oklahoma schools official is under fire for ties to an anti-trans influencer*. Them. https://www.them.us/story/ryan-walters-ron-causby-top-oklahoma-schools-official-under-fire-ties-anti-trans-influencer

Robertson, W. B. (2015). Mapping the Profit Motive: A Comparative Analysis of For-Profit and Non-Profit Charter Schools. *Education Policy Analysis Archives, 23*, 69–69.

Sippy, Z. (2021, April 16). *School integration was accelerated by this supreme court ruling on busing*. Teen Vogue. https://www.teenvogue.com/story/school-busing-integration-supreme-court

Socol, I., Moran, P., & Ratliff, C. (2018). *Timeless Learning: How Imagination, Observation, and Zero-Based Thinking Change Schools*. John Wiley & Sons.

SpeEdChange. (2012, May). https://speedchange.blogspot.com/2012/05/fried-chicken-n-watermelon-at-new-york.html

STEAM Academy. (n.d.). STEAM Academy. Retrieved March 30, 2024, from https://steam.fcps.net/

Steele, C. (1992). Race and the schooling of black Americans. *The Atlantic Monthly, 269*, 68–78.

Stitzlein, S. (2013). For-profit charter schools and threats to the publicness of public schools. *Philosophical Studies in Education, 44*, 88–99.

Suozzo, A., Glassford, A., Ngu, A., & Roberts, B. (n.d.). *Success Academy Charter Schools Inc, fiscal year ending June 2022* [dataset]. ProPublica. Retrieved March 30, 2024, from https://projects.propublica.org/nonprofits/organizations/205298861

Suozzo, A., Glassford, A., Ngu, A., & Roberts, B. (2013, May 9). *Success academy charter schools inc*. ProPublica. https://projects.propublica.org/nonprofits/organizations/205298861/202331329349308773/full

Tavenner, D. (2023, December 11). *Class Disrupted S5 E4: How America's Oldest Non-profit Aims to Drive the Future of Education*. https://www.the74million.org/article/class-disrupted-s5-e4-how-americas-oldest-nonprofit-aims-to-drive-the-future-of-education/

Taylor, K. (2015, October 29). At a Success Academy Charter School, Singling Out Pupils Who Have "Got to Go." *The New York Times*. https://www.nytimes.com/2015/10/30/nyregion/at-a-success-academy-charter-school-singling-out-pupils-who-have-got-to-go.html

Taylor, K., Frankenberg, E., & Siegel-Hawley, G. (2019). Racial Segregation in the Southern Schools, School Districts, and Counties Where Districts Have Seceded. *AERA Open, 5*(3), 2332858419860152.

Tewksbury, G. (2016). *CUNY Academic WCUNY Academic Works* (N. Michelli (Ed.)) [Ph.D]. City University of New York

Texas insists on discriminating against Black hair. (2024, March 4). *The Washington Post*. https://www.washingtonpost.com/opinions/2024/03/04/texas-crown-act-black-hair-discrimination/

The best national universities in America. (2024, February 6). US News & World Report. https://www.usnews.com/best-colleges/rankings/national-universities

The facts are in. Instead of promoting choice, much of the nearly $400 million for expanded Ohio school vouchers went to those already attending private schools: editorial. (2024, March 8). Cleveland. https://www.cleveland.com/opinion/2024/03/the-facts-are-in-instead-of-promoting-choice-much-of-the-nearly-400-million-for-expanded-ohio-school-vouchers-went-to-those-already-attending-private-schools-editorial.html

The Thomas B. Fordham Institute. (n.d.). The Thomas B. Fordham Institute. Retrieved March 30, 2024, from https://fordhaminstitute.org/about

US Indian Boarding school history. (n.d.). The National Native American Boarding School Healing Coalition. Retrieved March 30, 2024, from https://boardingschoolhealing.org/education/us-indian-boarding-school-history/

U.S. Senate: U.S. senate roll call votes 107th Congress - 1st session. (2023, August 14). https://www.senate.gov/legislative/LIS/roll_call_votes/vote1071/vote_107_1_00371.htm

Vallas, R., Robbins, K. G., & Odum, J. (2017, March 8). *5 Ways President Trump's Agenda Is a Disaster for People with Disabilities*. Center for American Progress. https://www.americanprogress.org/article/5-ways-president-trumps-agenda-disaster-people-disabilities/

Walker, T. (2024, February). *"no accountability": Vouchers wreak havoc on states.* https://www.nea.org/nea-today/all-news-articles/no-accountability-vouchers-wreak-havoc-states

Weber, M., & Baker, B. (2017). *NEPC Review: School District Reform in Newark and Assessment of Reform in Newark.* University of Colorado:NEPC. http://nepc.colorado.edu/thinktank/review-newark-reform

Wertheimer, L. K. (2023, September 28). The "anti woke" legislation making K-12 teachers in New Hampshire nervous. *The Boston Globe.* https://www.bostonglobe.com/2023/09/28/magazine/anti-woke-legislation-in-nh-schools/

Wikipedia contributors. (2024a, January 20). *Post hoc ergo propter hoc.* Wikipedia, The Free Encyclopedia. https://en.wikipedia.org/w/index.php?title=Post_hoc_ergo_propter_hoc&oldid=1197540932

Wikipedia contributors. (2024b, January 25). *Starve the beast.* Wikipedia, The Free Encyclopedia. https://en.wikipedia.org/w/index.php?title=Starve_the_beast&oldid=1198842067

Wikipedia contributors. (2024c, February 8). *Boston desegregation busing crisis.* Wikipedia, The Free Encyclopedia. https://en.wikipedia.org/w/index.php?title=Boston_desegregation_busing_crisis&oldid=1205049424

CHAPTER SIX:

A Bad 19th-Century Design is Threaded through Everything We Do. Cognition, Technology, and the Environment of School

This is Cubberley's sustained victory. Fifty years of teachers and administrators were trained to believe that the industrial-style schooling experiment was natural and inevitable. Counter-revolution after counter-revolution in carefully disguised support of wealth-preservation has sustained that belief.

When you believe that something is natural and/or inevitable—and that is backed by an authoritarian threat to anyone who disagrees, most will do very little to fight the system.

Let's return to the questions at the beginning of Chapter Two and consider the "everyday" of a child's or adolescent's life in school.

- Why do we have rectangular classrooms with a "teaching wall" at the front?
- Why do we line up student's chairs in rows so often?

- Why do we have lectures?
- Why are all in a class expected to be on the same page of a book?
- Why do we divide learners by age?
- Why do we grade them on a linear scale?
- Why aren't all children included?
- Why do we have notions of tardiness and truancy?
- Why do we have set daily schedules?
- Why do we line students up when they walk through a hall?
- Why is silence preferred?

Now, look at a kid's school day...

What happens as soon as you arrive at school? You follow the same path to the same classroom to the same seat day after day, as you are trained not to think, not to be curious, not to be creative.

You sit on brutally uncomfortable furniture—usually in a badly ventilated classroom designed by people instructed to save money at all costs—and wait to be told what to do. Thus, the training in being passive and subservient continues.

"Imagine you are 3 or 4 feet tall, a meter—give or take 10 cm—and you climb off this huge yellow bus (the vehicle that teaches you that seat belts are not important), or you climb out of mom or dad's car, and—you are at your school.

"Imagine you are 16 or 17, frustrated, tired, angry with the world, and you drive up to your school and walk toward the doors.

"Imagine you are 12, and home has its... umm, challenges. And you get off a chaotic school bus and walk toward your school."—Socol, Your School's UX. What is it? And where to start, 2016 (Socol, 2016)

If you do get interested in something, anything, you are interrupted continually—not by disruptive fellow learners—but by school adults who follow their own schedule, make their own announcements, and place their interests above yours at almost every minute. The tools of information and communication that have been part of your world since you could sit up and hold something are denied to you or so locked down as to make them virtually worthless. The "content" you are exposed to is deliberately irrelevant to both your current life and the life you will live. Finally, the pace is set by the needs of an invented "standard" white middle-class kid whose master's degree-holding mom brings cookies to school for the teachers. What have you learned? You have learned that you are not important, that you do not matter.

...and don't forget that 15-minute lunch hour, your complete lack of privacy, or the bullying environment (*SpeEdChange*, n.d.-a) your school works overtime to create. (*SpeEdChange*, n.d.-b)

Education-as-we-know-it is about building hierar-chies—among athletes, with grading, via teacher preferences, according to inherited wealth and parental power. When schools rank students, schools create unbalanced power relationships among students, and unbalanced power rela-tionships are the cornerstone of bullying.—Socol, Adult Communities and School Bullies, 2009 (*SpeEdChange*, n.d.-a)

Who wouldn't want to be part of this?

After school, you can either choose to raise your status among adults by playing football or becoming a cheerleader—assuming someone in your family can get you home—or you can just retreat into the misery of your second-shift homework assignment, which will be graded according to your socio-economic status.

Here is what is rare in most of those days—what Pam Moran and I call "the Four As." **The Four As** are what we believe every child needs from us every day: ***Acceptance, Access, Attention, and Abundance***. (This is a series of 3 posts on Medium) (Socol, 2019)

"***Acceptance*** *means every child is fully accepted for who they are. It doesn't matter if they're left-handed or severely multiply impaired, doesn't matter if they read slowly or if they climb well, doesn't matter if they like to work in noisy, active environments, or if they'd rather crawl under a table. They are all kids, and we owe every child the right to be accepted for who they are.*

"***Access*** *means all students can fully access the learning and the opportunities they need. Full access. If they can't read via alphabeti-cal code you still need to get them what's inside the books they want. If they can't sit still in your classroom you still need to make them comfortable in a way that allows them to stay and be fully involved.*

If they can't do your math facts worksheet but want to compute their batting average, you need to find a way that allows them to do that. When access—to books, or math, or art, or recess—is denied to a child, you are making them second-class citizens.

"**Attention** means we are firmly committed to the idea that children have important things to say about school stuff and not school stuff and that we need to hear them, see them, and understand them. Kids need our attention, and they will do whatever they must do to get that attention, good or bad. If we are in education, one of the most essential things we do is give children our attention. When we don't, we silence them, and that cannot be good. Let kids follow their passions and do things their way

"**Abundance** represents what we hope surrounds every child. That doesn't mean things—it means primarily what we can give without any financial strain. I remember this image from when we first gave one-to-one computers to our high school kids, it was just a time between classes, and I was at the bottom of a big central staircase in the middle of our 'most challenged' high school. A tall freshman came dancing down the stairs, holding his laptop, with headphones on, singing to himself. That's abundance—we could have given kids more limited computers with fewer choices and limits on downloading, we could have had rules about behaviors in corridors and on stairs, and we could have created a school culture where this kind of ninth-grader self-expression wasn't really accepted—but we made other choices. Abundance is about giving kids time, and slack when they need it, and opportunities, and second-third-fourth-fifth chances. And it's about making sure that we give kids all of the above.—Ira Socol, Semi-Charmed Kind of Life, 2019 (Socol, 2019)

We believe in movable furniture kids are empowered to rear-range—photo : Ira Socol

The principal of one of our high schools said when asked why he called his students "children," "My kids don't get to be children when they go home. They work, take care of siblings, take care of parents. When they come here, I want them to get to be children." That's abundance.

The Four As are not part of most school days because school was—I keep saying this—not designed for either children or adolescents. It was designed to create compliant citizens who would do the work of the 19th-century economy and not challenge the social structure.

Many of you reading this will say, "My school is not that bad," and often that will be true. I have worked in and visited schools across North America that do much better and try to do the right things. But before you say this with certainty, really observe. Don't just ask students (who have been trained in compliance since pre-school). Shadow a few kids every year. (*Stanford D.school*, n.d.) Shadow them all day, doing whatever they're doing. Ask other kids—every age kid, every kind of kid—to wear a video camera all day. Sit down one-on-one or with small groups and talk.

The best professional learning experience I ever had was listening to Chris Emdin interview a panel of our black and brown high school students in front of 300–350 teachers. We thought we had great schools—we'd really been trying. The kids shredded us on equity, culture, and environment as they described incredible moments of classroom disrespect. We'd done all the kinds of observations above and changed a world of rules and norms, yet we remained a long way from what our kids needed.

The school day plays out like this because it is an expression of the desires of the masters of American society during the 19th century.

Much of our school day—the norms we force on our children—was built on the beliefs developed by the Calvinist Protestants during the 16th and 17th centuries. Those who arrived in Massachusetts and would later begin the concept of American public education. To be more precise, these desires were built on the myths of those "founders of America" as adopted in order to sustain a ruling class. (Linker, 2009)

Before the 16th century, Europe was Catholic, agrarian, and locally determined. Sunrise and sunset defined the day. The feast days of the Catholic calendar of saints defined the year. The spoken word from the front of the church or cathedral defined God, morality, laws, and news.

Then, a change occurred, driven by four concurrent and complimentary new things. I do not believe that either Martin Luther or John Calvin saw themselves as doing anything but God's work, but their Reformation religious theories promoted a new understanding of society that would lead to industrial mercantilism, and their ideas spread through the power of new technologies.

Moving society away from Catholicism and the natural world. The village clock began marking time "efficiently." Image: Wikipedia (Wikipedia contributors, n.d.)

The new religions, along with new economic drivers and two inventions—the printing press and the mechanical clock—built a new form of society. (Boerner et al., 2021)

That new society encouraged people to move to cities—where jobs were—because wealth was equated with being among God's "elect." Those new jobs, which began to create wealth not associated with land and nobility, were constructed around those clocks—the new definers of the [work] day. The abandonment of the structure of saints removed feast days from the calendar and increased the work year.

The protestant religion spread rapidly as royal leaders found freedom from Rome's dictates and the power to control religion. It spread through books and the notion of fixed text. The prayer book and new Biblical translations were read by all together and were the same wherever one might go and not be subject to the whims of either priests or scribes.

"...the clock may have played a role in the spread of the Reformation, as it served as a coordinating device which created a sense for time, punctuality, and discipline that was key to the ideas of the Calvinist movements."—Boerner and Rubin, (Boerner et al., 2021)

Our acceptance of the mythic inevitability of, and the sanctity of, schools as we know them is far more religiously based than child development-based. Just as our notion of converting children not like us into adults just like us is far more religiously inspired than humane.

When these beliefs are embedded, offering learners those "Four As" or equitable opportunities becomes extremely difficult. When people hold tight to attitudes that layered on unexamined beliefs, the effort becomes impossible.

"[A]ttitude theory considers the way individuals base political decisions on normative assessments drawn from some underlying creed or set of values about "the good society." David Barker and Christopher Jan Carman wrote in 2000. "[P]erhaps the most thorough scholarly attention has been paid to individualism— the belief that each person should be self-reliant and free to pursue his or her interests, accepting full responsibility for the consequences of those pursuits... individualism was associated with incivility and social chaos by Europeans. However, in the United States individualism has always been revered as a moral virtue." (*EBSCOhost*, n.d.)

This sense of individualism as a moral virtue allows Americans— especially those who label themselves as "conservatives" but even many who call themselves "liberals"—to see the tree but not the forest when they look at "opportunity." Does Clarence Thomas prove that there is no discrimination against Blacks in America? Self-described conservatives may say "yes," but even as liberals say "no," they often fully embrace the stories of the "magical students" who rose from poverty, discrimination, and/or disability to succeed on the general terms of "whiteness' in the United States. You've heard the tale as often—the kid with dyslexia from an impoverished public housing, single-mom family who aced the SAT and got that scholarship from Harvard.

These stories are embraced and resonate because the "American Myth" argues that anyone can escape from poverty through the dint of individual effort. This effort revolves around two elements: hard work and good decision-making," according to J. F. Henry in 2007. (Henry, 2007) Henry then quotes President George W. Bush, who, announcing his cabinet after his election, stated, "People who work hard and make the right decisions in life can achieve anything they want in America."(Henry, 2007)

That, of course, is an article of faith. There is, and never has been, any evidence to support this on a rational basis. The vast majority of those born poor in the United States have ended their lives in poverty. African Americans consistently hold less wealth than white Americans. Those born with "disabilities" are far likelier to live in poverty than those without. It does not matter how hard they work or what decisions they make. Bush himself might not be the best example of a person whose work ethic lifted himself up.

These articles of faith allow Americans to see the Calvinist "elect"— those blessed by God with money and position—as people who "work hard" and make "the right decisions," even when the same behaviors are ignored or minimized in those from less privileged circumstances who fail to achieve wealth. "[I]t is an aspect of the Protestant Ethic and contains a distinctly moral assertion," Henry writes. "To succeed (usually meant in the context of income) is good, and success is determined in the main by these two factors. Hence, anyone not succeeding—the poor—are morally deficient in that they are lazy and/or make bad decisions. a merit-based reason for success in that it is the individual who is responsible for outcomes, and outcomes then are a measure of individual merit."

> "'I've said I've made mistakes in the past," he said. "People know that. They've thought about that." George W. Bush was arrested for drunk driving and skipped some military obligations, but when there are no negative consequences, there are no "bad decisions." (Mitchell, 2000)

> "A bad decision requires knowledge of consequences prior to the making of the decision. Were I to engage in theft but not be discovered as the thief, no bad consequences would befall me. Were I to be caught in the act, I would be punished, perhaps sent to jail; I clearly would have made a bad decision to steal, but only because the theft was detected. In the first instance, however, the decision was exactly the same, but it would not have been a bad decision as no negative consequence would have occurred."—J. F. Henry (Henry, 2007)

We are only fooling ourselves when we imagine that these religious beliefs—because they are just that—don't infiltrate everything that happens in schooling. A student who doesn't get their homework done is "lazy," not time-constrained by responsibilities at home or simply by the tasks of surviving. A student who doesn't get the assigned reading done has "made poor choices," it can't be that they might need audio versions of their books. A Black student with absent parents who curses in a corridor is treated differently by the typical building administrator than the white student whose mother is an attorney. An Autistic student is seen as not intelligent enough to be part of advanced classes because they are still developing their social and verbal skills. At the same time, the doctor's son is assumed to be on the AP track.

All of these scenarios shut down opportunities for learners outside the mainstream. All preserve the advantages of privileged birth. All are powered by intentional system design.

Sources:

Boerner, L., Rubin, J., & Severgnini, B. (2021). A time to print, a time to reform. *European Economic Review, 138*(103826), 103826.

EBSCOhost. (n.d.). Retrieved March 31, 2024, from https://web.p.ebscohost.com/abstract?site=e-host&scope=site&jrnl=01909320&asa=Y&AN=11304201&h=Qtpyl5wefd%2fUzDVAIyVPhl-RizeE1ryeGHcp5S8wtGb3BK%2bVCJVgeuyFMwIhbK%2bLGNY4jKqFKpTArmAhRyvUO-HA%3d%3d&crl=f&resultLocal=ErrCrlNoResults&resultNs=Ehost&crlhashurl=login.aspx%3fdirect%3dtrue%26profile%3dehost%26scope%3dsite%26authtype%3dcrawler%26jrnl%3d01909320%26asa%3dY%26AN%3d11304201

Henry, J. (2007). "Bad" Decisions, Poverty, and Economic Theory: The Individualist and Social Perspectives in Light of "The American Myth." *Forum for Social Economics, 36*(1), 17–27.

Linker, D. (2009, July 9). *Calvin and American exceptionalism.* The New Republic. https://newrepublic.com/article/50754/calvin-and-american-exceptionalism

Mitchell, A. (2000, November 3). THE 2000 CAMPAIGN: A DRIVING OFFENSE; Bush Acknowledges an Arrest for Drunken Driving in 1976. *The New York Times.* https://www.nytimes.com/2000/11/03/us/2000-campaign-driving-offense-bush-acknowledges-arrest-for-drunken-driving-1976.html

Socol, I. D. (2016, May 7). *Your School's UX. What is it? And where to start.* Medium. https://irasocol.medium.com/your-schools-ux-what-is-it-and-where-to-start-c9922768b01d

Socol, I. D. (2019, November 15). *Semi-Charmed Kind of Life (part one): Who kids are... and what kids need from us.* Age of Awareness. https://medium.com/age-of-awareness/semi-charmed-kind-of-life-part-1-who-kids-are-and-what-kids-need-from-us-dcb7dd8a02c4

SpeEdChange. (n.d.-a). Retrieved March 31, 2024, from https://speedchange.blogspot.com/2009/05/adult-communities-and-school-bullies.html

SpeEdChange. (n.d.-b). Retrieved March 31, 2024, from https://speedchange.blogspot.com/2010/07/lord-of-flies-how-adults-create.html

Stanford d.school. (n.d.). Stanford D.school. Retrieved March 31, 2024, from https://dschool.stanford.edu/shadow-a-student-k12

Wikipedia contributors. (n.d.). *Datei:Goslar-glockenspiel.jpg.* Wikipedia, The Free Encyclopedia. https://de.wikipedia.org/wiki/Datei:Goslar-glockenspiel.jpg

CHAPTER SEVEN:

Systemic Anachronisms that Limit
the Opportunities of Our Students.

Why does opportunity seem so elusive if a great educational system opens opportunities for its students? "Less than one in 13 children born into poverty in the United States will go on to hold a high-income job in adulthood; the odds are far longer for Black men born into poverty, at one in 40," John N. Friedman, an economist at Brown University, wrote in *The New York Times* in 2022, before claiming that "Education is the solution to this lack of mobility... with the right level of investment, education can not only provide more pathways out of poverty for individuals but also restore the equality of opportunity that is supposed to lie at America's core." (Friedman, 2022)

The key phrase is "with the right level of investment" because investment is elusive, specifically investment in the children who need it most. That investment must not just be financial; it must also be attitudinal.

"It is certainly not a new idea that education can change a child's life trajectory," Friedman continues, but unfortunately, that trajectory can shift in a positive direction, or it can shift the other way. Most often, unfortunately, the schools as we know them, *by design*, don't shift trajectories at all, instead setting them in stone.

A massive part of this, in contrast with Friedman's Ivy League pure focus on funding, is attitudinal. (Friedman, 2022) "At the center of these debates are interpretations of the gaps in educational achievement between white and non-Asian minority students as measured by standardized test scores," Linda Darling Hammond wrote in 1998. "The presumption that guides much of the conversation is that equal opportunity now exists; therefore, continued low levels of achievement on the part of minority students must be a function of genes, culture, or a lack of effort and will." Calling education in the United States "one of the most unequal in the industrialized world [where] students routinely receive dramatically different learning opportunities based on their social status," Hammond notes the obvious, "[That] educational outcomes for minority children are much more a function of their unequal access to key educational resources, including skilled teachers and quality curriculum than they are a function of race." (Darling-Hammond, 1998)

Create Your Own Mobility Animations

Pick any two demographic groups. You can sort by gender and by the income bracket in which children were raised. You can watch what happens to them as adult individuals, or in their adult households, in a variety of scenarios.

Follow the lives of [Black boys] and [   ] from [poor] • households, using their [household] • incomes as adults, and including kids of [all mothers, including immigrants ▾] :

Follow the lives of these **16,931** Americans and see where they end up as adults:

Two percent of Black males born into poverty end up as wealthy adults, in this New York Times *study, with only 23 percent reaching the middle class. For white males, almost half reach middle class or better, and ten percent reach wealth.* (Badger et al., 2018)

Funding matters, but educational funding is just one of our "faith-based" beliefs in systems designed for wealth preservation—a system built to benefit those who have. We live with a vast assortment of anachronisms—unquestioned beliefs in everyday practices - that continue to ensure unequal outcomes.

These anachronisms appear in systemic governance structures on every level, in the policies, procedures, and practices of educators and their institutions, in media reporting, and in the attitudes of parents and communities. Every one of these is something far beyond the level of "microaggression"—these are all assaults on our most vulnerable children.

Changing the System is Required

I have been saying for at least 20 years that the problems with schools are about something other than our teachers as individuals. It is not even about administrators. It is about a badly designed system locked in amber. It was created for all the wrong reasons, and it has consistently refused to be part of the present.

Anachronism One—Local Taxation and Local Control:

"The nation is hardly 'indivisible' where education is concerned. It is at least two nations, quite methodically divided, with... liberty for some... and justice ... only for the kids whose parents can afford to purchase it." Jonathan Kozol had it all exactly right when he published Savage Inequalities: Children in America's Schools in 1991. (Kozol, 1998) Nothing has changed for the better since.

I went through school in New Rochelle, New York, a city school district with 42 percent of students eligible for free lunches and another 4 percent eligible for reduced-price lunches. (2019, n.d.) In broad terms, the north—inland—part of the city and the immediate Long Island Sound shore are wealthy, while the southern end around the downtown is not. New Rochelle has a substantial tax base and a willingness to tax itself for schools, but it also faces the New York metro area's high costs of living. The schools there spend $24,640 per student per year. (2021, n.d.)

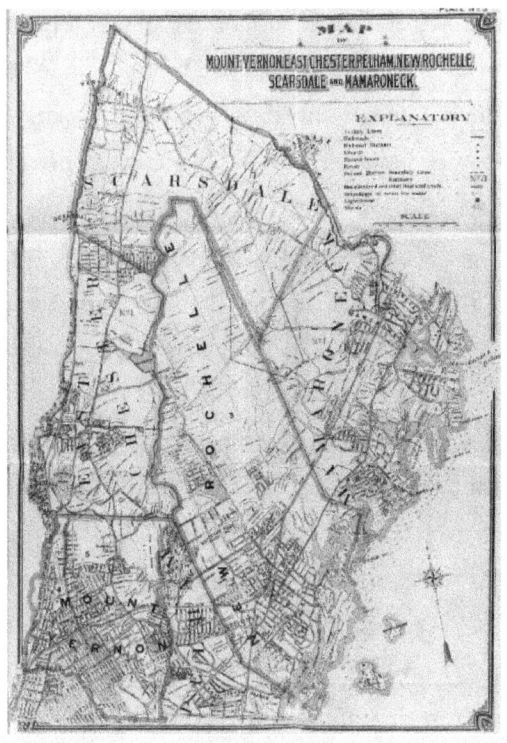

Scarsdale surrounds the "North End" of New Rochelle. Except for Mount Vernon, all the communities surrounding New Rochelle are whiter and wealthier. Map from 1900: Scarsdale Historical Society (Maps —, n.d.)

Surrounding the wealthy part of New Rochelle is the Town/Village of Scarsdale. Scarsdale has no students who qualify for free or reduced-cost lunches. (2018, n.d.) Scarsdale spends $30,842 per student per year. (2020, n.d.)

I have a good friend who was the Superintendent of Schools in a mile-square Michigan district—Godfrey-Lee—near Grand Rapids. That district has over 95 percent of students qualifying for free lunch (note: Governor Gretchen Whitmer and Democratic legislative majorities in Michigan have made lunch and breakfast free for all students statewide.) The Godfrey-Lee schools have about $11,000 per student per year to spend. (F-R Percentage for SY 21-22, 2023)

We do not need a deep analysis to see the pattern.

I am an absolute believer that "kids from poverty do not come to school knowing less, they know different." (I. D. Socol, 2016) The same is true for language learners, for the neurodivergent, those from differing races and cultures, the kids with trauma at home, and those with disabilities. In all these cases, it is our job to leverage what the kids bring to help them move forward on their own path.

We also all know that kids who come from homes in poverty, from traumatic situations, from other places on earth, and who are "not our standardized norm" have needs different and typically greater than the child who arrives at school in a Range Rover and goes home to a $1.8 million house. (32 Walbrooke Road, Scarsdale, NY 10583, n.d.) The net result of these combined disparities are inherited school funding and control systems that function as additional parts of our wealth preservation system that was designed to fail most children.

Schools in the United States are funded with inequity baked in because schools never became a priority for either the federal government or state governments. Schools did not become a priority for governments because the American concept is deeply rooted in a combination of self-interest and mythic belief. Our generic hero—as fictional as the ancient Greeks' Hercules—is a self-made, self-sufficient, self-educated man living in a self-sufficient community.

Within that framework, combined with the myth of equal opportunity, it only makes sense that the hero's self-sufficient family will be primarily responsible for raising and educating their children—perhaps in collaboration with neighbors who are just like the hero.

Public schooling was desired, not as a "whole society" responsibility (as in other 19th-century "modern" nations) but as the responsibility of the smallest units of government that could be found or developed.

This localization was rooted in the independent villages of colonial New England and the Calvinist churches at their center. The desires "to assure efficient education, to promote democracy, and to advance social cohesion, all swirled around the school district," Nadav Shoked wrote in 2017. "The district's supporters offered it as an institution better equipped, compared to existing local governments, to serve these goals." (Shoked, 2017)

Child-raising decisions were thus kept as close to the individual family as possible, satisfying the American mythic belief system. It satisfied the myth in the 18th century and still satisfied it in the 20th century—when my city's local elementary enrollment boundaries were matched to the local Catholic parishes. It satisfies it in the 2020s as localities nationwide choose to ban books.

"The school district is as much a staple of American law [because] it has been associated with a plethora of normative values," Shoked added. Those values include keeping tax money, not just control, "at home." If money is not kept close to home, "it raises the thorny issue of wealth redistribution. If school finance equalization is to take place within American schools, either additional money must be raised, or expenditures on children from wealthy areas need to be reduced. Given the immense obstacles to the latter option, these cases immediately raise the specter of increased taxes." (Reed, 2001)

Those "normative values" include the elephant in the classroom: racial segregation. If slavery is America's "original sin," then racism is in the design of its original DNA.

1956 Political Cartoon

Overwhelming evidence suggests that white Americans are uncomfortable if too many Black kids are in a classroom with their kids. They weren't in Topeka, Kansas in 1950, (Onion, 2009) or in New Rochelle, New York in 1960, (*Leveling Lincoln | PBS*, 2023) or in Boston in 1970, (American Experience | PBS, 2023), and they aren't now—whether in Brooklyn (Joffe-Walt et al., 2020), San Francisco (*Living Together, Learning Apart*, n.d.), or around Charlotte, North Carolina. (Smith, 2016)

And local control—often, since the 1980s, in the form of break-away segregation districts—helps reassure white parents that their children's learning will not be disrupted by children who are different and students labeled as "troubled." (Hannah-Jones, 2017)

"There will be no credible evidence in this trial of racial animus motivating the Gardendale (Alabama) Board of Education [to break away from a diverse county school district]," attorney Aaron McLeod told a federal court in 2017. "What the evidence instead will show is that the citizens of Gardendale cared so much about the education of their children that they raised their own taxes to enable their city to operate the schools their kids attend, and that is all that Gardendale is asking the court for today, to be allowed to operate its own school system for the sake of their children's education." (Hannah-Jones, 2017)

"Cared so much about the education of their children that they raised their own taxes to enable their city to operate the schools their kids attend." It is difficult to think of more carefully crafted racist code words.

> *"The town of Gardendale is 88 percent white, but its schools are now 25 percent black, in part because students bused in from North Smithfield, a working-class black community a few miles away, are zoned to schools located in Gardendale. Gardendale's secession would not eliminate black students from their schools, but by ensuring only students who lived in Gardendale could attend in the new district, it would significantly decrease their numbers."*—Nikole Hannah-Jones in The New York Times (Hannah-Jones, 2017)

State and local control of education—the United States didn't have a cabinet-level education department until 1953 (the Department of Health, Education, and Welfare), about 130–150 years after European nations had "Education Ministers"—allows incredible resistance to racial equality, racial opportunity, and racial equity. From the late 1950s through the 1970s, southern states (including Nikki Haley and Tim Scott's South Carolina, where neither could find systemic racism) engaged in "Massive Resistance," shutting public schools rather than integrating them. The white kids were invited to private "segregation academies"—the black kids were abandoned. (Carr, 2012)

Things have not necessarily changed much. "[LaToysha] Brown had started to wonder if separate could ever be equal. (Carr, 2012) She attended a nearly all-black high school with dangerous sinkholes in the courtyard, spotty Internet access in the classrooms, and a shortage of textbooks all around. Brown had never been inside Indianola Academy, the private school most of the town's white teenagers attend. But she sensed that the students there had books they could take home and walkways free of sinkholes." That was written for *The Atlantic* in 2012, and those academies continue to enroll most of the children of the white southern power structure. Yet, the same flight-to-private can be seen all across the north as well (Bento, 2021), and if not flight, then a twisting of the concepts of "merit" and "gifted" to segregate within schools—white kids are in gifted and Advanced Placement courses, black and brown kids are not. (Green & Waldman, 2018)

The Civil War "Ironclad" naval battle between the Union's Monitor and Pro-Slavery Merrimack redrawn—the South shut public schools—for years—to avoid court-ordered desegregation. (Battle of the Ironclads (U.S. National Park Service), n.d.)

The "local control" that Americans so cherish is a consistent engine of unequal and inequitable opportunity.

"In the first place God made idiots. This was for practice. Then he made school boards."—Mark Twain, *Following the Equator: A Journey Around the World* (1897) (Twain, 2020)

If America's population was not as mobile as it has proved to be, if America didn't have any national goals (which it may not have), and if America was not as fundamentally unequal as it is, this strange system might not have become as toxic as it has proved to be.

Toxic, though, it has remained with inequality—and a commitment to the failure of our most vulnerable children—built in by design.

Anachronism Two—Refusing to understand the cognitive changes driven by technological change:

We often complain about the passive nature of the internet and the disruption of mobile phone use. We must understand that (a) these are the tools of our kids' lives, and we owe it to them to help them figure out how to use their technologies well because (b) since Socrates (at least), we've been objecting to whatever new communication tools arise. (I. D. Socol, 2020)

Socrates was right about literacy. Reading is completely passive (if used without thought). Once on paper, print is fixed and cannot be updated or corrected (as digital text can be). It does not check for understanding and cannot be effectively challenged. Schools love fixed communication techniques—from printed books to lectures to TED Talks while Generations Z and Alpha know those limitations. "This book talks about a brontosaurus," a second grader complained to the school librarian. "I bet it thinks Pluto is still a planet."

Does human cognition change when communication technologies change? Of course, it does. No one doubts that the invention of complex oral language changed how humans learn and think. But didn't the arrival of cave paintings—and cave paintings were a huge jump because they introduced asynchronous storytelling—change learning and thinking? (I. D. Socol, 2020)

What about "interchangeable" symbolic language—pictographs, hieroglyphics, and alphabets? Now, consider how the arrival of photography—in changing what signifies something "real"—changed cognition. Film even more—the public's understanding of the motion picture as what represented reality was so strong that soon after its appearance, filmmakers had to fake the Battle of Manila in a New Jersey bathtub to show Americans that the Spanish-American War was real. All the "reality" tools of the past—woodcuts, lithographs, cycloramas—were no longer enough. (Robbins, 2017) "The movies became so identified with war news that Edison renamed his Projecting Kinetoscope the 'Wargraph' for the duration of the hostilities."

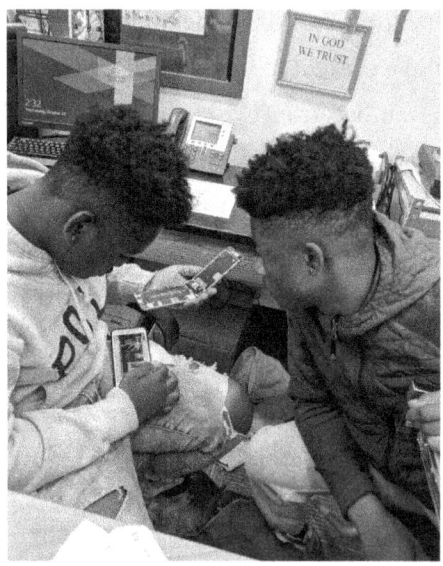

We believe in helping kids learn to control their technologies.
That doesn't happen when you ban stuff or lock things down.
– Photo: Ira Socol

The technological changes since 1900 have continued to alter human learning, cognition, and cognitive authority. (I. Socol, Fall 2007) Films of the 1960s and 70s used black and white—imitating newsreel footage—to represent reality. In the 1980s and 90s, the slightly faded off-color and shaky hand-held look of in-the-field videotape replaced that. In the aughts, the immediacy of the internet and the grainy look of early phone camera photos and videos became the thing. Do not just focus on the surface here. Our brains are trained from the beginning by the media we use and how we use it. If you teach via the cognitive construals of generations before your learners were born, you make yourself largely incomprehensible.

Arguments over contemporary technology in school and childhood sharpen these irreconcilable conceptions. Using correlative facts while ignoring anything that might shift responsibility onto adult behaviors, elite writers attack the information and communication technologies favored by younger generations.

Jonathan Haidt, a New York University professor, manages to blame everything happening to Generation Z on mobile phones without being able to provide one bit of causal evidence. "The decline in mental health is just one of many signs that something went awry [with Generation Z], Haidt wrote in *The Atlantic*. "Loneliness and friendlessness among American teens began to surge around 2012. Academic achievement went down, too. According to "The Nation's Report Card," scores in reading and math began to decline for U.S. students after 2012, reversing decades of slow but generally steady increase. PISA, the major international measure of educational trends, shows that declines in math, reading, and science happened globally, also beginning in the early 2010s... As the oldest members of Gen Z reach their late 20s, their troubles are carrying over into adulthood. Young adults are dating less, having less sex, and showing less interest in ever having children than prior generations. They are more likely to live with their parents. They were less likely to get jobs as teens, and managers say they are harder to work with. Many of these trends began with earlier generations, but most of them accelerated with Gen Z." (Haidt, 2024)

The answer, Haidt declares, "can be stated simply, although the underlying psychology is complex: Those were the years when adolescents in rich countries traded in their flip phones for smartphones and moved much more of their social lives online—particularly onto social-media platforms designed for virality and addiction." (Haidt, 2024)

Only after placing all the blame on the smartphone, which provides his headline and book blurbs, does Haidt admit that problem number one is "the decline of play and independence." (Haidt, 2024) He never mentions other factors, the collapse of any kind of political consensus in both the U.K. and the U.S., or the right-wing campaigns against childhood. The loss of faith in an economic future driven by the great recession. A stunning rise in the non-affordability of housing globally. The clear evidence of the existential threat of climate change that the young watch older generations block attempts to solve. The incredible rise of gun violence in schools in the United States. Or the persistent damage to childhood and adolescence done by increasingly "standards-based" education strategies, which, along with the increasing criminalization of adolescence, have made, for many, schools an irrelevant and hostile place.

No, Haidt argues, it is all about smartphones because, just like with funding inequities, looking at the solutions to these problems would require sacrifice on the part of Haidt's social class. He is not alone. NPR quotes a random woman who taught middle school in "the early aughts" to provide their anti-smartphone expertise. "I have talked to hundreds of parents, and no one has ever said to me, "I wish I gave my kid a phone earlier or I wish I'd given them social media access sooner. Never."" (M. Doucleff, 2023) NPR science correspondent Michaeleen Doucleff adds (M. Doucleff, 2014), "Smartphones, social media, and video games create large spikes in dopamine deep inside a child's brain. As NPR has reported, those spikes pull the child's attention to the device or app, almost like a magnet. They tell the child's brain that this activity is super critical way, more critical than other activities that trigger smaller spikes in dopamine, such as finishing homework, helping to clean up after dinner, or even playing outside with friends." (M. Doucleff, 2023)

Yes, a smartphone is more engaging than doing a worthless homework worksheet, which is no surprise, and yes, software developers are extraordinarily good at trapping the human brain—not just child and adolescent brains—but the problem is that neither the teacher nor Doucleff would have the same objection to a child being engrossed in a classic novel. It is not the dopamine hit they are worried about; it is the medium that provides that dopamine hit.

"'People in different cultures have strikingly different construals of the self, of others, and of the interdependence of these," Hazel Rose Markus and Shinobu Kitayama wrote in 1991. "These construals can influence, and in many cases determine, the very nature of individual experience, including cognition, emotion, and motivation."

"What might this all mean for cognition in education? How do we look at the ways these different "construals" control what occurs in the classroom? At how they impact what

occurs in every formalized learning environment? Or, indeed, how they affect what different parts of increasingly diverse cultures "know"? This is vital not simply because of racial, ethnic, religious, and lingual diversity, but because in periods of rapid change—such as this moment in time—different generations can become separate cultures, seeing the world in such significantly different ways that the very acts of cognition may no longer be mutually understandable. In schools, where one generation is "educated" by another, a communications gap of this sort can make almost everything impossible."—(I. Socol, Fall 2007)

These attitudes, viewing new technologies as a threat, disrespect students and ignore definitive technologically driven changes in cognition and cognitive authority. Yet this is a hill so many educators will choose to die on. William Alcott had to reassure teachers in his 1843 book introducing the newest technologies, "the black board and slate," "Let it not, for one moment, be imagined that I am desirous of substituting slates and black boards for books and all other implements; or a few lessons on these last, for hard study. Very far from it. What I would gladly do is to prepare the pupils of our common schools for the right use of books, and proper benefits of study... I have no doubt that much might be done towards securing a thorough English education, with nothing but the black board and slate, and a suitable course of oral instruction." (W. A. Alcott, 1843)

How is reality implied in this (highly disturbing) clip from Oliver Stone's 1991 film JFK? The images copy the faded Kodacolor look of amateur film in the 1960s. (Movieclips, 2012)

Anachronism Three—In defiance of research, we persist in the division of subjects and children according to the whims of long-dead old white men:

The division of children by age was not just a whim, it was a totalitarian invention to improve the art of beating children into submission. It is important to restate that the Prussian imperial education system was built to ensure—in those years after the defeats by Napoleonic France—that no Prussian soldier would ever disobey an order again. "Prussia," a French philosopher later wrote, "was not a country with an army but an army with a country." (Mortimer, 2004) The 1808 goal was that education would "forge a common culture and spirit of patriotism among all [in Prussia]," thus infusing the Prussian kingdom with the esprit de corps of the French Revolutionary era population without the interest in revolution or civil rights. (Levinger, 2002) That required repeated stamping of these ideas of nationalism, sacrifice of the individual, and obedience to the crown onto the young minds.

"The Puritans did believe that young children were more capable of intellectual activity and moral responsibility than we do today. As a result, while childhood was perceived as a distinct and separate phase of the life course, Puritans did not perceive a large intellectual or emotional gulf between older

children and adults. There was no sharp or clearly defined boundary, for example, between being a youth and becoming an adult. Although early Americans also acknowledged some differences between young and older children, the life course of children was not highly differentiated. Early Americans paid relatively little attention to the actual age of children and focused more on individual intellectual and physical differences."—(Angus, 1988)

Dividing children and adolescents by age is not a "traditional" system. Traditionally, in the one-room schoolhouse multiage model, "grades" represented a level a learner accomplished—the mastery learning model. When a student finished "third-grade reading," they showed their accomplishment to the teacher and moved on to "fourth-grade" work. The idea that all eight-year-olds would be in the same place academically would have seemed ridiculous.

"The typical school at the opening of the nineteenth century enrolled pupils of widely varying age, some as young as three, some as old as twenty, all taught in the same room by a single teacher."—(Angus, 1988)

The idea of these age-graded schools faced a great deal of opposition. In 1874, the St. Louis Superintendent "argued that annual promotions held back students who might be moving through the curriculum at a more rapid pace, and that many students, failing to be promoted a second time, withdrew and were permanently lost to the school." (Angus, 1988) In 1899, the New Castle, Pennsylvania Superintendent offered an alternative "plan of frequent promotions based on subject mastery, flexible enough to allow each student to be at different grade levels in different subjects," because the graded school did "not properly provide for the individual differences of the pupils." (Angus, 1988)

> *"No one dares deny that the children of every grade differ widely in age, in acquirements, in aptitude, in physical endurance, in power of attention, in home advantages, in the rate of mental development, in the time of entering school, in regularity of attendance, and in many other ways affecting their progress. . . . Because of the manner of grading and promoting, the graded school of today keeps all the children of each grade in intellectual lock step, not only month after month, but year after year, for their whole school lives. . . . Is not individuality of more importance than evenness of grading?"*—William J. Shearer, Elizabeth, New Jersey Schools Superintendent, 1899 (Angus, 1988)

In a time that worshipped efficiency, however, even the obvious failures of this system would not change the minds of political and economic leaders, much like today. In 1904 New York City determined that "39 percent of all elementary pupils were "retarded" (that is, overage) for their grade." (Angus, 1988) In 1908, Edward Thorndike found, "Of the children entering the public schools of our more favored cities... Less than 1 in 10 graduate from the high school. Only about a third graduate from an elementary school of seven grades or more... One main cause of elimination is incapacity for and lack of interest in the sort of intellectual work demanded by present courses of study." (Thorndike, 1908)

The only obvious solutions were to (a) blame the kids—especially immigrant children, or (b) fudge the statistics. "School authorities tended to decrease the number of non-promotions by their accounting practices. (Angus, 1988) School systems, for example, began passing large numbers of children with "conditional" promotions. Administrators recorded these students as promoted and at grade level, even if the students were later demoted. Administrators also changed the listing of students who were demoted but who subsequently left school from "nonpromoted" to "dropped." Finally, new students who were placed below grade level were listed as "transfers" rather than overage."

"Eventually, a system of "class" instruction emerged, much like the "chalk and talk" system that dominates today. Under this instructional arrangement, discipline became easier to maintain, and because of grade-level specialization, teachers could be effective with less training. This in turn allowed city school boards to hire more female teachers, which they could do at little more than half the salary of a male teacher."—
(Angus, 1988)

Detroit, however, chose solutions. Physical education, music, dramatics, and art were added as ways of both engaging students and offering more success possibilities, and by 1922, "boasted that 74 percent of its elementary students were either at or above grade level." (Angus, 1988)

"All of this time and effort and human resources spent to get the kids "where they should be" for their grade. But the grade is just based on age, and on these archaic standards of what kids are supposed to know by the end of this year in their lives. Who says? Think about when kids learn to walk. There is a huge range between when some kids first start to walk, and when doctors are concerned and start recommending therapy. Yet, once kids hit kindergarten, suddenly it is a narrow,

arbitrary window of what the students are supposed to know by the end of the year, and if they don't they are considered "behind."—Lisa Olsen, a teacher, on Medium, (Olsen, 2019)

When the schools I worked in moved to multiage spaces, up to 130 kids, K-5, working with six teachers in one big space, we found that we gave children what San Diego educators had called, "the gift of time." Kids chased their aspirational peers up the learning ladder, the need for pull-out special education services dropped dramatically—and when these often vulnerable children (including a large number from a refugee center) took our state tests, the multiage classes did as well as the wealthiest children in the county.

So long, 1900. This was part of a multiage classroom—K-5—with 130 students and six teachers. These became our most successful elementary spaces. Photo: Ira Socol

Anachronism Four—The division of subjects.

Separating content into discrete, separately taught subjects is the creation of the 1892 "Committee of Ten"—and is as counter-intuitive as it is accepted by most educators. (Elliott, 1893) "I'm not a science teacher," a high school faculty member wrote on Threads, "I'm a biology teacher." I responded, "Isn't chemistry important to biology? Isn't physics important to biology?" I should have added, aren't sociology and psychology important to biology?" That addition wouldn't have mattered because I got no response.

When I began graduate school, I finally became fully aware of the "content expert." Until then, I'd been extraordinarily lucky with teachers and professors who knew and were interested in many things, and I'd taken cross-curricular courses throughout my learning experiences. But one semester into grad school I realized how narrow the lives and interests of many "research faculty" had become. "I'm always surprised," I told friends, "that these people can figure out how to use the elevator to get out of the building in the afternoon." Their academic interests had become frighteningly small.

"As we know more, we see less."—Alison Gopnik (Alison Gopnik *Lantern v Spotlight*, n.d.)

That single-mindedness may—I assume—have research benefits. I think of the Curies standing by those pots for years, waiting for radioactive material to separate. More often, I would argue, it creates research that ignores the impacts of what is being studied on other things (as Yong Zhao says, educational research is never presented with side effects). (Zhao, 2017) So, it is not surprising that the Committee's over-educated faculty members wanted high school educators to mimic their own narrow approach to learning. (Seven of the Committee of

Ten were, or had been, university faculty or university presidents. Only one was a public school educator (page 4), and none came from a land grant university.) (Elliott, 1893)

0142. Writing Laboratory I
Fall, Winter, Spring. 0(0-2) [2(2-0) See page A-1 item 3.] ATL 0991 or admission by placement test; ATL 1144 concurrently.
An individualized program to develop composition skills by aiding students to discover how language functions in communication and by helping them to accept responsibility for learning to write correctly.

0152. Writing Laboratory II
Fall, Winter, Spring. 0(0-2) [2(2-0) See page A-1 item 3.] ATL 0142, ATL 1144 or approval of department; ATL 1154 concurrently.
Continuation of ATL 0142.

0162. Writing Laboratory III
Fall, Winter, Spring. 0(0-2) [2(2-0) See page A-1 item 3.] ATL 0152, ATL 1154 or approval of department; ATL 1164 concurrently.
Continuation of ATL 0152.

0991. Preparatory Writing Skills
Fall, Winter, Spring, Summer. 0(3-0) [3(3-0) See page A-1 item 3.] Admission by placement test.
Instruction and practice in writing. Emphasis on mastery of fundamental skills needed for a variety of writing assignments.

104. Writing for Science Majors
Fall. 3(3-0) Satisfactory grade in English proficiency exam; College of Natural Science majors. Interdepartmental with and administered by the Department of English.
Writing workshop for science students that develops and refines composition ability.

105. The Scientist as Writer
Winter. 3(3-0) ENG 104. Interdepartmental with and administered by the Department of English.
Study of various types of writing by scientists—

117. Use of Libraries
Fall, Winter. 1(1-0)
The use of libraries, with emphasis on MSU Library. Course will stress knowledge and use of bibliographic and reference resources.

121. Writing: American Expression
Fall, Winter, Spring, Summer. 3(3-0)
Satisfactory performance on the placement test.
Writing course to improve composition and critical reading abilities. Writings based on American literary and historical materials from Puritan times through the Enlightenment. Emphasis on unity and structure of essays.

122. Writing: American Expression
Fall, Winter, Spring, Summer. 3(3-0)
Three credits in the first term of any ATL sequence numbered 121 or higher or approval of department.
Writing course to improve composition and critical reading abilities. Writings based on American literary and historical materials of the nineteenth century. Emphasis on style and development of essays.

123. Writing: American Expression
Fall, Winter, Spring, Summer. 3(3-0)
Three credits in the second term of any ATL sequence numbered 121 or higher or approval of department.
Writing course to improve composition and research abilities. Writings based on American literary and historical materials of the twentieth century. Research project required.

131. Writing: Major Currents in American Experience
Fall. 3(3-0) Satisfactory performance on the placement test.
Writing course to improve composition and critical reading abilities. Writings based on materials concerning the individual's search for meaning in America. Emphasis on unity and structure of essays.

ical reading abilities. Writings based on American literature, painting, music, architecture and sculpture of the nineteenth century. Emphasis upon unity and development of essays.

143. Writing: American Humanities
Spring. 3(3-0) Three credits in the second term of any ATL sequence numbered 121 or higher or approval of department.
Writing course to improve composition and research abilities. Writings based on innovation in twentieth century American literature and the visual, plastic, musical, and dramatic arts. Research project required.

151. Writing: American Minorities
Fall. 3(3-0) Satisfactory performance on the placement test.
Writing course to improve composition and critical reading abilities. Writings based on minority literature from mythology to experiences of immigrants and ex-slaves. Emphasis upon unity and structure of essays.

152. Writing: American Minorities
Winter. 3(3-0) Three credits in the first term of any ATL sequence numbered 121 or higher or approval of department.
Writing course to improve composition and critical reading abilities. Writings based on minority literature from Reconstruction, Indian wars and end of European immigration. Emphasis upon style and development of essays.

153. Writing: American Minorities
Spring. 3(3-0) Three credits in the second term of any ATL sequence numbered 121 or higher or approval of department.
Writing course to improve composition and research abilities. Writings based on minority literature. Modern fiction and cultural pluralism emphasized; a research project is required.

Michigan State University has always run "American Thought and Language" (or its successors)), a first-year course sequence that links "English Language Arts" with History, Culture, and various other content areas.

As Ella Flagg Young tried to point out, this was nonsensical and led to students "flitting" from subject to subject without putting anything together. Yet, we've never stopped doing it.

Because Cubberley told everyone—convinced everyone—that the education system had not been either a political or an economic decision but had naturally "transformed" into "an institution for advancing national welfare," schools keep doing what they've been doing for far longer than a century—without ever considering whether what we do is good or bad for children. (Cubberley, 1920)

Anachronism Five—School as a Colonialist Project:

In most schools, students from the margins—Black, Brown, Immigrant, neurodiverse, disabled—continue to live under a colonial regime.

Colonialism? Yes, colonialism—the intent to convert students from who they are into little versions of the power elite—or not quite. This is the opposite of acceptance and Universal Design, which is why true Universal Design for Learning and true design for neurodiversity are such a difficult sell to educational leaders. The power elite doesn't want those different from themselves to ever quite "get there," instead, they want these children to live their lives chasing the idea of becoming someone else while never allowing them to be accepted as fully equal.

We know what power looks like: Bill Ackman's management team at Pershing Square Capital. No wonder African-American women leaders bother him so much. (Love Him or Hate Him, Ackman Now Runs the World's Top Hedge Fund, n.d.)

Part of the problem is that many of our leaders are the products of America's "Ivy League" universities. Deny all they want—and will—those attending elite schools do believe in their eugenic superiority. The ugly flip side of the "American Dream" meritocracy myth is that those who have elite status handed to them via generational wealth transfer have to believe in their eugenic superiority if they are not to see their status and privileges as unfair and unearned.

Those who believe in their superiority become colonialists through the moral (and liberal thinking) learning they are exposed to or simply through the immoral (and conservative thinking) they have observed in their parents and national leaders. Whatever the cause, many are fully willing to embrace what Kipling called the *White Man's Burden*, ("the white man's burden": Kipling) though very few will actually risk anything themselves to shoulder that burden, not even in political/career terms as Benjamin Disraeli or William McKinley (Wikipedia contributors 2024) might have. But they are fully willing to *"Take up the White Man's burden —, Ye dare not stoop to less —, Nor call too loud on Freedom."* (MIT visualizing cultures)

They are happy to do this because Cubberley made the American education system not just something for missionaries (Mann) and not something just for economic policy (Barnard) but literally "pleasurable" for those born to power, just as—in Edward Said's grand explanation, (Said 2012) Rudyard Kipling made British colonialism pleasurable for Britain's upper-class young men. (Cannadine 2002)

Edward Said (*1935–2003*) is an important author who has contributed to the understanding of this construction. Said was the leading intellectual bringing postcolonial literary theory together with politics and human actions "on the ground." In part, this series is inspired by something he said in a 2001 interview: *"But I don't write about just anything—I don't think I'm capable of doing that. I write about things that matter to me, and obviously one of those things is the idea of tribalism—one's origin, and the place that I was born in. But never without clarifying it in as dispassionate a way as possible, and always with some commitment to greater values—more universal values than just the ones of nation, tribe and family. Those issues would be issues of justice, oppression, giving a historical context when it's lost."*

For a wonderful appreciation, and place to begin, I recommend Terry Eagleton's review of Said's last book. (LENIN'S TOMB: Terry Eagleton on Edwar...)

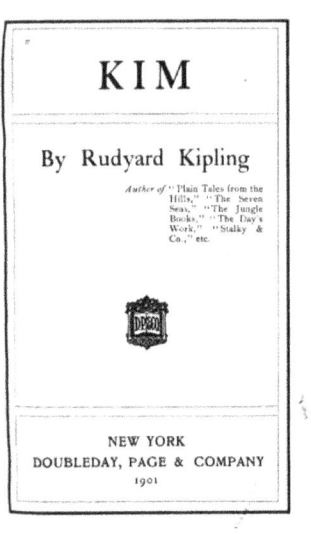

1901. Rudyard Kipling's book "Kim." colonialism as a joyful apprenticeship for Britain's wealthy aspirational class. ("the white man's burden": Kipling)

1899 Cartoon: The White Man's Burden

Cubberley does not sound joyful, he has none of the soaring oratory of Mann nor even the ability of Barnard to conjure the future, but he is clear and absolute:

It is also, as Said says regarding Kipling, an instrument of benign imperialism. "When the United States freed Cuba, Porto Rico, and the Philippines from Spanish rule, a general system of public education, modeled after the American educational ladder, was created as a safeguard to the liberty just brought to these islands, and to education the United States added courts of justice and bureaus of sanitation as important auxiliary agencies. As a result the peoples of these islands have made a degree of progress in self-government and industry in three decades not made in three centuries under Spanish rule." (The History of Education) (Cubberley 1920) We "comfortably" skip over the brutal Philippine War, (Wikipedia contributors 2024) the destruction of representative government in Puerto Rico, (Wikipedia contributors 2024) and the occupation of Cuba, in order to "prove" the perfect pro-gressivism of the system. (Sierra)

"It is the attempt to remould the school and to make of it a more potent instrument of the State for promoting national consciousness and political, social, and industrial welfare that has been behind the many changes and expansions and extensions of education which have marked the past half-century in all the leading world nations, and which underlie the most pressing problems in educational readjustment to-day. These changes and expansions and problems we shall consider more in detail in the chapters which follow. Suffice it here to say that from mere teaching institutions, engaged in imparting a little religious instruction and some knowledge of the tools of learning, the school, in all the leading nations, has to-day been transformed into an institution for advancing national welfare. The leading purpose now is to train for political and social efficiency in the more democratic types of governments being instituted among peoples, and to impart to the young those industrial and social experiences once taught in the home, the trades, and on the farm, but which the coming of

the factory system and city life have deprived them otherwise of knowing."—Cubberley, *The History of Education* (1919)

Said says "orientalism" and "adventure" allow the powerful to feel they are riding the wave of history—which is more appealing to self-identity than seeing yourself as a passive inheritor of wealth. (Said 2012) This explains what you hear about education from the elite, but also what you see from those aspiring to be seen as elite.

"See, "Black English" and "Spanglish" are really no fur-ther—linguistically—from "The Queen's English"(Wikipedia contributors 2024), than the American Southern Accent is, or the thick New England Accent is, our culture has simply decided that certain variations are OK because they embrace the power structure, and certain are not because they rep-resent threats to the power structure. Just as, in the United Kingdom, it is fine if you have an Edinburgh Accent, not fine if you sound like you are from Liverpool. Fine if you are clearly from Devonshire, not fine if you are clearly from Glasgow. None of this is about competency or fluency or understand-ability, rather, it is completely, and only, about power."—Ira Socol, Pygmalion (SpeEdChange, 2011)

"Through analyses of colonial schooling, anthropology, and the formation of academic subjects instrumental in the expansion of empire (history, geography, science, language and literature), Will-insky argues that education was and is the research and development arm of imperialism. Drawing on contemporary classrooms and mate-rials, he considers how schools continue to educate the young within the "colonial imaginary." Through primary texts, recording students' voices, and examining schooling itself, John Willinsky, in *Learning to Divide the World*, argues that teaching imperial legacies in multicultural education balances the achievements of "Western" (European and North American) culture with the facts of the divided world those achievements created. (Learning to Divide the World, 2011)

Colonialism in schools—everything from "the canon" to behavior rules—is as destructive to our learners as it has been to colonized people the world over—forever.

All these anachronisms share the same origin—they are wealth preservation structures created to sustain the economic status quo. If we still use them, we are all complicit. Yet these are not the only anachronisms that reinforce this situation; our daily actions do the same as Chapter Eight will describe.

Sources:

32 Walbrooke Road, Scarsdale, NY 10583. (n.d.). Trulia Real Estate Search. Retrieved March 31, 2024, from https://www.trulia.com/home/32-walbrooke-rd-scarsdale-ny-10583-33035217

2018. (n.d.). Retrieved March 31, 2024, from https://data.nysed.gov/studenteducator. php?year=2018&instid=800000034927

2019. (n.d.). Retrieved March 31, 2024, from https://data.nysed.gov/studenteducator. php?year=2019&instid=800000035159

2020. (n.d.). Retrieved March 31, 2024, from https://data.nysed.gov/expenditures. php?year=2020&instid=800000034927

2021. (n.d.). Retrieved March 31, 2024, from https://data.nysed.gov/expenditures. php?year=2021&instid=800000035159

Alcott, W. A. (1843). *Slate and Black Board Exercises* (p. 7). Mark H. Newman.

Alison Gopnik Lantern v Spotlight. (n.d.). Retrieved April 2, 2024, from http://alisongopnik.com/ lantern_v_spotlight.htm

American Experience | PBS. (2023, September 11). *The Busing Battleground | Full Documentary | AMERICAN EXPERIENCE | PBS.* Youtube. https://www.youtube.com/watch?v=S2Hm8jqByvU

Angus, D. (1988). Historical Development of Age Stratification in Schooling. *Teachers College Record, 90*(2), 211–236.

Badger, E., Miller, C. C., Pearce, A., & Quealy, K. (2018, March 27). Income Mobility Charts for Girls, Asian-Americans and Other Groups. Or Make Your Own. *The New York Times.* https://www. nytimes.com/interactive/2018/03/27/upshot/make-your-own-mobility-animation.html

Battle of the ironclads (U.s. national Park service). (n.d.). Retrieved March 31, 2024, from https://www. nps.gov/articles/battle-of-the-ironclads.htm

Bento, A. (2021). When and where residential racial segregation matters for the Black self-employment rate. *The Review of Black Political Economy, 48*, 455–480.

Carr, S. (2012, December 13). In Southern Towns, "Segregation Academies" Are Still Going Strong. *The Atlantic.* https://www.theatlantic.com/national/archive/2012/12/ in-southern-towns-segregation-academies-are-still-going-strong/266207/

Cubberley, E. P. (1920). *The History of Education: Educational Practice and Progress Considered as a Phase of the Development and Spread of Western Civilization.* Houghton Mifflin.

Darling-Hammond, L. (1998, March 1). *Unequal Opportunity: Race and Education.* Brookings. https:// www.brookings.edu/articles/unequal-opportunity-race-and-education/

Doucleff, M. (2023, July 12). So your tween wants a smartphone? Read this first. *NPR.* https://www.npr. org/sections/health-shots/2023/07/12/1187130983/smartphone-tween-safe-alternatives

Doucleff, M. F. M. (2014, September 15). Michaeleen Doucleff. *NPR.* https://www.npr.org/ people/348778932/michaeleen-doucleff

Elliott, C. (1893). *Report of the Committee on Secondary School Studies.* National Educational Association .

Friedman, J. N. (2022, September 1). Opinion. *The New York Times*. https://www.nytimes.
com/2022/09/01/opinion/us-school-social-mobility.html

F-R percentage for SY 21-22. (2023).

Green, E. L., & Waldman, A. (2018, October 16). "You Are Still Black": Charlottesville's Racial Divide
Hinders Students. *The New York Times*. https://www.nytimes.com/2018/10/16/us/charlottes-
ville-riots-black-students-schools.html

Haidt, J. (2024, March 13). End the Phone-Based Childhood Now. *The Atlantic*. https://www.theatlantic.com/technology/archive/2024/03/
teen-childhood-smartphone-use-mental-health-effects/677722/

Hannah-Jones, N. (2017, September 6). The Resegregation of Jefferson County. *The New York Times*.
https://www.nytimes.com/2017/09/06/magazine/the-resegregation-of-jefferson-county.html

Joffe-Walt, C., Snyder, J., Koenig, S., Drumming, N., Glass, I., Ewing, E. L., Lissy, R., & Nelson, S.
(2020, July 23). Introducing: Nice White Parents. *The New York Times*. https://www.nytimes.
com/2020/07/23/podcasts/nice-white-parents-serial.html

Kozol, J. (1998). *Savage Inequalities*. HarperCollins.

Leveling Lincoln | PBS. (2023, April 10). https://www.pbs.org/video/leveling-lincoln-wmrarj/

Levinger, M. B. (2002). *Enlightened Nationalism: The Transformation of Prussian Political Culture,
1806-1848*. Oxford University Press.

Living together, learning apart. (n.d.). San Francisco Chronicle. Retrieved March 31, 2024, from
https://www.sfchronicle.com/schools-desegregation/

Love him or hate him, Ackman now runs the world's top hedge fund. (n.d.). Retrieved April 2, 2024,
from Bloomberg.com

Maps. (n.d.). Scarsdale Historical Society. Retrieved March 31, 2024, from https://www.scarsdalehistor-
icalsociety.org/maps

Mortimer, G. (2004). *Early Modern Military History, 1450-1815*. Springer.

Movieclips. (2012, October 6). *The Zapruder Film - JFK (6/7) Movie CLIP (1991) HD*. Youtube. https://
www.youtube.com/watch?v=2nmGS8rVuIM

Olsen, L. (2019, November 15). *It's Time to Ditch the Archaic Idea of Age Based
Grade Levels*. Age of Awareness. https://medium.com/age-of-awareness/
its-time-to-ditch-the-archaic-idea-of-age-based-grade-levels-7f0494efddb4

Onion, A. (2009, October 27). *Brown v. Board of Education* History. https://www.history.com/topics/
black-history/brown-v-board-of-education-of-topeka

Robbins, D. L. (2017). War, Modernity, and Motion in the Edison Films of 1898. *Journal of Latin American Cultural Studies, 26*(3), 351–375.

San Antonio Independent School District v. Rodriguez, 411 U.s. 1 (1973). (n.d.). Justia Law. Retrieved
March 31, 2024, from https://supreme.justia.com/cases/federal/us/411/1/

Shoked, N. (2017). An American Oddity: The law, history, and toll of the School District. *Northwestern
University Law Review, 111*, 945–1024.

Smith, C. (2016, October 3). The Desegregation and Resegregation of Charlotte's
Schools. *The New Yorker*. https://www.newyorker.com/news/news-desk/
the-desegregation-and-resegregation-of-charlottes-schools

Socol, I. (Fall 2007). *Irreconcilable Authority Cognitive Theory Culture and Technology in the 21st Century Classroom.*

Socol, I. D. (2016, December 16). *You must see your school as a home of opportunity.* Medium. https://irasocol.medium.com/you-must-see-your-school-as-a-home-of-opportunity-6c7532b43e6f

Socol, I. D. (2020, January 4). *The Width of the World.* Medium. https://irasocol.medium.com/the-width-of-the-world-8f7cab56a16b

Stealth Inequalities.pdf. (n.d.).

Thorndike, E. (1908). *The Elimination of Pupils from School.* Department of the Interior: Bureau of Education.

Twain, M. (2020). *Following the equator, complete.* Ray of Hope. https://www.gutenberg.org/files/2895/2895-h/2895-h.htm

Zhao, Y. (2017). What works may hurt: Side effects in education. *Journal of Educational Change, 18*(1), 1–19.

CHAPTER EIGHT:

Daily Anachronisms that Limit
the Opportunities of Our Students.

The systemic anachronisms in chapter seven form a structure of barriers to opportunity around our students. This is exacerbated by the intentional and unintentional enforcement of ancient patterns that rob children of possibilities every day.

The "every day" and "every hour" norms in most schools provide an assaultive background for many students who come from races, ethnicities, social classes, and neural constructs outside the privileges reinforced by our educational system. These are typically described as "microaggressions," but for those on the receiving end, they are not, in any way, small. (Steketee et al., 2021)

Whether or not these actions, norms, rules, and policies are intentional acts of aggression, the impact on the receiving student is the same. "Aversive racists sympathize with minority groups and endorse principles of racial equality while simultaneously holding often non-conscious feelings of superiority, discomfort, anxiety, and fear. Aversive racism can manifest as microaggressions," wrote Keels, Durkee, and Hope in 2017. They quote Sue, Capodilupo, Torino et al. (Sue et al., 2007) describing the 'brief and commonplace daily verbal, behavioral, and environmental indignities, whether intentional or unintentional, that communicate hostile, derogatory, or negative racial slights and insults to the target person or group," before noting that making it all worse is "this dismissal of people of color's experiences of racial-ethnic discrimination is one aspect of aversive racism and is evidenced in the gulf between Whites' and Blacks' perceptions of the persistence of discrimination." (Keels et al., 2017)

In a 2023 research project, Mary K. Humphreys wrote about how this extends to students with disabilities in everything from the "burdens" claimed by the school and teachers when accommodations are sought to the normalized joking about disabilities common among students and teachers to "a common ableist belief is that disability accommodations are simply "special privileges," a belief that can result in being either jealous or suspicious of someone truly needing that accommodation." (Humphreys, 2023)

These daily assaults separate students from non-privileged situations from their peers and consistently deprive them of opportunities. Every time we tell a student not to run in a hallway, or say that they cannot leave the room without you giving permission, or say that they are late, or over-enforce grammar rules on speech or casual writing, or insist on documentation and diagnosis before allowing the use of Universal Design for Learning tools, we are reinforcing our societal hierarchy. (Ralabate, 2011)

Anachronism One—We remain committed to discomfort:

Brighter task lighting in a dimmer room—the "Reading Room" of the New York Public Library Research (42nd Street) Branch. Carrère and Hastings 1911. (Wikipedia contributors, 2024) *Unlike the "modern" factories from before The Great War, working and learning spaces were typically created with a range of lighting. This room still has its table lamps, sunlight, and gentler overall lighting.* (Main Reading Room, the New York Public Library, n.d.)

School furniture tends to be beyond awful—despite better choices being available. Learners are rarely afforded choices—which are essential to comfort. (Ackers, n.d.) Lighting is typically terrible because schools long ago embraced German factory lighting design (Fox & Guagnini, 1999)—one overall level—which is bad for both eyesight and attention (our eyes relax when they can move from brighter task lighting to dimmer room lighting, improving mood and productivity). (Newsham et al., 2005) We resist human-sized designs and accept the work of terrible architects who have yet to realize that young kids are not very tall. We rarely provide the three things researchers—and William Alcott in the 1830s—know boost attention: sunlight, fresh air, and continuous large muscle movement. (*Spaces In Motion Web.pdf*, n.d.)

Classrooms were designed to mimic strict protestant churches, where sitting still on uncomfortable seats was part of obedience training. If your school still works that way, you are letting one particular religion control the learning environment. It is also vital to understand that, when uncomfortable, 90 percent of a person's brain focuses on that discomfort. (The rest is either angry or sleepy.)

Trapping students in locked classrooms is also an obedience training invention. Alcott believed that five minutes of sitting still was the limit for most students, that they should go outside every 20 minutes, and that the school's garden was more important to learning than the classroom, but as he knew, even in the 1830s, he was going against the grain of international education. Whether in the U.S., England, or Japan, schools, according to Jansen, Marius, and Stone, 1967 (*Gilgoric.pdf*, n.d.), students are "taught firstly—and most importantly—the virtue of obedience to superiors in order to preserve social stability." We've all heard the argument that "kids need to get used to it." In other words, to accept being miserable as an adult employee, one must begin to build up a tolerance for that from childhood, which is all about training rather than learning.

> *"To sit still, at times—entirely still—if not continued too long, is one form of doing something; and I consider it as much a part of the teacher's duty to form his pupils to the habit of sitting still, as to teach them spelling and reading. Not of course an hour at a time, or half an hour, or a quarter, even. To some children, five minutes would be long enough; and to most, ten minutes would he the full extent of what would be useful,"* —(W. A. Alcott, 1842)

> *"But I have not found this deathlike silence in a school room either useful or necessary. True, I have sometimes required it of my pupils. But at other times, I have permitted more of the hum of business. If there were a difference at all in the results, I think the last mentioned course the best."* —(W. A. Alcott, 1842)

Comfort promotes attention. Movement promotes attention. Attention to engaging tasks allows complex learning to happen, and choices prepare learners for the choices they will make all their lives. On the other side of the ledger, blocking sunlight puts kids to sleep. Sitting still puts kids to sleep. Bad furniture drives kids to want to leave.

I worked in a school system that said, "Every learner should be able to enter any learning space and choose where, how, or if to sit." Simple things like moving teacher desks away from windows and not using windowsills as storage can offer both choices and sunlight to our children. Rooms of various sizes, created with transparency, can allow students to choose grouping conditions for their work. Accepting that students should choose different environments for different tasks develops agency and responsibility. We must get ourselves out of an imagined past to believe in science and children.

Making a classroom choice-driven and comfortable can be done for nothing (found furniture). Here, a middle school classroom furnished with a "street find" couch and old office chairs from a government surplus warehouse. – Photo: Ira Socol

Or you can pay for it… four old middle school science class-rooms joined into a series of different-sized spaces. Solar Tubes brought sunlight into what had been windowless 1970s spaces. - Photo: VMDO Architects.(VMDO Architects, n.d.)

Anachronism Two—Homework:

I will always argue that homework is an engine of inequity. Whether it is a simple math worksheet, a textbook assignment ("do the 33 problems at the end of chapter 12"), or the never-going-away science fair project, homework measures the socioeconomic status of the learner's home far more than it measures anything else.

"Students, as I noted at the start, "go home" to radically variable environments. Some head home to houses with university-educated parents with the time and inclination to support their learning, others to university-educated parents with an inclination to do their work for them, others to university-educated parents who are either not home or are 'not present' in their children's lives," I wrote in 2012. "Many more go home to homes without the parental resources or skillsets to support student learning or go home to houses where the children themselves have real responsibilities—including child and/or parent care and/or employment—essential to their survival within a family unit. Further, home resources vary dramatically. There are broadband—everybody has a computer at home—homes, and there are disconnected homes..." (*SpeEdChange*, n.d.)

> "Contrary to the popular view today, homework has not always been viewed as a vital element in academics. During the late nineteenth and early twentieth centuries America had a strong "antihomework" movement. For example, Rice's (1897) study concluded that laborious devotion by children to their spelling homework bore no relation to later spelling ability. He decried what he termed mechanical schooling and argued that time spent on homework could be better spent on other activities. Others went as far as to say that homework was harmful to the mental and physical health of children (Bok1900). Perhaps the height of this movement was in 1901 when the California state legislature passed a law abolishing homework for children under the age of fifteen and limited it in public high schools (California Civil Code 1901)."— (Eren & Henderson, 2011)

Homework is another of our "tradition" myths. A few still believe that Abe Lincoln "did his homework by firelight," an unlikely scenario because (a) he probably did not attend school for more than a dozen months in his life; (b) because the only books he came across were from his stepmother or a neighbor (his schools were "ABC schools" which taught the alphabet and Bible verses via hornbooks); and (c) because the idea of "homework" had yet to be invented. (Russell, 2009) Any time early 19th century children had outside of their limited school hours was spent working on their family farm or in their family's cottage industry. However, if self-described traditionalists can root this myth in sacred American history, then their desire to naturalize this educational strategy is fulfilled.

LINCOLN WORKING, BY THE FIRELIGHT.

At least this image shows an adult Lincoln and describes this as "work," not "schoolwork." (File:Photograph of Abraham Lincoln wo...)

Homework began to be a part of education in the 1880s-1890s as America's new middle class grew, and those parents began sending their children to public schools. Suddenly, schools had students who did not need to do chores before and after school—it was a status symbol to have children without chores—so homework became a way of keeping children out of trouble while declaring parental wealth. This other import from Prussia—homework in the mid-19th century Volksschulen was a method of the government controlling family life in urban areas prone to revolutions (Who Invented Homework? The History of...)—became controversial immediately, with everyone from physicians to the Ladies Home Journal attacking the concept. (Mehta 2009)

"When are parents going to open their eyes to this fearful evil? Are they as blind as bats, that they do not see what is being wrought by this crowning folly of night study?"—(Bok 1900)

Anachronism Three—Learning by the Clock:

The school day, the school week, the school year, and the "Carnegie Unit" of seat time are all absurd ways to measure or organize human learning.

Absurd is the wrong word. These are mechanical (the ticking of the clock), Calvinist (human control over the natural environment), industrial (efficiency above all), and capitalist (we won't pay teachers for their achievements or per student; we will pay them as little as possible for occupying our children for as long as possible) ways to measure and organize "learning."

In the natural world, learning is timeless, driven by curiosity and just-in-time needs. The day is structured around the sun's rising and setting, as well as the weather. Learning is always conjoined. Understanding *Macbeth* becomes stronger with knowledge of the ascension of James VI/I to the English throne. To understand *The Great Gatsby* requires knowing the American economic system and its myths. Understanding biology requires comprehension of chemical reactions and the physics behind muscle movements. Since humans are individuals and members of a cooperative society, no act of learning is the same for everyone.

Our academic time, though, is very much the stuff of the first years of the 20th century—when the Carnegie Unit was developed, everything needed to be measured in time. "Ford's new Highland Park assembly plant began producing cars with an efficiency that was unheard of at that time. Initially, the chassis was assembled in 12 hours and 8 minutes, but by 1914, it only took 93 minutes to assemble a new Model T." (Model T)

The great capitalist advantage of "wage slavery" over older compensation models (sharecropping in the U.S., European peasantry, and artisan compensation) was that in those old systems, excess production directly enriched the worker, while with hourly wages, excess production directly enriches the owners. This book is not the place to dive deeply into Marxist or any economic theory, but educators should consider how they are compensated and how their students are "compensated" for their work through credits and grades. In both cases, time has become the primary thing measured, though obviously, other choices exist. The Carnegie Unit was explicitly tied to university educator pension plans—in other words—compensation. In early educational environments, teachers—tutors—were paid by each student. In the Carnegie model, all the excess (more students jammed into that classroom) benefits of the ruling class, even when the ruling class is described as "taxpayers."

93 hours to assemble a Model T... 120 hours to learn Chemistry or Shakespeare.

"The incentive to adopt the Carnegie unit as a standard of [university] admission was purely financial and void of academic consideration. The Carnegie unit was not only a financial incentive, but it was an appropriate tool for educational institutions during the Industrial Era," wrote Heidi Nickel in 2003. (Carnegie Unit and School reform .pdf) "Factories needed workers who could listen to instructions, absorb bits of isolated information, and regurgitate those bits of information when necessary." The strange point is that the Carnegie Unit specified radically different understandings of academic time for secondary and tertiary education. As university courses trended toward the now standard 45 hours of instruction per credit, high schools were locked into a 120-hour formula. (This appears most absurd when viewed through the Advanced Placement lens, where 120 hours in a high school classroom plus massive amounts of homework represents

45 hours of university instruction plus no more than 45 hours of work expected outside that instructional time.)

"Reforms [in the operations of secondary schools] are extremely difficult to implement because the Carnegie unit has become a deeply embedded fundamental notion of "good" practice in the minds of parents and children," Nickel adds, while quoting Robert Marzano: "They are often afraid that if credits and grades are abandoned, their school will not be considered a 'real' school ...[T]he public perceives certain defining characteristics of school as those things that they have come to think of as 'real school.' Any attempt to alter 'real school' ... is very difficult even when the alteration will clearly produce better results."

"These phobias of changing policies are inhibiting schools from making needed changes," Nickel continues. "If the Carnegie were eliminated, many organizational and instructional changes would follow. Many concepts would be better understood if they were not taught as discrete units." (Carnegie Unit and School reform .pdf)

That the Carnegie Unit fails to provide a rational structure for education isn't new information. In 1954—just a year after the U.S. Department of Health, Education, and Welfare was established—the department published a 58-page report challenging the use of this 120-hour definition of learning.

Referring to the Carnegie Unit in their 1954 reportto the Department of Health, Education, and Welfare—70 years ago as this is written—as "the concept of serving time in the classroom," Tompkins and Gaumnitz determine that the unit of measurement has "fallacies." "[T]he diploma means only that a pupil has attended high school for four years," they say, while admitting that the unit "interferes with good education," makes daily schedules "inflexible," and "restricts the development of a more functional curriculum based upon students' abilities, interests, and life needs."

"Those urging the reexamination of the Carnegie Unit as a useful means of measuring pupil progress point out that those time allotments reduce high-school graduation to a question of covering certain bodies of subject matter regarded as approximately equal to one another, and suggest that each pupil achieve in each a similar degree of mastery [or at least the recallable knowledge of 65 percent of the material]. Followed blindly, as it often is, they say that this concept (1) asks few questions about a pupil's ability to master the required bodies of knowledge, (2) pays too little attention to what he already knows, (3) forgets conveniently that some learn the same facts or skills in a fraction of the time required by others, (4) fails to reconcile wide variations in teaching skill and efficiency, and (5) ignores the many other facts about teaching, learning, testing, and marking which do not conform to such a simple, quantitative formula as the Carnegie Unit."—Tompkins and Gaumnitz, 1954. (Carnegie HUD report 1954.pdf)*

Eliminating our ties to a historic structure that was known to be outmoded long before almost everyone in our school buildings was alive seems like a no-brainer, and yet Daniel Buck—remember Chapter Four—and his friends find this measure of "doing time" their sole definition of achievement. (Eden 2024)

Anachronism Four—Non-Actionable Assessment:

What is assessment? Why do we give grades? What are students supposed to understand about grades?

Assessment has a purpose. Evaluation has a purpose. The concept of "mastery"—as in "I can do this"—has a purpose. But does linear measurement have a place in human learning? Like so many of these anachronisms, that idea is less traditional and less inevitable than we imagine.

"When you assess something, you are forced to assume that a linear scale of values can be applied to it. Otherwise no assessment is possible. Every person who says of something that it is good or bad or a bit better than yesterday is declaring that a points system exists; that you can, in a reasonably clear and obvious fashion, set some sort of a number against an achievement."—Peter Hoeg (Høeg 1994)

Linear evaluation in formal education appeared first at Yale in 1785. Ezra Stiles, the college president, wrote about the results of an exam: "Present at exam. 58. Sick 2. Out of To 11. Of these 58, 20 Optimi, 16 2d Opt., 12 Inferiores (Boni), 10 Pejores' (Stiles, 1901, p. 154)." (Tocci, 2008) This looks a lot like the 4.0 scale I knew in university situations (not at Pratt Institute, which was Pass/Fail with written evaluations)—4.0 = Optimi, 3.0, Second Optimi, 2.0 = Inferiores, whether Pejores equals 1.0 or does not matter. Either grade gets a student in trouble.

"Good grades are met, usually, with relief, as in, "whew... got through that." Bad grades are met with either, "the teacher sucks," or, "the teacher hates me," and both are valid conclusions given that grading is "an absolutely uncalibrated instrument." (Finkelstein, 1913) Because no two teachers utilize the same measures in the same way, and because so much subjective judgment goes into grading anything, along with so many things unrelated to skill or knowledge gain—attendance, behavior, homework, et al—that kids literally have no idea what a grade means."— (Socol 2019)

However, linear grading did not enter the larger educational conversation for years. "Grading as a system was particular to Yale for 28 years, though there is no clear evidence of its use each year. The approach was simplified and quantified in 1813 to a numerical scale, 1–4 [the order was reversed with 1 being "best"]," Tocci writes. In "the 1830s, Harvard started a similar system, first using the 1–4 scale and seven years later changing to a 1–100 scale. In 1869 the faculty at Harvard voted to de-link students' conduct from academic measurement and award grades only for scholarship, arguing that gentlemanly behavior should be accorded a different evaluation beyond straight calculation (Smallwood, 1935)."—Tocci, 2008

None of this offered useful information for the learner. That lack of actionable information—along with that "absolutely uncalibrated" issue—remains the problem today. A ranking tells you nothing unless you understand all that is being ranked, and a percentage is worthless unless you know what was not accomplished. Explaining the Pass/ Fail grading in Pratt's School of Architecture, Structural Engineering professor Y.S. Lee said simply, "No one leaves my class knowing 95 percent of what makes a building stand up." (Legacy 2003)

What might an "A" mean anyway? Is it 95 percent? As in, 'U.S. Supreme Court Justice Clarence Thomas received an A in Constitutional Law. He only missed three questions: He did not seem to understand the First, Second, or 13th Amendments.'

Or, 'She received an F, a 58 percent. She knew everything and was ahead of the class, but because of the zeroes the teacher gave her for undone homework and a missed test, she failed.'

In neither case does the grade itself tell us anything important. The student will not be clear about anything without the accompanying narrative assessment, a person reading the transcript will likewise know nothing, and the grade itself offers no actionable evaluative assessment—there is nothing in either "A" or "F" that might push either learner to use their intrinsic curiosity and commitment to get better. Clarence Thomas takes his A to the Federalist Society, and because he parrots what those rich people say—the privilege of the compliant—he gets to the top. The learner with the F knows nothing beyond the teacher being "an unfair idiot."

The A-F, or 1–100 (which allows students to be ranked 60 points below failure at the teacher's whim), or 4.0 grading systems are all sorting mechanisms—gatekeeping mechanisms. It is part of the whole structure of limiting opportunity to those who already are privileged.

> "Horace Mann expressed concerns that students would be too focused on class rank and may, "incur moral hazards and delinquencies" as they chased extrinsic motivation. His solution was to show progress of a student overtime through monthly report cards, as to show growth and development. In general, early reformers saw report cards as a way to inspire intrinsic motivation while still tracking a student's progress."—Chris McNutt, (McNutt)

The privileged will already know how to behave like upper-middle-class white kids. They'll know how to get their homework done by educated mothers and fathers, they'll be driven to school and get there on time—and if they have trouble with any of that, they will have doctors' notes, and disability evaluations, and parental excuses that are accepted without question. They will also attend schools that attract(perhaps) better teachers with greater resources—higher wages, fewer challenges, and safer neighborhoods. They will win this grading game.

> "What should the mark really represent? Should the mark be based upon ability or performance, or even upon zeal and

enthusiasm?... Marks may be based upon performance, upon ability, or upon accomplishment. The last named is, save under unusual circumstances, the quality on which the marks should be based."—Isidore Finkelstein of the Cornell Educational Laboratory, 1913. (Finkelstein 1913)

"The end result of that journey—the 100-point grading system in its current permutation—is a "badly lopsided scale that is heavily gamed against the student," Youki Terada (2023) quotes researchers James Carifio and Theodore Carey of the University of Massachusetts–Lowell. "When the original 100-point scale prevailed, grades were centered around the midpoint, and a failing grade and a passing grade had equal weight... when the centerpoint shifted upward, there was simply less area in which to succeed: Roughly 60 percent of the grading scale was now dedicated to failing marks, and the implications of a very low grade or a zero became catastrophic." (Terada 2023)

The original Danish title of this book about 'inclusion gone wrong'—De måske egnede—translates to the Jeffersonian "for those who might be useful."

"But never at any time has a code of practice been laid down for the awarding of points. No offense intended to anyone. Never at any time in the history of the world has anyone—for anything ever so slightly more

complicated than the straightforward play of a ball or a 400-meter race-been able to come up with a code of practice that could be learned and followed by several different people, in such a way that they would all arrive at the same mark. Never at any time have they been able to agree on a method for determining when one drawing, one meal, one sentence, one insult, the picking of one lock, one blow, one patriotic song, one Danish essay, one playground, one frog, or one interview is good or bad or better or worse than another."—Peter Høeg, *Borderliners,* (Høeg 1994)

In a 2015 study, Carifio and Carey found that "for many students... receiving a zero was demoralizing—not corrective. (Carifio and Carey 2013) "The assigning of even a small number of catastrophically low grades, especially early in the marking term, before student self-efficacy can be established, can create this sense of helplessness," Terada continued in an Edutopia article, "putting students in an impossible situation and discouraging them for the rest of the grading period. Giving students a lifeline out of a ruinous situation keeps them engaged and motivated to do better, the research suggests." (Terada 2023)

Finally, Terada doubts the "real life norm" argument. "There are times when deadlines must be strictly enforced, but for the most part, employers are typically forgiving of extensions and late work, recognizing that "assigned deadlines can be stressfully tight, compromising output quality." (Terada 2023)

"Feldman says we also don't want to include non-academics in grades—things like messy binders and not coming to class with a pencil, or the one that is commonly factored

in: late work. A student who writes an A-quality essay but hands it in late gets her writing downgraded to a B, and the student who writes a B-quality essay turned in by the deadline receives a B. There's nothing to distinguish those two B grades, although those students have very different levels of content mastery."— (Terada 2023)

Lory Hough, in a 2023 article on The Harvard Graduate School of Education site, quotes Grading for Equity author Joe Feldman, "Traditional grading also invites biases... especially around behavior. (Hough) When we include a student's behavior in a grade, we're imposing on all of our students a narrow idea of what a 'successful' student is." But that is just another way to reward "acting white." (Buck 2010)

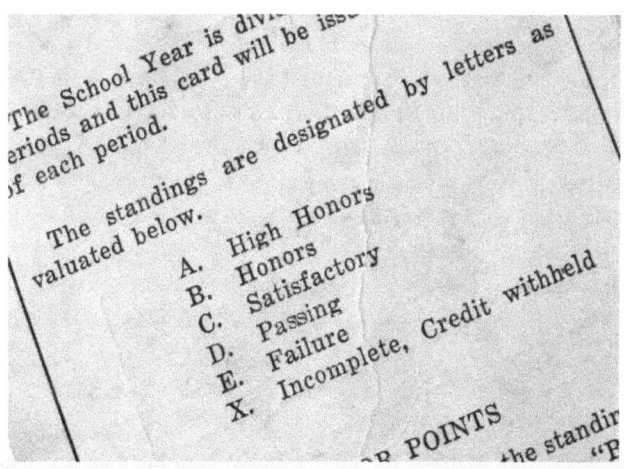

Mount Holyoke College grading in 1897. F hasn't been linked to "failure" yet.

All these anachronisms share the same origin—they are wealth preservation structures created to sustain the economic status quo. If we still use them, we are all complicit.

Sources:

Ackers, J. (n.d.). Redefining Ownership in Flexible Learning Environments: Empowering Students to Shape Their Educational Journey. *VSAmerica.com*. Retrieved April 15, 2024, from https://vsamerica.com/blog/redefining-ownership-flexible-learning-environments

Alcott, W. A. (1842). Slate and Black Board Exercises for Common Schools. *Connecticut Common School Journal (1838-1853)*, *4*(8), 69–84.

Alcott, W. A. (1969). *Confessions of a School Master*. Arno Press.

Eren, O., & Henderson, D. (2011). Are we wasting our children's time by giving them more homework? *SSRN Electronic Journal*. https://doi.org/10.1016/J.ECONEDUREV.2011.03.011

Fox, R., & Guagnini, A. (1999). Laboratories, Workshops, and Sites. Concepts and Practices of Research in Industrial Europe, 1800-1914 (Concluded). *Historical Studies in the Physical and Biological Sciences: HSPS / Office of History of Science and Technology, University of California, Berkeley*, *29*(2), 191–294.

gilgoric.pdf. (n.d.).

Humphreys, M. (2023). *Examining the Prevalence of Disability Stigma in Schools Among High School Students With Disabilities* (M. O'Malley (Ed.)) [Ed Specialist , California State University]. https://search.proquest.com/openview/dd131fa4a96f47fdb969d5e6d2538585/1?pq-origsite=gscholar&cbl=18750&diss=y

Keels, M., Durkee, M., & Hope, E. (2017). The Psychological and Academic Costs of School-Based Racial and Ethnic Microaggressions. *American Educational Research Journal*, *54*(6), 1316–1344.

Main reading room, the New York Public Library. (n.d.). NYPL Digital Collections. Retrieved April 15, 2024, from https://digitalcollections.nypl.org/items/510d47e0-d8bc-a3d9-e040-e00a18064a99

Newsham, G., Arsenault, C., Veitch, J., Tosco, A. M., & Duval, C. (2005). Task Lighting Effects on Office Worker Satisfaction and Performance, and Energy Efficiency. *LEUKOS*, *1*(4), 7–26.

Ralabate, P. K. (2011). *Universal Design for Learning: Meeting the Needs of All Students*. https://doi.org/10.1044/leader.FTR2.16102011.14

Russell, N. (2009, September 24). Trace the history of the hornbook. *Columbia Daily Tribune*. https://www.columbiatribune.com/story/lifestyle/around-town/2009/09/24/trace-history-hornbook/21540703007/

Spaces In Motion Web.pdf. (n.d.).

SpeEdChange. (n.d.). Retrieved April 15, 2024, from https://speedchange.blogspot.com/2012/01/changing-gears-2012-rejecting-flip.html

Steketee, A., Williams, M. T., Valencia, B. T., Printz, D., & Hooper, L. M. (2021). Racial and Language Microaggressions in the School Ecology. *Perspectives on Psychological Science: A Journal of the Association for Psychological Science*, *16*(5), 1075–1098.

Sue, D. W., Capodilupo, C. M., Torino, G. C., Bucceri, J. M., Holder, A. M. B., Nadal, K. L., & Esquilin, M. (2007). Racial microaggressions in everyday life: implications for clinical practice. *The American Psychologist*, *62*(4), 271–286.

VMDO architects. (n.d.). VMDO Architects. Retrieved April 15, 2024, from https://www.vmdo.com/

Wikipedia contributors. (2024, April 11). *New York Public Library Main Branch*. Wikipedia, The Free Encyclopedia. https://en.wikipedia.org/w/index.php?title=New_York_Public_Library_Main_Branch&oldid=1218462457

CHAPTER NINE:

Can America Embrace its Children and Help Them Grow?

"Robert F. Kennedy had come [to an Eastern Kentucky school] to learn about rural poverty. Instead, his arrival petrified the students, who sat riveted to their ancient desks with their heads down, afraid to even look at the great man and his entourage.

"He sized up the problem. Instead of making a speech for the media, Kennedy moved quietly among the students, stopping to reassure them. He'd squeeze a hand, murmur in an ear. "What did you have to eat today?" he asked one girl. "I know you're scared," he told a boy, "but it's gonna be all right.""—Rick Hampson, *USA Today*, 2018, "RFK's visit to Appalachia, 50 years later: How Kennedy country became Trump country" (Hampson, 2018)

Bobby Kennedy (the real one) in Appalachia in 1966. No other elected US leader has ever tried to make vulnerable children the heart of his work. Image: (File: Robert F. Kennedy NYWTS.jpg, 1966)

Those of us involved in American education struggle with a massive problem. As much as I dislike the terms "industrialized economies," "advanced nations," and "first world," let's simply say that among nations that might be described in those ways, none treats children worse than the United States. It is not even close.

We like "our children"—via tribal and family links—but we don't like "other people's children" (Delpit, 2005). Perhaps we see "other people's children" as threatening because, in the game of evolutionary genetics, every other child is a potential competitor. Perhaps it is, and has been, the wild irrational fear of "communism" (which might be defined as "higher taxes on those with 90 percent of the national wealth"). *Business Insider* noted that in 1971, "a rogue's gallery of Republicans persuaded President Richard Nixon to veto [a bill that would have provided for universal child care], citing the threat of communism to the American family unit." About the Republicans forcing the COVID-Era child subsidies to expire, that publication found it "hard to locate anything but abject hatred for kids in this decision."

Maybe it is simply political disregard for a group of citizens who cannot vote. "Collectively," Nicholas Kristof wrote in *The New York Times* in February 2024, "we mistreat America's children, especially by the standards of other wealthy countries. When we're formulating policies for children as a whole rather than coddling our own little angels, we fall scandalously short. We prize children in the abstract but, as a society, tend to ignore their needs. Children are more likely to go hungry or live in poverty in America than in most of our peer countries, and they are also much more likely to die young — because of drugs, guns, accidents, and an inequitable health care system."

As a society, we are reluctant to feed our hungry children (Iowa and other states refused federal money in 2023 to feed kids). (Jordan, 2023) We refuse to give them enough time with their parents (no parental leave, no mandatory vacation days, no mandatory sick leave, no effective minimum wage laws, so many parents must have three or four jobs to survive, only unpaid family leave). We refuse to ensure that every family has access to preventative health care. Families least able to afford it pay higher tax rates than our wealthiest citizens. Some states have decided to be extremely cruel to any child who is different. And education funding goes primarily to people with the most money.

The United States is a brutal place that prioritizes almost anything, from billionaire sports team owners to lunatics who think they must walk around with military weapons to make up for—I don't know... a lack of testosterone?—to tax cuts for the world's wealthiest individuals, over providing safety and opportunity to children.

How Much Governments Spend On Child Care for Toddlers

Annual public spending per child on early childhood care

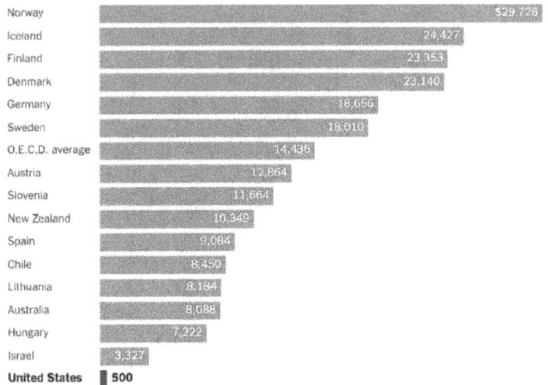

Norway	$29,726
Iceland	24,427
Finland	23,353
Denmark	23,140
Germany	18,656
Sweden	18,010
O.E.C.D. average	14,436
Austria	12,864
Slovenia	11,664
New Zealand	10,349
Spain	9,084
Chile	8,450
Lithuania	8,184
Australia	8,088
Hungary	7,222
Israel	3,327
United States	500

Source: Organization for Economic Cooperation and Development and Elizabeth Davis and Aaron Sojourner for the Hamilton Project

"If you have children in America, it is up to you to keep them safe, healthy, and well cared for. This philosophy shapes government policy in some obvious ways: The U.S. is one of the only countries in the world without guaranteed paid maternity leave. (Miller, 2021b) Compared with the rest of the OECD, an international coalition of 38 nations—most of them wealthy—it spends far less on direct cash benefits for families (which the U.S. briefly experimented with more broadly during the early pandemic but then abandoned), as well as on early education and child care. Statutory paid vacation, sick leave, caregiving leave, and pension credits for caregivers (Jankowski, 2011)are all common (Paid Sick Leave to Protect Income, Health and Jobs through the COVID-19 Crisis, n.d.) in OECD countries but absent in America."—Stephanie H. Murray (Murray, 2024)

Our schools have been designed to fail certain children and certain adolescents. That's the history I have been trying to put before you. The design begins at birth, travels through a refusal to support child care ("In the developed world, the United States is an outlier in its low levels of financial support for young children's care."), and ends up with an educational system more focused on denying opportunity than creating it. (Miller, 2021a) (Miller, 2021b)

Conceptually that is a vital topic, but we need to see the trees in that forest. We need to look closely at the many tiny tools of oppression and exclusion that chase those students into failure or just out the door.

The forms through which life realizes itself, whether school, family, society, church, or state, tend to fix themselves, and to check the life which grows through them. This is natural and inevitable. A considerable part of man's effort must be spent in readjusting the forms of life to the growing conditions of life. Man lives in advance of the customs of society, the laws of the state, the creeds of the church, and the methods and statutes of the school. When the tension becomes too great, as it does naturally and periodically, the old forms must be readjusted, or new ones substituted. It will be evolution or revolution. = Arnold Tompkins (Tompkins, 1895)

From our buildings to our schedule, to our furniture, to the technologies we prefer, to the ways we spend money (and raise money), to every policy we have in place, to teacher training, to professional development, to our practices and philosophies, we are either welcoming all learners to opportunity or we are doing something different.

Children on the margins—on the borderline in Peter Høeg's words—find themselves not just unloved, not just the victims of microaggressions, but fully under attack.

"The rules of the culture of power are a reflection of the rules of the culture of those who have power. This means that success in institutions-schools, workplaces, and so on—is predicated upon acquisition of the culture of those who are in power. Children from middle-class homes tend to do better in school than those from non-middle-class homes because the culture of the school is based on the culture of the upper and middle classes—of those in power. The upper and middle classes send their children to school with all the accoutrements of the culture of power; children from other kinds of families operate within perfectly wonderful and viable cultures but not cultures that carry the codes or rules of power.—Lisa Delpit, *Other People's Children: Cultural Conflict in the Classroom,* (Delpit, 2005)

Black children have faced a war against them since the Reagan Administration, if not the Nixon Administration, as the Republican Party adopted its "Southern Strategy" to remake itself as an electoral coalition devoted to racism and segregation. (Cultures, 2018) "A Nation at Risk: The Imperative for Educational Reform, (The National Commission on Excellence in Education, 1983) the Reagan administration report on the state of American education... cast a long and dark shadow over young Black people of my generation," Dr. Bettina Love, a professor at Columbia University's Teachers College, writes in her 2023 book Punished for Dreaming. (Love, 2023) "Together with Reagan's war on drugs, [this] set in motion the merging of prisons and schools under the guise of "getting tough" on education. "Getting tough" was a euphemism for "punishment," sold to the public as high-stakes testing, school choice, vouchers, charter schools, and school safety. At the same time, police officers were placed in schools along with metal detectors, police dogs, and surveillance equipment to control the students they now openly called thugs and criminals."

All of that remains in place, now strongly supported by many white "liberal" parents who, frustrated by their inability to get the nation to stop letting everyone carry a military weapon, have embraced police in schools, metal detectors, and harsh discipline for anyone "disruptive."

> *"Republican-appointed judges released southern states and localities from school desegregation and voting rights mandates—and now resegregation of schools has taken hold in the South as well as in the nation."*—Ferrel Guillory, 2023 (Cultures, 2018)

While black students are assaulted daily by an escalating disciplinary structure set in motion—typically—by a student somehow offending the white suburban standards of politeness held by a few teachers, and an entire major political party attacks LGBTQ+ students, (*Mapping Attacks on LGBTQ Rights in U.S. State Legislatures in 2024*, 2024) students with disabilities find themselves either ignored and abandoned (Lander, 2023) or as pawns in the profitable games of the "disability-industrial complex"—caught between school spending, technology, and behavior preferences on one side and whatever corporate entity has last talked to over-active parents on the other. (Douce, 2019)

"Whatever you are teaching, you are teaching everything"

When the environment changes, what we teach changes. Here, part of a group of 60 high school students who worked with 4 core subject teachers and a CTE teacher with no bell schedule in flexible spaces). The students spent each morning in this program, got 5 credits, and had the afternoons for electives. photo: Ira Socol

The end result is that every day, millions of kids go to schools that are not just unwelcoming and unaccommodating but fully hostile. Wealthy and powerful parents can solve that—bringing legal pressure and paying for private schools—but the children of the powerless are trapped.

"Whatever you are teaching, you are teaching everything," I say this in many conversations with educators because, as adults or as leaders, we too often forget that children learn very little from the things we say—although they may learn they are worthless from the words of adults—they learn from watching us and from the experiences we craft for them. School is, unfortunately, a set of experiences in which children learn...

- Their place in the social hierarchy.
- That rich is better than poor.
- That white is better than black or brown.
- That thin is better than fat.
- That fast—on the playground or in the classroom—is better than slow.
- That strong is better than weak.
- That compliance matters more than capability.
- That bullying (I. Socol, 2009)—or even violence—is not just acceptable, it works.
- That boys matter more than girls.
- That neurotypical is better than neurodiverse.
- That being typically abled is better than dealing with any disability.
- That being good at math, English, social studies, and certain sciences is better than being good at art, music, theater, dance, or anything else.
- But... that playing a sport well might be the most important thing of all and makes you far more valuable than a kid who plays chess, raps, or sits in a corner and writes stories.
- That having two parents—one male, one female—is better than any other family possibility.

Then we teach a few other things in many schools...

- That mobile phones are not essential tools students will need to choose, adapt, and use well throughout their lives. "They are just too distracting."
- That access to information and stories is reserved for those who read alphabetic text well.
- That if something is printed on paper, it is more believable than something expressed on a screen, in a video, or through music or art.

- And yet, we also teach that big tech companies know more than anyone in the building. Schools and teachers brand themselves with the Apple, Google, and/or Microsoft logos. Schools and districts commit to huge contracts with corporate vendors and consultants and babysit students with badly designed—but highly profitable—"learning" apps.
- That the history of white people is more important than the history of the vast majority of the earth's people.
- That having wealth and/or power makes what you say more important than what someone without wealth and power says.
- That children's needs, decisions, desires, and choices are always less important than the conveniences of adults.

That's all on top of the well-known "adults lie," "adults have left us a mess to clean up," and "adults are always hypocrites," the things kids have always learned.

If you think about a student's day, and especially if you shadow a student (which every school leader should do multiple times a year with different types of learners) (Stanford D.school, n.d.), you will see all these things taught every minute. They are not—usually—said out loud, at least not where people think they will be overheard, but the messages will come across loud and clear.

"I am a biology teacher. I am not a Science teacher."—anonymous social media post 2024.

Will Richardson pointed out a few questions in 2016.
- "Do kids learn better when we separate out the content into different subjects, or is it just easier for us?
- "Do kids learn better when we have every one of them pretty much go through the same curriculum in the same way, or is it just easier for us?

- "Do kids learn better when we have them turn off all of their technology in school, or is it just easier for us?
- "Do kids learn better when we assess them all the same way, or is it just easier for us?
- "Do kids learn better when we decide what they should learn and how they should learn it, or is it just easier for us?
- "Do kids learn better in 50—or 90-minute blocks, or is it just easier for us?"

Then Richardson added, "Sadly, "doing the right thing" for our kids in schools is difficult. In education, our structures, our histories, our nostalgia for trying to do the "wrong thing right" runs deep. Regardless of how we got here (and the story is complex) (Watters, 2015), we are profoundly wedded to what now constitutes this "education system" that dominates our learning world. (Watters, 2015) The roles and expectations of students and teachers and administrators and parents are so clearly reinforced by our own experience, our cultural representations, and by those who have millions of dollars invested in the status quo that any serious suggestion that we might be doing the "wrong thing" is simply layered over by a new initiative, a new technology, a new curriculum, or a new success story to avoid having to grapple with the more fundamental question."

"During the days of the one-room schoolhouse, a teacher ... was able to effectively reach 30 children ranging in age from 5 to 16 because each child's education was based on an individualized lesson plan. Mastery learning was the norm; children did not move on until they mastered the topic they were studying. Progress may have been slow or even non-existent, but no one expected children simply to move at a pace set by the teacher. Today, technology gives teachers the abil-

ity to again offer every child an individualized learning plan and to implement mastery learning using an abundance of resources. It allows teachers to find materials that motivate individual students, to have those materials immediately at hand when they are needed, and to devise activities that match students' unique learning styles."—Bethany M. Baxter (Baxter, September-October 2000)

Changing schools is possible. Creating great schools is possible. Helping every young person move ahead is possible. People have been doing that since long before William Alcott collected his observations, and they are doing that today. But every expansion of opportunity is a political challenge to those determined to keep success to themselves.

"Education is the most political thing we do, it is the fight for our future." (I. D. Socol, 2020)

Education is either about social reproduction or it is about opportunity. Those with wealth, power, and status prefer social reproduction—for both self-interest and parental self-interest. Those without—unless they've been co-opted by those who stoke religious/pseudo-religious hatred—desire opportunity

What this means is that those who are liberal or leftist but who have wealth, power, and/or status are never quite "all-in" on education as opportunity. Yes, professors of education promote progressive ideas, but they do that from segregated enclaves closed to opportunity—Palo Alto, California; Cambridge, Massachusetts; Ann Arbor, Michigan; Boulder, Colorado; Evanston, Illinois; even places like East Lansing, Michigan and State College, Pennsylvania. (*For Professors, Segregation Begins at Home*, 2019)

They also do that while ensuring that their children have every conceivable advantage over the children of have-nots.

"Regardless of their stated beliefs, many academics are disinclined to tear down these policies and practices, from which they have benefited enormously. It's no secret that many people residing in highly educated college communities have deeply internalized beliefs about intelligence and merit, as defined by performance on standardized achievement tests. The path to their own elite opportunities began with their selection into advanced ability groups in elementary reading and math, to their assignment to gifted and talented programs in the middle grades, to their enrollment in tiered courses in high school."—Emdin, Moran, and Socol (*For Professors, Segregation Begins at Home*, 2019)

It is obviously not just professors. Take a look at the websites for two New York City public schools separated by two miles and a lot of demographics. There is PS 20, "The Clinton Hill School," (PS 20 the Clinton Hill School — Cluster Specialists, n.d.) serving what are now the highly upscale parts of Fort Greene in Brooklyn (it was far less upscale when I lived there), with Dance, Art, Music, and French among the offerings, and there is PS 124—definitely not a deeply impoverished community but a place lacking in status—which does have a dance teacher and an intervention teacher, but not art, or music, or French, and where the website begs for contributions. (PS 124, n.d.)

The parents of PS 20 kids are far-left by American standards. Their member of Congress is Hakeem Jeffries (Wikipedia contributors, 2024b), and their State Assembly member is the Democratic Socialist Phara Souffrant Forrest, who received 99.4 percent of the vote in the last election. (Wikipedia contributors, 2024c) However, they send their children to a school filled with opportunities unavailable to most Brooklyn children, and they aggressively fund-raise and lobby the Board of Education to keep that true.

Thus, when it comes to fundamental—revolutionary—change, changing funding mechanisms and teacher pay, changing attendance boundaries, altering the school year, adding UDL technologies and strategies for every child, giving every child the learning opportunities wealthy "gifted" kids get—you will find it very difficult to build a coalition.

"Why would I want more kids to get an advanced diploma? Then my kid's diploma would be worth less."—A University of Virginia faculty member at a local school board meeting.

This is all part of a long historical pattern that blocks revolutionary success. You might look at the Revolutions of 1848 Podcast (33 chapters in the Revolutions podcast series). (Seaquence, 2023) In part 7.33 of that series, Mike Duncan points out that a primary cause of the failure of the movements that swept Europe that year was the inability of the "liberal conservatives"—who were fighting for representative government and civil rights—to work with the "radical left"—which was seeking socio-economic changes to benefit workers and the poor. When the "liberal conservatives" initially gained power, they refused to go along with the social agenda—rights to jobs, housing, and food—of the "radical left." (Wikipedia contributors, 2024a) That split the forces of revolution and made the job of the counter-revolutionaries easy.

Of course, they refused to go along. The "liberals" were people with wealth and status. Upending the economic order threatened wealth and status, and humans are—and always have been—motivated primarily by self-interest. Those who transcend that form the tiny minority that are our heroes.

"Most Americans have been to school and know what a "real school" is like. Congruence with that cultural template has helped maintain the legitimacy of the institution in the minds of the public. But when schooling departed too much from the consensual model of a "real school," failed to match the grammar of schooling, trouble often ensued. If teachers did not maintain strict discipline and consistently supervise students in class, if traditional subjects were neglected, if pupils did not bring report cards home, reforms might be suspect."—Tyack and Cuban, *Tinkering toward Utopia,* 2009 (Tyack & Cuban, 1995)

There is, however, another conceptual battle that underlies all of these debates: Everyone believes they have legitimate expertise in education—in a way that is only creeping into other professional fields, such as medicine, at this point in history.

We allow all kinds of uninformed people to pronounce themselves as "experts." You know these people. They're all over the (Donahue, 2023) and Education sections of *The New York Times.* (Ashford, 2024) They're lobbying every state legislator—Blue or Red—to go along with faux science. (Reinking et al., 2023) They're constantly babbling on YouTube, LinkedIn, and other social media platforms.

We do this largely because we still believe in that American misreading of Calvinism, that wealth proves that God has you as one of his "elect." (Wikipedia contributors, 2024d) We also, as humans, crave certainty—no matter if that certainty is not grounded in reality. We are certain animals. We believe in Gods we cannot see. We believe in unprovable health assumptions. We believe in our lifestyles, our upbringings, and those we see as successes.

"As I explained, the "science of reading" movement is grounded in the media and parent advocacy (specifically focusing on dyslexia)—advocates who have no expertise or background in literacy—but is essentially a thinly veiled resurrection of the tired intensive phonics versus holistic approaches to teaching reading."—Dr. Paul Thomas, (Thomas, 2021)

There are far too many philosophical academic papers and books on human certainty, and reading these can be somewhere beyond painful, but let's just say that whether humans were certain that Apollo rode across the sky in a golden chariot, that the only comprehensible government was an autocracy, that classical economics was right about the absolute nature of the demand curves, that "Trump is on my side," or that "the only way to measure merit is a multiple choice test," it is, unfortunately, not different to those individuals than certainty about the Big Bang, or Einstein's explanations of gravity, or the understanding that everything is made up of atoms. This is because, in the words of "Mr. Certainty," Ludvig Wittgenstein, "I did not get my picture of the world by satisfying myself of its correctness; nor do I have it because I am satisfied of its correctness. No: it is the inherited background against which I distinguish between true and false. In other words, I take in what I am learning and judge it against what I already know." (Moyal-Sharrock, 2007)

If you know that traditional school is good, the evidence you absorb will confirm that. If you know that "reading instruction in the United States is bad," you will judge what you see against that background. If you know "some people are superior to others," evidence will, in your eyes, suggest that is true.

The modern scientific era increased our belief in certainty. As human knowledge exploded, it suggested that there is a single correct answer to every question. So, there must be one correct way to teach reading, one correct way to attend school, and one correct way to manage a classroom. "[T]he whole time I studied education, I thought about ... my high school experiences," writes Bettina Love in *Punished for Dreaming: How School Reform Harms Black Children and How We Heal.* "Why was our education made up of a series of barriers that we, as children, were expected to jump over? Why, instead of learning, were we punished with low expectations, physical violence, surveillance, standardized testing, and frequent suspensions? For us and Black kids like us, school, instead of being a place of learning, was a place of harm. I now know that each barrier was intentional and put there to punish Black folx for fighting for racial equality in public education." (Love, 2023)

"I think of school as a disease that I've been cured of"—a Spanish educational reformer during a work session in Virginia, 2019.

This certainty serves the pursuit of racism, ableism, nativism, and colonialism, no matter how we dress it up. As a commenter on Twitter once wrote in response to my opposition to "The Science of Reading," "You're just like anti-vaxxers, you're anti-science." He was absolutely certain in his white, ableist beliefs about literacy, and by assigning the word "science" to his own biases, he reifies this for himself and those he speaks to.

Yes, there is objective certainty—that which is based on scientific evidence—and there is a kind of "faith certainty"—that which is taught by human interaction, religion, nationalism, propaganda, family, and today, social media. In the social sciences, however, with the double-blind studies medicine depends on impossible, the objective can be very subjective. The University of Chicago Department of Economics (Department of Economics Homepage, n.d.) cannot disprove Marxist

Economics, yet they are certain Marx was wrong. (Basu & Brooks, n.d.) Those advocating various educational strategies, including myself, can provide evidence, but those with differing world views easily discount that evidence.

> *"First is the modernist view of scientific solution—a belief in the inevitability of human progress through science. These decision-makers enter the debate with a belief that each adaptation in the educational system has been "progressive," and thus that the education system which they succeeded in was "near perfect"—the result of centuries of continuous improvement. A bit of "tinkering" will thus result in "perfection." Their authority flows from certainty and the promise of being led to such perfection. The second problem is the idea that success is quantifiable and that the idea of it applies to all of us equally. The third problem is the leaders presuming that their framing of experiences is both correct and applicable universally."*—Why is everyone an expert on education? (Thompson et al., 2011)

Cubberley brought certainty to education in the United States. More specifically, he brought the idea of certainty through his manufactured historiology. The "colonial imaginary" Cubberley brought into full flower in American schooling, taking disparate intentions—moral and commercial, religious and imperial—and merging them into a coherent whole that the American intellectual elite could fully enjoy and feel good about. As Wilson sent Americans off to fight to "make the world safe for democracy," Cubberley sent them to build the American ideal: "The problem of the twentieth century, then, and probably of other centuries to come, is how the constructive forces in modern society, of which the schools of nations should stand first, can best direct their efforts to influence and direct the deeper sources of the life of a people, so that the national characteristics it is desired to display to the world will be developed because the schools have instilled into every child these national ideals." (Cubberley, 1920)

The world, and all within America, would be reconstructed on the American ideal, which we would all be certain about. The young vanguard of American society would, then as now, be prepared carefully to accomplish this vision.

Our problem is that the world that Cubberley was certain about, whether his observations were valid at the time or not, has vanished. That turn-of-the-20th-century, second industrial revolution, eugenics, Social Darwinism, women cannot vote, prohibition will solve all social issues, segregation is good, Calvinist nose-to-the-grindstone world was his backdrop and determined his truths, as it did for that long-ago ruling class he was advising.

With that worldview, Cubberley, like Jefferson and Barnard before him, laid out a path to Americanness and Whiteness, knowing that most could not follow it. Intending that most could not follow it. The design made it impossible for others to ever catch up. The further you were from the expressed ideal at the start, the further behind you would remain. (English, 2002)

The persistence of certainty in that design, when the United States clearly no longer needs 80 percent of its working population devoted to mining, assembly lines, and other manual labor, when we no longer (at least publicly) embrace our racism, our misogyny, our anti-Catholicism, our antisemitism, when we no longer all go to offices every day or prevent women from having civil or commercial rights, demonstrates the power of the myths that Cubberley reified.

At School

1900: Reading in the School of the Future (Corrigan, 2013)

The names Alcott, Hopkins, Young, Dewey, Holt, and Postman have largely been forgotten, but we must re-introduce them to our educators and our leaders. The works of these thinkers and observers remind us of both the mythic fantasy we have regarding schools and our long history of trying to do better for our children. They help us remember that we have had and do have small wins—wins that change the lives of children. They allow those trying to do the right things today to build on past accomplishments, rather than wasting energy on re-inventing the long ago invented.

"Most Americans have been to school and know what a "real school" is like. Congruence with that cultural template has helped maintain the legitimacy of the institution in the minds of the public. But when schooling departed too much from the consensual model of a "real school," failed to match the gram-

mar of schooling, trouble often ensued. If teachers did not maintain strict discipline and consistently supervise students in class, if traditional subjects were neglected, if pupils did not bring report cards home, reforms might be suspect."—(Tyack & Cuban, 1995)

Most adults' vision of "school" is very much fixed. Why wouldn't it be? These Conceptualizations have been beaten into people for 13, 17, 20 years or more. In the general mind, school consists of a school day in a school building with school classrooms, school teachers, school books, school rules, and school boredom because that is all they know.

"How do you know they're doing anything?" Observers in our multiage spaces (in this case, 130 K-5 students with 6 teachers) often could not figure out what was happening. The student agency was not school-as-they-knew-how-to-see-it. – photo: Ira Socol

When they see something different, they cannot make sense of what they are experiencing.

When we, in a Virginia system, began eliminating many of these constructs, visitors expressed bafflement.

Three students, third and fourth graders, were walking through the doors from a multiage space to the playground. "Do you know where they're going?" A visitor asked a teacher. "No," the teacher answered, "but I'm pretty sure they do."

Visitors to our multiage elementary spaces—120–150 learners K-5 in large complex spaces with 6–8 teachers—simply had no idea what was happening or even how to look at the scene. They could not see the learning without continuous teacher talk, large group structures, age separations, assigned seats, or most rules. "What am I looking at? Why isn't anyone giving instructions?" a visiting school leader asked.

Similar questions arose in a middle school language arts classroom without much "traditional" furniture or "traditional" assignments, in a high school classroom with multiple teachers and no bell schedule, in our Mechatronics classrooms with full learner-created contexts, in our high school music studios, and on and on.

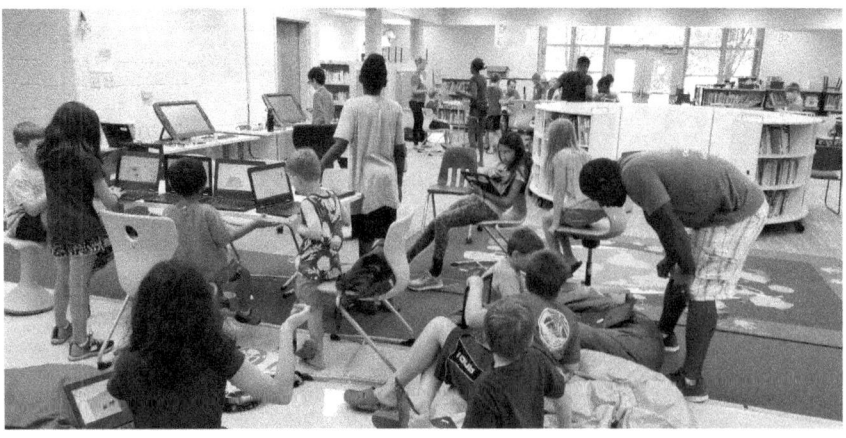

All ages of students gathered for CoderDojo each summer in a mass week-long program. We paid teachers to come work in these kinds of environments with master educators. This immersive professional learning offered an opportunity to understand and prove the power of student-determined learning. (by the way, 5-year-olds grasped the full number line—negative integers included—and slope/intercept during these weeks) - photo: Ira Socol

The unfamiliar is automatically assumed to be a "lesser alternative," maybe good for "those kids." "Unfortunately, I think most of that would also have an overall negative impact on student learning and wellbeing," a self-described progressive British educator responded when I described these innovations. The investment in "the familiar" that educators make is massive. When we make massive investments in anything, we tend to defend those choices to all because otherwise, we feel like we have made a massive mistake.

"For their part, teachers also have had an investment in the familiar institutional practices of the school. They learned these as students, and as they moved to the other side of the desk, they often took traditional patterns of organization for granted as just the way things were. It was one thing to add on a popular innovation at the border of the school- say a new vocational wing or dental examinations and quite another to ask teachers, faced with the job of controlling and instructing a large number of students, to make fundamental changes in their daily routines... The institutional character of the school, then, influenced the chances that a particular reform would

be incorporated into the educational system, how it would be implemented, and how the public and teachers would view the results. Both general beliefs in the broader culture about what a "real school" was and the hold of standard operating procedures on staff and students put a brake on innovators who sought basic changes in classroom instruction."— (Purkey & Smith, 1985)

Still raking winners from the rubbish

The change that must come first is in attitude. Even those with the best intentions can barely restrain themselves from picking out a few winners; as Jefferson said, "Twenty of the best geniuses will be raked from the rubbish annually and be instructed at the public expense."

I perhaps blew a $10 million grant from a foundation seeking to create "super [high] schools" when I—with the support of my team—refused to change our proposal from a program that would have transformed four high schools—for all our students—to the foundation's preferred single school. "We're not going to create one great high school and three mediocre high schools," I said during a contentious phone call before adding, "I think you miss the point; you don't have to give out money to create great high schools. I can take you to great places across the country. What I can't show you, and you can't show me, is a system of great high schools, and that's what we need."

If the richest people in America, if the most powerful people in America refuse to put the effort into making things right for every child and every adolescent, it will be impossible to get there. It's not just their grant-making. It's their full-scale tax-avoiding exploits, their massive contributions to politicians whose very platforms are inequality and inequity, their happiness at disinvesting in the communities that need them most, their constant preference for obscene executive pay and corporate profits over doing the right things for children.

If our "liberal intelligentsia," those we most hope would serve as allies, fail to recognize their role in this struggle and refuse to accept that they might stop supporting colonial actions, we all move toward hopelessness. "For many who consider themselves members of liberal or radical camps, acknowledging personal power and admitting participation in the culture of power is distinctly uncomfortable," Love writes. "[W]hite colleagues and instructors [do] not perceive themselves to have power over the nonwhite speakers. However, either by virtue of their position, their numbers, or their access to that particular code of power of calling upon research to validate one's position, the white educators had the authority to establish what was to be considered "truth" regardless of the opinions of the people of color, and the latter were well aware of that fact." In the simplest terms, as Chana Joffe-Walt stated at the beginning of *The New York Times* podcast series, Nice White Parents, "If you want to understand why our schools aren't better, that's where you have to look. You have to look at white parents." (Joffe-Walt et al., 2020)

And if our "mainstream media" keeps telling people that Elon Musk, Jeff Bezos, and Bill Ackman are somehow "important" and thus worthy of news stories about their opinions, they are fully com-

How Loud Billionaires Convert Their Wealth Into Power

Feb. 5, 2024

By William D. Cohan

How? They do it through your newspaper. (Cohan, 2024)

plicit. Stop looking at those with money, *New York Times*, and start asking who is doing the work humanity needs done.

A very long time ago I told an NYPD mentor that I'd joined the police department because I wanted "to do something good for once." He challenged me on the self-deprecating "for once" while referring to the "do something good" as "delusional."

"Delusional?" I asked.

"Of course," he answered, "but it's a delusion most of us operate under."

Perhaps hoping to change education in the United States is equally delusional, but if so, it is another delusional driver of my life's work. On the other hand, I know that my efforts—alongside thousands of others—have made real differences in the lives of real children.

"He was definitely worth all of the rule-breaking I did for him! Heck, the rule-breaking I did has paid off for just about every kid over the years," a former colleague wrote to me about a year ago amidst a tragedy. (I. D. Socol, 2022) She is so right about that. When we have a system designed to fail children, we have no moral choice other than to engage in systemic rule-breaking on behalf of the next generations.

"Most school curricula are based on a set of assumptions which the experimental program rejects. For example, most school programs assume (1) that knowledge is best presented and comprehended when organized into "subjects," (2) that there are "major" subjects and "minor" ones, (3) that subjects are things you "take," and that once you have "had" them, you need not take them again, (4) that most subjects have a specific "content," (5) that the content of these subjects is more or less stable, (6) that a major function of the teacher is to "transmit" this content (7), that the practical place to do this is in a room within a centrally located building, (8) that students

learn best in 45-minute periods which are held five times a week, (9) that students are functioning well (i.e., learning) when they are listening to their teacher, reading their texts, doing their assignments, and otherwise "paying attention" to the content being transmitted, and (10) that all of this must go on as a preparation for life.

"In other words, we are assuming (1) that learning takes place best not when conceived as a preparation for life but when it occurs in the context of actually living, (2) that each learner ultimately must organize his own learning in his own way, (3) that "problems" and personal interests rather than "subjects" are a more realistic structure by which to organize learning experiences, (4) that students are capable of directly and authentically participating in the intellectual and social life of their community, (5) that they should do so, and (6) that the community badly needs them."—Neil Postman, Alan Shapiro, James Gaddy proposal for an alternative high school, (Postman et al., 1969)

When I was in grad school, frustrated by a general lack of revolutionary thoughts around me, I pursued the topic of "How American schools came to be as they are" because I needed to know the why behind our everyday activities. I began by tracking the winners. Yes, I featured Alcott, but it was mostly a rogue's gallery of people from Barnard to Cubberley—the men who created the schools I have hated since I was six years old.

I say, somewhat accurately, that the School-Without-Walls alternative high school I attended (created by Postman, Weingartner, and a heroic teacher named Alan Shapiro) saved my life. (Wikipedia contributors, 2023) *I remember watching hundreds of tributes to my late mother pour in—over 30 years after her retirement—with endless comments about how her multiage second-third-grade open classroom changed lives. I have watched fabulous educators in New York, Michigan, Virginia, Nevada, Pennsylvania, Florida, Kentucky, Wisconsin, Illinois, Massachusetts, Vermont, and beyond bend and break the rules, taking significant professional risks to make the lives of kids—especially the kids on the margins—better, really better. This is important work.*

Since then, I've become much more enthralled with the people who fought for children. I had to. I needed inspiration for the challenging days of my professional life as I worked with many others to change schools into places celebrating childhood, adolescence, curiosity, creativity, invention, play, authentic communication, and opportunity for all.

The history is what it is. The future need not be what we have now. We have voices and more agency than we allow ourselves to comprehend. And we will not—in the end—regret fighting for something better.

Sources:

Ashford, G. (2024, January 3). As Literacy Lags, Hochul Proposes Changing How Schools Teach Reading. *The New York Times.* https://www.nytimes.com/2024/01/03/nyregion/new-york-schools-reading-hochul.html

Basu, D., & Brooks, C. (n.d.). *The basics of Marxist economics.* Retrieved April 19, 2024, from https://jacobin.com/2023/03/karl-marx-capital-economics-introduction-profit-surplus-value-labor-deepankar-basu-interview

Baxter, B. M. (September-October 2000). *The technology source archives - returning to the one-room schoolhouse.* Technology Source. http://technologysource.org/article/266/

Cohan, W. D. (2024, February 5). Opinion. *The New York Times.* https://www.nytimes.com/2024/02/05/opinion/ackman-billionaires-musk-trump-social-media-x.html

Corrigan, P. T. (2013, September 12). *What did the future of learning look like 100 years ago?* Teaching & Learning in Higher Ed. https://teachingandlearninginhighered.org/2013/09/12/what-did-the-future-of-learning-look-like-100-years-ago/

Cubberley, E. P. (1920). *The History of Education: Educational Practice and Progress Considered as a Phase of the Development and Spread of Western Civilization.* Houghton Mifflin.

Cultures, S. (2018, October 31). *Southern Strategy.* Southern Cultures. https://www.southerncultures.org/article/southern-strategy-from-nixon-to-trump/

Delpit, L. (2005, October 21). *Other people's children.* The New Press. https://thenewpress.com/books/other-peoples-children

Department of economics homepage. (n.d.). Retrieved April 19, 2024, from https://economics.uchicago.edu/

Donahue, T. (2023, October 23). Opinion. *The New York Times.* https://www.nytimes.com/2023/10/23/opinion/grade-inflation-high-school.html

Douce, D. (2019, August 5). *Advocating for students with dyslexia in public schools.* International Dyslexia Association. https://dyslexiaida.org/advocating-for-a-child-with-dyslexia-within-the-public-education-system/

English, F. W. (2002). On the Intractability of the Achievement Gap in Urban Schools and the Discursive Practice of Continuing Racial Discrimination. *Education and Urban Society, 34*(3), 298–311.

File:Robert F. Kennedy NYWTS.jpg. (1966, February 4). Wikimedia. https://commons.wikimedia.org/wiki/File:Robert_F._Kennedy_NYWTS.jpg

For professors, segregation begins at home. (2019, January 21). Kappan Online. https://kappanonline.org/professors-college-towns-segregation-emdin-moran-socol/

Hampson, R. (2018, February 12). RFK's visit to Appalachia, 50 years later: How Kennedy country became Trump country. *USA Today.* https://www.usatoday.com/story/news/politics/2018/02/12/rfks-visit-appalachia-50-years-later-how-kennedy-country-became-trump-country/310267002/

Jankowski, J. (2011). Caregiver credits in France, Germany, and Sweden: lessons for the United States. *Social Security Bulletin, 71*(4), 61–76.

Joffe-Walt, C., Snyder, J., Koenig, S., Drumming, N., Glass, I., Ewing, E. L., Lissy, R., & Nelson, S. (2020, July 23). Introducing: Nice White Parents. *The New York Times*. https://www.nytimes.com/2020/07/23/podcasts/nice-white-parents-serial.html

Jordan, E. (2023, December 22). Iowa rejects millions in federal summer food aid for children. *Gazette*. https://www.thegazette.com/state-government/iowa-rejects-millions-in-federal-summer-food-aid-for-children/

Lander, B. (2023, August 28). *NYC Comptroller Report Finds DOE Fails to Deliver Mandated Special Education Services to Thousands of Children Even As Claims Spending Surged Tenfold*. Office of the New York City Comptroller Brad Lander. https://comptroller.nyc.gov/newsroom/nyc-comptroller-report-finds-doe-fails-to-deliver-mandated-special-education-services-to-thousands-of-children-even-as-claims-spending-surged-tenfold/

Love, B. L. (2023). *Punished for Dreaming: How School Reform Harms Black Children and How We Heal*. St. Martin's Publishing Group.

Mapping attacks on LGBTQ rights in U.s. state legislatures in 2024. (2024, January 16). American Civil Liberties Union. https://www.aclu.org/legislative-attacks-on-lgbtq-rights-2024

Miller, C. C. (2021a, October 6). How other nations pay for child care. The U.s. is an outlier. *The New York Times*. https://www.nytimes.com/2021/10/06/upshot/child-care-biden.html

Miller, C. C. (2021b, October 25). The World "Has Found a Way to Do This": The U.S. Lags on Paid Leave. *The New York Times*. https://www.nytimes.com/2021/10/25/upshot/paid-leave-democrats.html

Moyal-Sharrock, D. (2007). Wittgenstein on Psychological Certainty. In D. Moyal-Sharrock (Ed.), *Perspicuous Presentations: Essays on Wittgenstein's Philosophy of Psychology* (pp. 210–235). Palgrave Macmillan.

Murray, S. H. (2024, January 5). Why Parents Struggle So Much in the World's Richest Country. *The Atlantic*. https://www.theatlantic.com/family/archive/2024/01/america-failed-parents-rich-countries-raising-kids/677023/

Paid sick leave to protect income, health and jobs through the COVID-19 crisis. (n.d.). OECD. Retrieved April 17, 2024, from https://www.oecd.org/coronavirus/policy-responses/paid-sick-leave-to-protect-income-health-and-jobs-through-the-covid-19-crisis-a9e1a154/

Postman, N., Gaddy, J., & Shapiro, A. (1969). *3I Program: Proposal, 1970*. http://www.joshkarpf.com/3i/proposal1969.html

Postman, N., & Weingartner, C. (1969). *Teaching as a Subversive Activity* (p. 3). Dell Publishing.

PS 20 the Clinton hill school — cluster specialists. (n.d.). PS 20 The Clinton Hill School. Retrieved April 18, 2024, from https://www.ps20.org/clusterteachers

PS 124. (n.d.). PS 124. Retrieved April 18, 2024, from https://www.ps124brooklyn.org/

Purkey, S. C., & Smith, M. S. (1985). School Reform: The District Policy Implications of the Effective Schools Literature. *The Elementary School Journal*, *85*(3), 353–389.

Reinking, D., Hruby, G. G., & Risko, V. J. (2023). Legislating Phonics: Settled Science or Political Polemics? *Teachers College Record*, *125*(1), 104–131.

Richardson, W. (2016, March 17). *We're trying to do "the wrong thing right" in schools.* Modern Learning. https://medium.com/modern-learning/ we-re-trying-to-do-the-wrong-thing-right-in-schools-210ce8f85d35

Seaquence. (2023, September 18). *Mike Duncan's Revolutions - 10.4 - Historical Materialism.* Youtube. https://www.youtube.com/watch?v=281K_OkxFis

Socol, I. (2009, May 10). Adult Communities and School Bullies. *SpeEDChange.* https://speedchange. blogspot.com/2009/05/adult-communities-and-school-bullies.html

Socol, I. (2010, July 23). *Lord of the Flies: How Adults Create Bullying.* SpeEdChange. https://speed-change.blogspot.com/2010/07/lord-of-flies-how-adults-create.html

Socol, I. D. (2020, June 4). *Education is the most political thing we do, it is the fight for our future.* Age of Awareness. https://medium.com/age-of-awareness/ education-is-the-most-political-thing-we-do-it-is-the-fight-for-our-future-315b85dc51d

Socol, I. D. (2022, October 25). *Eric Lee Hahn — not an honor roll kid.* Teachers on Fire Magazine. https://medium.com/teachers-on-fire/eric-lee-hahn-not-an-honor-roll-kid-639730704008

Stanford d.school. (n.d.). Stanford D.school. Retrieved April 18, 2024, from https://dschool.stanford. edu/shadow-a-student-k12

The National Commission on Excellence in Education. (1983). *A Nation at Risk: The Imperative for Educational Reform (A Report to the Nation and the Secretary of Education United States Department of Education)* (D. Gardner (Ed.)). CreateSpace Independent Publishing Platform.

Thomas, P. (2021, April 23). *Dismantling the "science of reading" and the harmful reading policies in its wake.* Medium. https://plthomasedd.medium.com/ dismantling-the-science-of-reading-and-the-harmful-reading-policies-in-its-wake-d15d9fe6d8e0

Thompson, G., Socol, I., & Lasic, T. (2011). Why is everyone an expert on education? *Human Edublogs.* https://www.academia.edu/5970631/ Why_is_everyone_an_expert_on_education_Thompson_Socol_Lasic_

Tompkins, A. (1895). *The Philosophy of School Management.* Ginn.

Tyack, D. B., & Cuban, L. (1995). *Tinkering Toward Utopia* (p. 10). Harvard University Press.

Watters, A. (2015, April 25). *The invented history of "the factory model of education."* Hack Education. https://hackeducation.com/2015/04/25/factory-model

Wikipedia contributors. (2023, February 6). *Alan Shapiro (education reformer).* Wikipedia, The Free Encyclopedia. https://en.wikipedia.org/w/index. php?title=Alan_Shapiro_(education_reformer)&oldid=1137887081

Wikipedia contributors. (2024a, March 21). *Mike Duncan (podcaster).* Wikipedia, The Free Encyclopedia. https://en.wikipedia.org/w/index.php?title=Mike_Duncan_(podcaster)&oldid=1214793052

Wikipedia contributors. (2024b, April 2). *Hakeem Jeffries.* Wikipedia, The Free Encyclopedia. https:// en.wikipedia.org/w/index.php?title=Hakeem_Jeffries&oldid=1216956733

Wikipedia contributors. (2024c, April 4). *Phara Souffrant Forrest.* Wikipedia, The Free Encyclopedia. https://en.wikipedia.org/w/index.php?title=Phara_Souffrant_Forrest&oldid=1217290123

Wikipedia contributors. (2024d, April 11). *Predestination in Calvinism.* Wikipedia, The Free Encyclopedia. https://en.wikipedia.org/w/index. php?title=Predestination_in_Calvinism&oldid=1218423992

AN AFTERWORD:

These were never good ideas,
and these were never good intentions.

"Now, in fairness, it's always easier for the defenders of the status quo to stick together. The status quo is a tangible, existent thing. It's here and now, it's what exists. Unity of purpose is simply defending what exists, protecting how things are. And not only that, they have the tangible resources to protect themselves, because what they are defending are those tangible resources. Meanwhile, the fight to replace the status quo means creating something new that presently exists only in the imagination. It's a blank slate of infinite possibilities. It's a utopia, approachable from an infinite number of paths, some of them leading in wildly different directions: up, down, around or behind, to this valley or that mountaintop or that

paradise by the sea. And because there are an infinite number of places to go and an infinite number of ways to get there, the critics of the status quo, the enemies of the status quo can divide into an infinite number of factions, while the defenders of the status quo can just sit tight and stay put. It's literally all they have to do. It's all they want to do. It's all they ever will do." - Mike Duncan *Revolutions/10-103-the-final-chapter/*

If we never change our underlying beliefs, we will never change our behaviors or results.

Americans face many challenges in these times of so many fundamental transformations and yet show little evidence of any national commitment to re-designing the fundamental structures that define our ability to meet the future. This is equally true of our constitution, our electoral systems, our economic rules, and our educational system.

Whether the cultural fears are about climate change, radical inequalities in both resources and rights, violence, disrespect, or interpersonal cruelty, our society seems to refuse to face the fact that all these problems remain beyond solutions because of the beliefs expressed by our unquestioned systems.

The foundations of those unquestioned systems were built in the 17th and 18th centuries by people committed to inequalities and inherent selfishness, based on failings of our human nature and constructed with religiously held beliefs in the superiority of the few. Those factors became the foundation of the American mythic determination that our personal rights and privileges—whoever you are—allow us to violate the rights and privileges of everyone else. Education is indeed just one part of the cultural structure that establishes that fact, but it is an essential part.

Within that cultural construct, our schools have been intentionally designed to fail the majority of children and adolescents for specific economic reasons. They have been designed to fail the future through worship of the past. That's the history I've been trying to put before you.

> *"The forms through which life realizes itself, whether school, family, society, church, or state, tend to fix themselves, and to check the life which grows through them. This is natural and inevitable. A considerable part of man's effort must be spent in readjusting the forms of life to the growing conditions of life. Man lives in advance of the customs of society, the laws of the state, the creeds of the church, and the methods and statutes of the school. When the tension becomes too great, as it does naturally and periodically, the old forms must be readjusted, or new ones substituted. It will be evolution or revolution."* = Arnold Tompkins, 1895

Conceptually, that is the point. However chaotic and confusing the history of our education system may appear, it is part of an economic and social system that operates ruthlessly to protect the interests of those in power. That represents a daunting challenge in its entirety, but we do need to see the trees in that forest. We need to look closely at the many tools of oppression and exclusion, big and small, systemic and personal, that chase those students into failure and then out the door.

From our buildings to our schedules, our furniture, the technologies we prefer, the ways we spend money (and raise money), the policies we have in place, our teacher training and professional development, in all our practices and philosophies, we are either welcoming all learners to opportunity or we are doing something different.

If we are not welcoming all learners, if our schools are not "homes of opportunity," we need to stop saying "I can't" and "Yeah, but..." and "We tried that before..." We also must stop saying, "It's too hard," and

"But we don't get any respect," and even, "We don't get paid enough," because, though it is hard, and you don't get the respect or money you deserve, this is still about giving the best possible future to our children—and I don't think there's any higher or more important aspiration on earth.

I am not a Marxist-Leninist type of revolutionary. There is too much brutality in Lenin's theory of change and perhaps too much certainty in the writings of Marx. I do, however, share certain traits identified with romantic revolutionaries. I believe in the possibility of revolution, I believe in the possibility of a successful and humane revolution, and I believe in revolutionary sacrifice.

I also acknowledge that revolutions need a courageous spearpoint and that not everyone can take on that role. Courage, I have learned across my life, is rarer in fact than in our hopes. Courage is also easier when one has less to lose. I have no right to ask anyone to do what they cannot do. No one has that right. We should, though, have the right to ask all not to be counter-revolutionary, to get out of the way of those driving change, and to follow the leaders when the risks are lower.

"For reason in revolt now thunders
And at last ends the age of can't.
Away with all your superstitions
Servile masses arise, arise
We'll change henceforth the old tradition
And spurn the dust to win the prize."
— The Internationale—written in French by Eugène Pottier, in the aftermath of the Paris Commune, June 1871—translated to every language in many ways. This version is ascribed to Charles H. Kerr.

I've seen all the "can'ts" in action, in all kinds of places, since 1970, and I can guarantee you that (a) these are not true—learner-centered, child-focused, humane solutions are possible, (b) students do better in every way—all students, even on standardized tests—when we make these key changes, (c) students are happier, learn more, become much less confrontational and "better behaved" in learner-centered, humane environments, (d) teacher and administrator stress is reduced significantly, and (e) all involved lead more balanced, healthier lives as we see improved long term life success.

Middle School kids prep for a state math exam the school hasn't passed in years. (Note: they passed after this) - photo: Ira Socol

High schools "without walls," "without classes or classrooms," with "student-determined context"? Yes, yes, and yes. Elementary classrooms with 120–180 K-5 learners and six or eight teachers, with no "teacher voice" or "teaching wall"? Yes, and yes. Middle schools without bells and with a focus on students making and building? Yes. Schools without linear and/or comparative grading? Yes. Schools with mastery focus instead of a clock focus? Yes.

A study of displacement in an open classroom, multiage elementary school. – photo: Ira Socol

I've seen these transformations in urban schools, suburban schools, and rural schools. In schools filled with generational wealth and schools filled with generational poverty—where every kid got not only free lunch and breakfast but family dinners sent home.

My observations confirm what William Alcott, Louisa Parsons Hopkins, Ella Flagg Young, John Holt, and Neil Postman all knew—there is a different way.

Students in a high school "without classes or classrooms"—built above a brewery in a start-up business incubator—work together. – photo: Pamela Moran

History can be a cautionary tale, a theory of human progress, or a straitjacket that stops us from moving.

Don't put on that straitjacket.

Instead, make changes and redraw the design so it includes. No, everything probably can't change at once—but we ask learners to change and adapt their thinking every day, and we can demonstrate the importance of that type of mindset by adopting it ourselves. Pick a few from the "menu" below and start your own revolution.

- Turn off your bells; everyone knows what time it is, and the factory whistle is long gone everywhere but the school.
- Take a real look at discipline—which is always weaponized against students on the margins and usually weaponized

against adolescence itself. Ask your students to build your discipline database, so you truly understand what is happening in your school. (When a teacher gives a student a zero grade for non-compliance, they will deny that is discipline—they will never report it to you. But the student knows exactly what is happening.)

- Ignore—out loud or silently—the Carnegie Unit and seat time. How "time on your ass" became accepted as a measurement of learning is so bizarre—if they knew it made no sense in 1906 and in 1954, why are we still there 120 years later? Learning exists outside of time, and on unique personal schedules. Believe that, and operate your school as if you understand that.

- Put your school on human time. Secondary schools should never start before 9:00 am—every bit of research confirms that. And double your "passing times" between class sessions. The calmest high school I ever worked in had 10 minutes between classes (and a coffee bar open in the central cafeteria). The hallways weren't rushed; kids got food and drink, used the toilet, talked to the teachers, who were all out in the corridors, and checked in with friends.

The evidence from the accumulating body of literature suggests that later school start times result in longer, higher-quality sleep. We used longitudinal methodology to follow changes to sleep, mood, health, and academics in a high school that delayed start time by 45 minutes. Initially, students lengthened sleep by 20 minutes. At one year follow-up, total sleep time returned to baseline, although the timing of sleep was significantly and persistently delayed. Lasting reductions in tardiness and disciplinary incidents were observed despite a lack of change in total sleep, suggesting a delay in sleep period can in itself improve daytime behaviors. Longer sleep times, coupled with delayed timing, may be necessary to improve mood, health, or academic performance. sleep. Other benefits include improved attendance and retention rates, elevated mood and motivation, and in some cases, better academic performance. A decrease in vehicular accidents has also been reported." —Thatcher and Onyper, 2016

- Give kids the chance to enter their learning spaces and decide for themselves where, how, or if to sit. This is step one in moving away from being a colonial-white-preferences school and toward opportunity for all, including all students we might classify as neurodiverse.

- Replace your "Gifted" and "Intervention" programs with what our educators began calling "Talent Developers"—staff that worked with every learner to leverage their abilities and build their educations. Never limit the best learning opportunities or creative breaks to your "high performers." If you do, you'll never know the potential that your biases hide from your view.

- Go multiage. Children and teens learn best from aspirational peers, those kids able to do "the next thing" well. They embed their new knowledge best when they teach others. But most importantly, our children deserve what San Diego multiage educators call "the gift of time." The time that matches their pace of development. U.S. educators rightly protested the notion of dividing children up by "born-on date" because they knew how that formula turns successful children into failures (she might be ready for sixth-grade math, but if she cannot read well enough, Florida, Mississippi, and too many other places will keep her in third grade permanently). If you've never watched a K-5 or K-6 classroom, you haven't been able to see the wonders of natural human learning within a school.

- Build disciplinary expectations and school norms—especially dress codes and hallway behaviors—with kids, with every kind of kid involved. This is one of those basic "consent of the governed" things Americans forget when working outside the adult middle class.

- Have students run your Professional Learning sessions (with or without teachers), and never hold a Professional Learning session or Faculty Meeting that does not look like the kind of engaging learner-centered pedagogy you want to see.

- Eliminate Zeroes. Whatever your grading system is, there is no room for grades below failure— punishment grades that destroy incentive by making recovery impossible. If you can, stop linear grading and comparative grading. Those are tools of oppression, methods of limiting opportunity, and wealth preservation systems that reward those "born on third base."

- Adopt Universal Design for Learning as your model. Disability or not, students need the tools, strategies, and structures they need—not what adults assume. This not only opens opportunities but also builds lifespan capabilities.

- Celebrate those "4As," Acceptance, Access, Attention, and Abundance. These are what kids need. Stop thinking that any child "needs to be fixed" or that any child arrives at your school "behind." They are who they are, and they are where they are, and we, as nurturing adults, must meet the child we have before us, wherever they are.

- When building or renovating a school, reject the design vocabulary spelled out by Henry Barnard before the U.S. Civil War.

Abandon rectangular classrooms, single-teacher classrooms, and double-loaded corridors. Even a square classroom (preferably with a door in the center of a wall) begins to eliminate the "look straight ahead" mode. Build with transparency in mind. Big outside windows, ways to see into classrooms. And make your cafeteria and Library an all-day "Central Parks."

- The best school security comes from making sure that every student feels safe, comfortable, and welcome. We do this by giving them more of our attention than we expect them to give us. Administrators need to be in front of the school every morning, greeting kids and being ready to listen to them. Teachers need to be in the halls between classes, and ready to listen. We don't sabotage kids with zeros or any noncompliance grading, and we don't bully kids with honor rolls, exclusive courses, or by making one student extracurricular activity more important than others.

  So, given the above, think two times, or five, before buying any standard school security systems. Research shows that the main impact of metal detectors is making kids feel unsafe (after all, doesn't their presence announce danger?) Avoid complex alert systems; if kids have their phones, you can send emergency alerts to everyone instantly, just as university campuses do. (This also eliminates the need for the wild distractions of P.A. announcements.)

- Know that if you are not anti-racist, you are acting in racist ways. The same is true of being ableist. In our society, we have work to do, and our children are watching us to see if they think we care.

- Make sure that your school is a home of opportunity. A school "has to first be a home—the kind of home the children may not have at home. A place that is relentlessly safe, that is both calming and exciting, that offers unconditional love, and that offers boundless opportunity. That 'home' must be supportive and accepting, loving and encouraging, and it must provide the biggest possible window onto the world, onto the universe."

Ultimately, we can write a history that looks like progress. We have the chance to design our schools in ways that bring kids in, put learners at the center, and embrace both a real understanding of human differences and the belief that we can move every young person toward a future in which they can thrive.

Let's finally bury Barnard and Cubberley and focus on our kids and their futures.

Sources:

Duncan, M. (2022, July 4). Revolutions 10.103 – the final chapter. *Revolutions Transcripts*. https://www.jacobmercy.com/Revolutions/10-103-the-final-chapter/

Dunster, G. P., de la Iglesia, L., Ben-Hamo, M., Nave, C., Fleischer, J. G., Panda, S., & de la Iglesia, H. O. (2018). Sleepmore in Seattle: Later school start times are associated with more sleep and better performance in high school students. *Science Advances*, *4*(12), eaau6200.

Lo, J. C., Lee, S. M., Lee, X. K., Sasmita, K., Chee, N. I. Y. N., Tandi, J., Cher, W. S., Gooley, J. J., & Chee, M. W. L. (04 2018). Sustained benefits of delaying school start time on adolescent sleep and well-being. *Sleep*, *41*(6), zsy052.

Pottier, E. (1871, June). *Lyrics: The International* (C. Kerr (trans.)). Marxism in Music. https://www.marxists.org/history/ussr/sounds/lyrics/international.htm

Reeves, D. B. (2004). The Case Against Zero. *Phi Delta Kappan*, *86*(4), 324–325.

Schools, L. C. P. (2024, February 21). *Highlights: DISCOVER 2024*. Youtube. https://www.youtube.com/watch?v=qyEVINOfpRs

shanmugamlakshmanan. (2008, August 22). *Reds Internationale*. Youtube. https://www.youtube.com/watch?v=c13q2wYZr_0

Socol, I. D. (2016, December 16). *You must see your school as a home of opportunity*. Medium. https://irasocol.medium.com/you-must-see-your-school-as-a-home-of-opportunity-6c7532b43e6f

Socol, I. D. (2019, November 15). *Semi-Charmed Kind of Life (part one): Who kids are... and what kids need from us*. Age of Awareness. https://medium.com/age-of-awareness/semi-charmed-kind-of-life-part-1-who-kids-are-and-what-kids-need-from-us-dcb7dd8a02c4

Socol, I. D. (2021, May 26). *Racism is written through the heart of every school hallway, not just every American street*. Educate. https://medium.com/educate-pub/racism-is-written-through-the-heart-of-every-school-hallway-not-just-every-american-street-a5cedbeacd00

Socol, I. D. (2022, December 5). *Toolbelt theory still matters*. Teachers on Fire Magazine. https://medium.com/teachers-on-fire/toolbelt-theory-still-matters-c8e0e3d8936

Socol, I. D. (2023, September 7). *Student reported discipline will begin the change your school needs*. Teachers on Fire Magazine. https://medium.com/teachers-on-fire/student-reported-discipline-will-begin-the-change-your-school-needs-6e3c2d2d2654

Tompkins, A. (1895). *The Philosophy of School Management* (Google Books; p. 10). Ginn and Company.

Wikipedia contributors. (2024, September 2). *The Internationale*. Wikipedia, The Free Encyclopedia. https://en.wikipedia.org/w/index.php?title=The_Internationale&oldid=1243581114

FROM EAST LANSING, MICHIGAN AND CHARLOTTESVILLE, VIRGINIA, 2011.

Toward the end of my dissertation writing process, I began my work with Dr. Pamela Moran in Albemarle County, Virginia. That became a story of tremendous success in re-imagining learning for 14,000 students in 26 schools. Despite the inevitable backsliding in the years since Dr. Moran and I left, the innovations and attitudes developed over a radical decade of change continue to improve the school experience for thousands of children.

As with every revolutionary period, the tale is one of both possibility and frustration, but it is important to me to end this book with optimism despite the history I have described. What follows was the

Epilogue of that old document. I would probably write it differently today, but its original form carries its own power.

Epilogue

It is a late September afternoon in Charlottesville, Virginia, and the sun has come out for the first time during the eight days of my visit there. The temperature leaps, as does the color spectrum and charm of this ancient American valley where Jefferson lived, worked, and built schools, digs itself out from under the clouds.

I am heading toward the airport for my flight back to Michigan with Dr. Pamela Moran, the superintendent of the Albemarle County Public Schools, my focus during this time. I am driving, and she lifts a thick, black-covered binder with large white words on its front from her briefcase. I am assuming it is some form of frustrating policy manual, but instead, as she opens it and begins to read, I discover a 20-year-old manuscript by Dr. Daniel Walsh of the University of Illinois: a history of a battle a generation ago over the direction of these schools. It is the tale of a battle lost, and Dr. Moran — in 1991 a young elementary school principal working to transform a small rural southern school into something inclusive and child-centered — begins to cry as she reads a line about her former boss, the man who then held the job she holds now, vomiting blood before the acrimonious school board meetings which led to his resignation.

She pauses. "So many people were hurt so badly," she says. "People now have followed me back out onto this limb, and I'm so afraid it will all happen again."

Dr. Moran — Pam — recovers. But, as Walsh has noted about that past superintendent, I have glimpsed something we rarely see, the private pain, the private persona behind a public figure. "Researchers have examined ideas and values," Walsh writes, "but too often in the process, the people who have the ideas become trivialized, reduced to selected actions or answers. Ideas and values do not struggle. People do, in their day-to-day lives. Their struggles are seldom coldly intellectual, rather they are emotional and ideological and economic. Their struggles become personalized... Ideas do not develop ulcers, cry in frustration, find themselves unable to sleep at night. They do not experience pain and fear and anguish. These things only people do" (Walsh, unpublished manuscript, 1991, pp. 8–9).

The Albemarle County Public Schools are a large organization with perhaps an outsized level of importance and scrutiny. The division covers 768 square miles of central Virginia, has over 13,000 students, over 2,400 employees, and 26 schools. It surrounds the University of Virginia, and many of the faculty at the Curry School of Education send their children to these schools. Because of the university, Charlottesville is filled with political and research organizations. Because of the proximity to Washington, D.C. what happens here is reported far beyond the mountains which rim the county.

Yet above all, the schools of Albemarle County, Virginia are people. They are people from many places and every social class. They are children and parents and grandparents. They did "well"/are doing "well" in school or they did/are not. They live on grand ante-bellum farms or in shacks or trailers, suburban houses and crowded apartments. They learn, in my experience and counter to the work of the University of Virginia's Daniel Willingham, in a very wide range of ways.

They are people who believe, who strive, who try. And if they are working in these schools they are doing so, almost unanimously, because the lives of children are very important to them.

We stop for iced tea. I say to Pam, "Like any leader who brings people into a battle, you worry about them. If you didn't, you'd be a lousy leader." Then I tell her a couple of stories from the past week. I tell her that these principals, librarians, and teachers I have been working with are already on the front lines, as she was 20 years ago. They struggle daily with state and federal mandates, with other teachers and administrators who "don't get it," with parents who want to reproduce themselves in their children, and who thus want school today to look exactly as school "did then," with those in the community who want to reserve educational success and the opportunities which come with that for their own children.

"They are on this path with you," I tell her. "Because they want to be here."

This is true of Michael, the young third-grade teacher who hated school and now leads a classroom filled with academic choices, behavioral choices, and comfort choices. Where students draw their ideas on the floor and tables, choose their technologies, and Skype with people from around the world. It is true for Brian and Chad, two very different middle school teachers in two very different middle schools, whose classrooms filled with "Special Needs" students seem completely without limitations. It is true of Matt, a former Teach for America teacher, now, years later, principal of an economically challenged elementary where every student, from pre-K to grade five, leads their parent-teacher conferences, discussing their own learning with both understanding and bravery. It is true of Joan, who has created a high school library so inviting that it is not only filled with students long before and long after school but often with students who cut class to work there.

If I, Pam, and the educators I am working with in Albemarle County, are in combat with Henry Barnard and Ellwood Cubberley, we will first see that historically, from the 1840s to today, we have lost the battles. American schools are not what William Alcott envisioned, nor John Dewey, nor Neil Postman, nor Alan Shapiro. But it cannot be seen as nothing but defeats. For the classrooms, school corridors, and school libraries I have been in this week are nothing like what Barnard or Cubberley envisioned either.

I say that 15 years after the destruction of this division's first experiment with child-centered education, she became superintendent, the rebel taking power again. I say that what we are doing now is far more advanced than what they were doing then. I note that simply the fact that the two of us have significant influence on these schools is a sign that Cubberley doesn't always win.

This transformation, in fact, is as transformative in style as in outcome. Learning from the redesign of the late 1980s, Dr. Moran has rejected most top-down approaches, and together, the superintendent, her cabinet, principals, teachers, and I have expanded the "Toolbelt Theory" approach into a school-building-centered series of 'seed' projects, building redesign around the mix of a school's specific needs and its physical, faculty, and student attributes. Principals meet and dream. School librarians meet and dream. Teachers spend long nights on Twitter re-imagining lessons and spaces. Every part of this process, from the diverse backgrounds of the central office cabinet to the surprising number of principals who were trained in special needs education, is as 'anti-Cubberley' as the classrooms, libraries, and school corridors illustrated here.

His specter does always haunt me, however, and just a few days before, I watched a small group of wealthy and politically connected people from one corner of the county assault Dr. Moran and her "trendiness" at a board meeting. "When will they actually learn something?" one asks of students who seem to be happy. "Students will still need to look things up on microfiche when they get to college," says another, critical of the interest in contemporary technologies. For Dr. Moran and others who remember the history that Walsh has chronicled, there is great fear.

For me, however, there is something else. If my war with Cubberley began when I was in second grade — mocked and hit and locked in the closet because of my struggles with reading and classroom rules by a teacher trained in the Cubberley tradition — then I must look at a second grader I met in Albemarle County's Greer Elementary School.

He sat at a round table near the center of a comfortable classroom, where children were working on many things in many ways. Sitting next to him was a girl who was finishing her reading of the entire Harry Potter series. But this boy could neither read nor write the words of the lessons on Ancient Egypt which were the work of the class. If you looked very hard, you could figure out that the symbols he created, which might have been "ppr," meant "papyrus."

Still, he was a full member of the class, fully honored by the teacher and the students, and he was learning along with everyone else by whatever means worked for him. When I pulled out my phone and, using the browser, showed him papyrus growing in the pool by the Temple of Dendur at New York City's Metropolitan Museum of Art. As he took the phone into his hands and zoomed into a living experience, he smiled with the thrill of understanding, of connection.

I have tried to tell these educators that this is a brutal and endless war. Few things arouse political passions as education does, for it is a struggle for the future. Those who, from Henry Barnard then to the billionaires of today, stand for the economic and social status quo (softened by charity) will always have more resources at hand than Alcott or Dewey or Dr. Moran, but sometimes we do create change. That change, the change in the lives of all of our children, is something we will keep fighting for.

ACKNOWLEDGMENTS.

In my life, written words can pour out, but writing – the ideas that matter – comes slowly. The learning behind the writing is a never-ending social process that is both mine and ours. "Ours" being the key word, I have far more people to thank than I possibly can.

First, Jill, my wife, who has been there for me, for us, and has always put up with my crazed, unquiet brain, which isn't an easy task. Thank you Jill.

And Pam Moran, who has supported and pushed this work since it was a dissertation in progress. She also introduced me to a school system ready for the future, and as that system's leader, gave me the chance to help create learner-centered, creative, and innovative learning spaces for every kind of student, no matter what age, neural structure, disability, economic background, family life situation, race, or home language. In Albemarle County, Virginia we proved that this history can be overcome. She pushed me to rewrite this in a readable, updated form, edited and footnoted the project, and would not let it remain unfinished.

A special "thank you" to Scott Mcleod, for his generosity in writing this book's foreword.

But this book has been the work of many over a period of time longer than this century. It begins with three Grand Valley State University professors, Edward Cole, Ivo Soljan, and Jonathan White, who let me see how history controls the present in ways we often refuse to see. The work continued with educators in West Michigan who showed me very different choices in everything about K-12 learning.

At the Michigan State University College of Education, I was lucky to meet an incredible cohort of faculty and graduate student peers who allowed me to organize my thinking historically, philosophically, environmentally, and even artistically. Professors Lynn Fendler, Yong Zhao, Punya Mishra, Rand Spiro, Troy Mariage, Avner Segall, and the late Susan Peters and Cleo Cherryholmes, transformed my thinking, and that is proof of learning. My peers, Adam Greteman, Leigh Graves Wolf, Paula Frederica Hunt, Nomalanga Grootboom, Terri Gustafson, Paula Frederica Hunt, Sara Beauchamp-Hicks, Carrie Anna Courtad, and so many others, opened my world through their remarkable range of experiences and interests.

There is my Irish contingent, John Heffernan, Pam O'Brien, Catherine Cronin, Conor Galvin, Mary Loftus, Bernie Goldbach, Hellie Bullock, Stephen Howell, and others, because, as they say, "If you've never seen anything but green, do you know what green is?" Their unique perspective has enriched my understanding. Too much educational research in the United States, whether on reading instruction or school organization, fails to look beyond the limits of our national borders.

The teachers and principals I worked with during an incredible decade of innovation in Albemarle County, Virginia, taught me so much. Academics and other education leaders have been so generous with their time, and their contributions are massive.

And yes, kids, whether six weeks old or 25, watching, listening to, and talking with kids is the most important educational research of all.

There are so many that if I begin to name names, I will inevitably miss people who are very important to me. I do hope that you know who you are, and please understand how grateful I am for all you have done, all that you are doing, and all that you will do.

\-   Ira David Socol

THE AUTHOR.

Ira David Socol is an educational change leader and proponent of Universal Design for Learning with extensive experience in assistive technology and learning space design. A co-author of *Timeless Learning: How Imagination, Observation, and Zero-Based Thinking Change Schools*, and *Education Reimagined: A Space for Risk*, Socol has significantly impacted school system redesigns across the United States. He currently works as Senior Provocateur and Learning Environment Specialist at Socol Moran Partners, advising school systems, architects, states, and educational organizations. His expertise includes reimagining learning spaces, adopting universal design practices, integrating assistive technology, and promoting student-centered education for children who will live into the 22nd century.

Before all that, he was a kid who hated the structure of school and an adult with the same attitude. Dyslexic and ADHD, he found school, whether in elementary or doctoral, uncomfortable and irrelevant to his curiosities, interests, and needs, except for a Neil Postman-designed alternative high school "without walls." After attempting universities twice, he served as a New York City police officer and finally found his way back to college and back into K-12 schools supporting learners with differences.

Invited into Michigan State University's education Ph.D. program, he began digging into the "unasked questions" behind our educational practices and found that our schools were, quite literally, designed to fail 80 percent of students while preserving the wealth disparities in the nation. These studies led to his role as an important innovator of learner-centered-learning, and to this book.

www.ingramcontent.com/pod-product-compliance
Lightning Source LLC
Chambersburg PA
CBHW070548130626
46556CB00001B/61